# THE
# RIKSDAG
## IN FOCUS

*Swedish History in a Parliamentary Perspective*

STIG HADENIUS

SVERIGES RIKSDAG
THE SWEDISH PARLIAMENT

STIG HADENIUS is professor of journalism at Stockholm University. He received his doctorate in history at Uppsala University in 1964 and was for many years assistant professor of political science at Göteborg University.

© Stig Hadenius and the Swedish Riksdag, 1997

*Editorial group:* Björn Asker, Marianne Carlbom, Ulf Christoffersson, Margareta Eliason, Anders Forsberg, Gunnar Grenfors, Linda Linder, Stefan Lundhem, Anders Norberg and Andreas Tjerneld

*Special acknowledgements:* Gunnar Åselius, Anders Claréus and Torgny Nevéus

*Translation:* Marie Clark Nelson

*Graphic design:* Gary Newman

*Cover photomontage:* Anders F. Rönnblom

Printed in Sweden by Berlings, Arlöv 1997

ISBN 91-88398-21-8

# Contents

# Preface

THE SWEDISH PARLIAMENT – THE RIKSDAG – has a long history stretching back half a millennium in time. But Sweden did not become a democracy, in the true sense of the word, until this century. It was first in 1921 that all citizens, women as well as men, were eligible to vote and thus had the opportunity to influence their own future and that of their children.

*The Riksdag in Focus: Swedish History in a Parliamentary Perspective*, written by an experienced scholar, describes the development of the Riksdag and of democracy during these centuries. Thus this book is also an account of Sweden from an underdeveloped, undemocratic agricultural country to the free and peaceful welfare society of today.

Democratic debate and the desire to reach long-lasting solutions have deep roots in Swedish society. The willingness to listen, respect for the arguments of others and the striving for compromise and mutual understanding have characterized this development from the early meetings of the lords and the parish councils to today's contract negotiations and the agreements reached across the bounds of political blocs.

Reaching agreement takes time. Democracy never has quick answers. But history has shown us that democratic methods are unsurpassed for attaining long-term sustainable social development.

The future of democracy is dependent on our dedication and our involvement, based on experience and knowledge of the past. Therefore this book concerns us all.

*Birgitta Dahl*
Speaker of the Riksdag

# CHAPTER 1

# The Swedish Riksdag

## Some Perspectives

**M**AY 1935 MARKED THE GRAND quincentennial celebration of the Swedish Riksdag. Festivities took place both in Stockholm and in the town of Arboga, where the first Riksdag was supposedly held. Members of foreign parliaments were invited, and 3,600 representatives of the country's cities, towns and local governments assembled at Stockholm Stadium. The King, the government and the Riksdag used the occasion to stress the importance of the representative body for the Swedish people.

The original Arboga Meeting was held in 1435 during a dramatic period in Swedish history. Erik of Pomerania ruled over a union consisting of Sweden–Finland, Norway and Denmark. He had been designated King of the Nordic Realms by his predecessor, Queen Margareta. There was, however, strong dissension among and within the countries.

After 1434 there was open hostility to the union King and his men in Sweden. German and Danish sheriffs had been installed in fortresses throughout the country, and they were accused of exacting unreasonable taxes and committing outrages against Swedes. Engelbrekt Engelbrektsson from the mining district of Bergslagen became the spearhead of this revolt. What really lay behind the unrest is lost in the shadows of the past. It has later been described as a struggle not only between Swedes and foreigners,

Bronze tablet designed by Erik Lindberg on the occasion of the 1935 celebration of the quincentenary of the Arboga Meeting. The tablet is mounted in the Riksdag Building.

"The tyrannical sheriffs' harshness and extortion" is the subject of this illustration taken from *Historia de gentibus septentrionalibus* (History of the Nordic Peoples) by Olaus Magnus. The work was written during the exile of the former Archbishop and printed in Rome in 1555.

*On the opposite page:* The building where the Riksdag meets today was completed in 1904. Nearly four decades had passed since the dissolution of the Estates. In the decoration of the main entry the architect Aron Johansson included representatives of the four Estates, which he placed directly below the statue of Mother Svea.

The Arboga Meeting is described in the Chronicle of Karl Knutsson, which gained its final form in the 1450s. The modifications made in an earlier version can be seen on the page shown here. Engelbrekt's role at the meeting was toned down. At the same time the ruling King, Karl Knutsson Bonde, received a more prominent place.

but also between common people and nobility. We know very little about the role Engelbrekt actually played.

As part of the struggle against Erik of Pomerania, a summons was issued to a meeting in Arboga in 1435. It is this meeting that has later been acclaimed the first Swedish Riksdag. The participants included a number of councilors of the realm, some of the country's wealthiest and most prestigious lords (estate owners and bishops), as well as burghers and perhaps even some peasants. Engelbrekt was chosen by those assembled as Protector of the Realm (*rikshövitsman*), the country's military leader.

It is not known what other decisions were made in Arboga or what forms the meeting took. The most informative source is the Chronicle of Karl Knutsson, which was largely a propaganda piece written in opposition to Erik of Pomerania. Medieval chronicles spread the news of the times; they were sung or read at gatherings or by the fireplace during long winter evenings. Such chronicles were meant to be entertaining, but also had the goal of spreading specific interpretations of events or rallying support for certain issues.

Just as today's TV-series, the chronicles pitted "good" against "evil," and the subtleties of reality were vastly simplified. The authors of the chronicles were the PR-men of their day, and they possessed considerable talent both as storytellers and as promoters of their employers.

Whether or not the Arboga Meeting should be called Sweden's first Riksdag depends on how the few sources from that era are interpreted and what criteria are applied. The term *riksdag* itself does not appear until a little over a hundred years after the Arboga Meeting. Drawing on the

Erik of Pomerania in a drawing from 1424.

common European experience, the Swedish historian Herman Schück has listed a number of criteria that must be met for a representative body to be considered a parliament, a riksdag.

- The assembly should represent the entire country; even those living far from the meeting place should be represented.
- All social groups regarded as free, that is, not under the jurisdiction of "lord or master," should be represented. This definition also includes the peasants, which was unique to the Swedish representative body.
- The groups in the representative body should function independently as "Estates" or "Houses," so as to insure the participation of all groups in the decision-making process. No groups should function merely as rubber stamps.

## Engelbrekt – Warrior and Politician

ENGELBREKT ENGELBREKTSSON is one of Sweden's most noted figures from the Middle Ages. He was from the mining district of Norberg in Bergslagen, but he had his origins in a German family that is believed to have immigrated to Sweden during the 1360s. His days of glory lasted from 1434 to 1436, when he led a revolt against Erik of Pomerania. He was a skillful rebel leader, who probably learned the art of war serving with Erik when the latter fought in Germany. After his death Engelbrekt was worshipped as a saint, and many made pilgrimages to his grave in Örebro.

The Chronicle of Karl Knutsson describes very dramatically how Engelbrekt was brutally murdered with an axe and pierced by fifteen spears in 1436 on an island in Lake Hjälmaren. Engelbrekt's death, however, had nothing to do with his struggle against Erik of Pomerania; nor was it concerned with the domestic political conflicts in which he was involved. The murderer was a personal enemy.

The murder was to play a significant role in the historical writings concerning Engelbrekt. He was soon depicted as a hero and a martyr. For nineteenth century historians and those in the beginning of the twentieth century he symbolized the ancient struggle for national freedom against foreign intruders.

Engelbrekt was not only a warrior; he was also a politician. He was not a man of the people; he belonged to the nobility. At the Arboga Meeting in 1435 he was elected a member of the Council of the Realm. The motives for his struggle may be debated. The fact that Erik of Pomerania was German and that the sheriffs were German and Danish was not of any great significance. As we have seen, Engelbrekt was himself of German origin. More important were certainly the high taxes which the sheriffs exacted and the policy of Erik of Pomerania which favored neither the privileged classes, the peasantry nor the iron exporters of Bergslagen.

Bror Hjorth's statue of Engelbrekt, which crowns one of the stairways in the Riksdag Building, was completed in 1935 and is very much in keeping with that era's interpretation of the rebel leader. We know nothing about Engelbrekt's actual appearance.

- The assembly should have competence and continuity; its meetings should be held regularly, and its position should be duly considered. The meetings should not only serve as support for a government or King, but should also make decisions concerning taxes and laws and, ultimately, take a stand on questions of war and peace.

If Herman Schück's definition is applied, the Arboga Meeting cannot be considered a riksdag. Few of the criteria are entirely met.

During the Middle Ages a number of assemblies were held which may be interesting to study, even though they do not fulfill these conditions. They were important to their contemporary world and forerunners of the Riksdag which was to come.

## A Celebration for National Unity

The uncertainty which still exists concerning the origin of the Riksdag also left its imprint on the 1935 quincentenary. Professor Sven Tunberg, an historian, was among the celebration speakers, and, according to the pseudonym Åbergsson in *Dagens Nyheter* (the Daily News – a major Stockholm newspaper), he held one of the most noted lectures.

As the "historical expert" he began by giving assurances that the Arboga Meeting really was the first Riksdag. Thereafter he acclaimed Engelbrekt:

The Post Office commemorated the quincentenary with a series of stamps related to the history of the Riksdag. The artist was Olle Hjortzberg.

> Our thoughts and our reflections go today to the hour of birth of the Swedish Riksdag. Seldom has our country found itself in a more precarious position than at that time, threatened both from without and from within. Only radical intervention could bring aid, which roused and summoned the bonded power of the soul of the Swedish people, roused and summoned it for the preservation of the Swedish kingdom's independence in the face of the fatal powers of destruction. That intervention and that aid came with Engelbrekt.
>
> Nor have accusations and disparaging voices been lacking in regard to his person and his deeds. Above all, attempts have been made to assert that his importance has been exaggerated, but one thing is certain: Engelbrekt saved the Swedish realm when it was obviously endangered, and it was he who with his life's work ushered the Swedish Riksdag onto the stage.

The Speaker of the Second Chamber, the Social Democrat August Sävström, delivered the best speech, according to Åbergsson. He also praised Engelbrekt for "his breakthrough in arousing among Swedes a sense of unity, a feeling which resulted in a demand for national independence and freedom." Åbergsson continued:

> For the Swedish Riksdag, said Mr. Sävström, the work of Engelbrekt implies massive responsibility in united service of the nation and the people. With feelings of reverence and gratitude we therefore hail the great statesman on this historic ground. It is good for a people to have collective memories to unite

The press gave wide coverage of the Riksdag quincentennial celebration. Here is the front page of *Dagens Nyheter*, May 28, 1935.

them. Such memories can form an invisible link underlying all differences of opinion, if properly understood.

In spite of the assurances of Professor Tunberg and the Speaker of the Second Chamber, in 1935 there were those who doubted whether the Arboga Meeting had really constituted a riksdag, and there is reason to ponder why such lavish festivities were held on this much-disputed date. The fanfares, the lofty speeches and the quincentennial banquet perhaps had less to do with the 1435 assembly than with the prevailing spirit in the early 1930s. The Riksdag wanted to demonstrate its ancient roots; it wanted to show that it was firmly anchored in the past.

The first two decades of the twentieth century had brought about profound changes in Sweden's political life.

- Universal and equal suffrage was introduced. It occurred gradually and after many conflicts, but in 1921 the first truly democratic election was held. All women and men had then in principle been granted equal suffrage in elections to both the Riksdag and the local assemblies.
- The Crown acknowledged the parliamentary system. The government was no longer dependent on the King, but rather on the Riksdag, for the exercise of power. The long struggle which the Crown and the conservatives had waged against this new order was definitively decided in favor of the Riksdag.

Axel Wallenberg's commemorative medal from the 1935 Riksdag quincentenary emphasized Engelbrekt's role at the Arboga Meeting.

The political reforms, however, did not lead to immediate improvements within the country. The 1920s became a decade of instability. Participation in elections was low, about 50 percent, although the promoters of universal and equal suffrage had maintained that the vote was important to so many. There were numerous strikes, and the country was led by minority governments unable to carry out their programs. There was disappointment over the fact that the democratic ideals that had been the object of such a long struggle produced so few results once they had been realized. It was in this atmosphere that a decision was made to support a comprehensive book project on the history of the Riksdag and to celebrate the quincentenary.

## Stability in Times of Unrest

During the 1930s the social climate in Sweden changed for the better. Agreements were reached in the political field and on the labor market which led to stability and increased strength instead of the splintering and rivalries of the 1920s. The development in Sweden was positive in contrast to that of many other European countries where dictators and other antidemocratic forces seized power. It became important for a small democratically run country such as Sweden to clearly mark its independence and its national identity. The Riksdag quincentenary became a symbol of a new and strong Sweden where the King, the government and the elected representatives of the people in the Riksdag and in local assemblies stood side by side.

Sweden was to be proud of its Riksdag – five hundred years of unbroken rule by the people. And Engelbrekt was very suitable to serve as one of the fathers of the country. The descriptions from the 1930s portrayed him as a plain man from the mining district who, with the help of the Swedish peasantry, drove out the foreign sheriffs. The quincentennial celebration served the purposes of both the King and the various political parties.

The celebration of Engelbrekt and the Arboga Meeting may be taken as an example of how history is often used by later periods. Engelbrekt had national roots, which the King and the conservatives could emphasize, and popular roots, which the Social Democrats could bring to the fore. The conservatives had long had a "monopoly" on national ideals in Sweden, as illustrated by the so-called Farmers' Demonstration of 1914. In a spirit of nationalism Sweden's farmers showed their support for the King and a stronger defense policy and their opposition to the groups which were working for parliamentarism and democracy. King Gustaf V met the farmers in the Palace Yard and spoke in elevated tones of "my army" and "my fleet." A conflict existed between the power of the aristocracy, represented by the King, and popular power, as it was manifested in the Riksdag majority. The Liberal Prime Minister Karl Staaff had to resign; the Crown had won for the time being.

At the Riksdag quincentenary in 1935 the King used a completely different tone than in his Palace Yard speech:

> The jubilee, which the Riksdag is now celebrating, is a reminder that Sweden is an old monarchy, and yet the Riksdag has a five hundred year tradition in the realm.
>
> In times of unrest, not least during Engelbrekt's rebellion, Swedes have found their most valuable heritage in the law of the land as an expression for both the country's independence and the people's preservation of domestic social peace.
>
> It was on this foundation that both the national monarchy and the Swedish Riksdag developed. The Crown took the lead initially in matters concerning the common good of the country and the people. But eventually the influence of the Riksdag on national policy and the importance of its initiative grew in various areas of social life.

This five crown silver piece with an image of Gustaf V was minted for the quincentenary of the Arboga Meeting of 1435.

The King finally acknowledged popular rule. Through Speaker August Sävström the Social Democrats also showed their support both for the Swedish Riksdag and for royal power in the form that it had taken since the breakthrough of parliamentarism and democracy. Sweden was a united country both outwardly and inwardly. The conflicts were over, and the common task became most important.

## On Parliaments

On the occasion of the quincentenary Iceland's parliament presented this work of art to the Riksdag. It was painted by Asgrimur Jónsson and represents Thingvellir, where the Icelandic parliament, the Althing, assembled every year from 930 until 1798.

IN ANCIENT ATHENS all free men (women and slaves were excluded) assembled in the city square and made decisions concerning taxes and war and peace, and they determined who should administer these decisions. These assemblies were democratic; the votes of all present were counted and the majority ruled.

In Sweden we can find equivalents of these Greek assemblies in the medieval village meetings where all free men gathered to make decisions which concerned the common good. However, for questions regarding the province or the entire country it was not practically possible for all inhabitants to meet in one place. Thus some form of representation was necessary – an assembly of people who spoke and made decisions for various groups in society.

In the Nordic countries the Icelandic parliament has the oldest history of all representative bodies. As early as 930 the leading men of Iceland met at Thingvellir to pass judgement and to make laws.

Today nearly all countries have parliaments of some kind, but their functions vary considerably. Democracy is not a prerequisite for such a body. There are many parliaments where the members are not selected according to democratic principles, and for several centuries the Swedish Riksdag was not democratically chosen. Nor is parliamentarism necessarily the rule: the composition of a government does not have to be dependent upon the power distribution in the parliament. In the USA the President appoints his Cabinet without considering the party in power in the federal representative body, the Congress.

There are countries where the parliament has power only on paper, while a dictator rules, and there are others, such as the USA, which have a division of power between a president, a representative body and a supreme court.

In Sweden, according to the Instrument of Government, the fundamental power resides in the Riksdag. In the first chapter the document states:

> All public power in Sweden proceeds from the people.
>
> – – –
>
> The Riksdag is the foremost representative of the people.

However, reality does not always correspond to what is found in laws and constitutions. In the Soviet Union the representative body, the Supreme Soviet, had significant power according to the constitution, even under Stalin's rule. The same was true of the German *Reichstag* under Hitler. In practice these parliaments had nothing to say.

The word *riksdag* is derived from German and is now used only in Sweden, Finland and Estonia. In Sweden until 1866 it denoted the actual meeting. The institution was called "the Estates of the Realm" or simply "the Estates". It consisted of four Estates: the Nobility, the Clergy, the Burghers and the Peasantry. During the absolute monarchy at the end of the seventeenth century and in the beginning of the eighteenth reference was sometimes made to "His Majesty's Estates." With the reform of the system of representation in 1866 the term *riksdag* came to have a dual meaning. It still designated the meeting, but now also the institution. According to the 1974 Instrument of Government the word *riksdag* is restricted to the organ of the state.

The 1974 Instrument of Government. This simple printed document may be compared with the lavish design of its predecessors (see, for example, the 1719 Instrument of Government on p. 78).

# CHAPTER 2

# Representation but No Riksdag

S WEDEN was a sparsely settled agricultural country with a few small towns during the Middle Ages. Fortresses and manors existed, but they were comparable neither to those found on the continent nor to those which were to be erected during Sweden's Age of Greatness in the seventeenth century. Waterways provided the major means of communication. The roads which did exist were most often mere paths for mounted riders. It was the waterways that allowed speedy transportation over long distances. When Engelbrekt crossed Lake Hjälmaren by boat on his journey from Örebro to Stockholm, he was following a customary route.

Bands of highwaymen reigned in the great forests, but the waterways could also be dangerous. Even Erik of Pomerania made a living by piracy, when he made his home in Visby on the island of Gotland after his removal from the throne.

The transportation difficulties and communication problems of the past should be kept in mind when looking at the history of the Riksdag. Journeys to the meeting places were expensive, difficult, dangerous and very time-consuming. Thus meetings were held in various parts of the country, but still areas far distant from the meeting place were often poorly represented, especially Finland's interior. (Finland was part of Sweden from the Middle Ages until 1809.)

Lake Mälaren was an important waterway. It was the main link between major medieval towns such as Strängnäs, Västerås, Sigtuna and Stockholm. In the picture the remains of Alsnö House can be discerned in the foreground.

*On the opposite page:* Although many meetings of the lords and other gatherings were held in locations outside Stockholm during the Middle Ages, the city was the center for politics and trade. The painting in *Storkyrkan* in Stockholm showing a parhelion dates from 1535 and is one of the oldest known depictions of the city.

## Medieval Sweden

In medieval Sweden the land was owned by the Crown, the Church, noblemen and peasants. In the fifteenth century more than half of the land was in the hands of free peasants who were under obligation to pay taxes to the Crown. Others cultivated Crown lands, church lands or the lands of the nobility.

The farms were clustered in villages, and the villages were largely self-sufficient. Butter and hides were products that were sold, while only a limited number of items were bought. Salt was absolutely necessary for preserving fish and meat, and hops for brewing beer.

The peasants in the villages were highly dependent on one another. Village life was carefully regulated by special statutes which were sometimes written, sometimes part of the oral tradition. There were rules concerning the division of common catches from hunting and fishing or about what should be done if a peasant became ill and could not harvest his crop or take part in the common work. A village elder saw that the rules were followed. He was appointed by the peasants, usually for one year at a time.

Sweden had no serfs directly bound to noblemen, as were found in a number of other European countries. Even the peasants who cultivated farms owned by the Crown, the nobility or the Church were free to move. The difference between them and the peasants who cultivated their own land was that the former did not pay taxes to the Crown, but rather fees to the landowner.

However, both in the countryside and in the towns and cities there were people who did not own property and who did not have any legal rights, as did the burghers and the peasants. Bondage had been abolished by King Magnus Eriksson during the fourteenth century "in honor of God and the Virgin Mary and for the

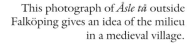
This photograph of *Åsle tå* outside Falköping gives an idea of the milieu in a medieval village.

As were other Hanseatic towns such as Lübeck and Reval (Tallinn), Visby was surrounded by a wall. The wall was built at the end of the thirteenth century, when there were conflicts between the burghers in the town and the peasants in the surrounding countryside.

tranquility of the souls of our fathers." Yet many people, vagrants, outlaws and others, lived outside the minutely regulated medieval society.

Towns and cities were usually separated from the surrounding countryside only by some form of fence or ditch. Tolls were collected at the town gates. Stockholm, Visby and Kalmar were surrounded by walls patterned after those found on the continent. In the countryside the peasants were largely self-sufficient, and they bartered for the few things they needed from the world outside. In the towns and cities money was used, and their residents alone possessed trading rights. Local government also differed from that of the countryside with its parishes and hundreds. Towns had two mayors and a number of councilmen. These officials were elected at the "general council meeting" which was open to all who were designated as burghers.

The burghers were divided into guilds. Here we see Tord the Master Mason in a miniature found in the 1487 bylaws of the Stockholm Guild of Masons.

Many Germans immigrated to Stockholm and other Swedish towns and cities during the Middle Ages. This influx left its mark both on local government and on the guild system. Under the guild system different kinds of craftsmen were organized in special craft associations. The painters had their guild, and the shoemakers theirs.

The church at Varnhem Monastery in the province of Västergötland was built during the second half of the twelfth and beginning of the thirteenth centuries. The monasteries were not only religious centers but were also largely responsible for sick care and education.

The Archbishop was the foremost spokesman of the Swedish Church and, as such, Jakob Ulvsson had himself portrayed on this sumptuous chasuble which he donated to Uppsala Cathedral in 1482.

The differences between the towns and the countryside were not always so great. Many people in the towns were also self-sufficient. For example, the burghers kept their own animals. The center of the town was the main square and the town hall. The towns were small but came to life during the regular markets and fairs or during royal visits.

Sweden was a Roman Catholic country during the Middle Ages, and the Church was in principle subordinate to the Pope in Rome, but regents and certain noblemen also had a great deal of influence over clerical appointments. The country was divided into dioceses, each ruled by a bishop and a cathedral chapter. The bishop often belonged to the secular nobility and was powerful, not only because of the control he exerted over the priests and others within the diocese, but also because he had income both from his own property and from church lands. Each parish and town had one or more priests, who in the beginning of the Middle Ages were appointed by the parish residents or by the town's burghers, but later by the diocese.

Education and health care were in the hands of the Church, which was also responsible for many of the country's contacts with the rest of the world. Monasteries were important for education, and convents even provided the opportunity for girls to attend school.

The office of the Archbishop was one of the most important political and economic posts in the country. The bishops sat on the Council of the Realm, and there was little control exerted by the Pope in Rome. Sweden was far from the center of Catholicism, which left room for both the clerical and secular nobility to use their own discretion.

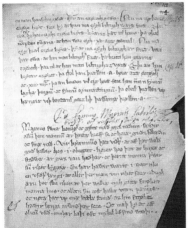

Saint George and the Dragon in *Storkyrkan* in Stockholm is a monument to the victory in the Battle of Brunkeberg in 1471. The sculpture group was made by the renowned North German sculptor Bernt Notke, who was commissioned by Sten Sture the Elder. It was dedicated in 1489. Saint George is represented here as a typical knight of the era.

The Church and the monasteries and convents were exempt from taxation. They were also under the jurisdiction of their own legal code, canon law. The influence of the Church increased, particularly toward the end of the Middle Ages; it became a state within the state. Open struggles between the clergy and representatives of secular power often occurred.

The existence of a secular group exempt from dues to the Crown was mentioned for the first time in the statute which King Magnus Ladulås (Barnlock) passed on the island of Alsnö in Lake Mälaren in 1280. This document guaranteed tax exemptions to his own armed retinue and that of his brother Bengt. The same applied to the squires of the Archbishop and of the bishops, as well as to all men who served with their mounts. Military developments prompted the organization of this tax-exempt group. The old peasant armies needed horsemen who were trained and who possessed modern equipment. In return their lands were freed from taxation.

The four Estates – the Nobility, the Clergy, the Burghers and the Peasantry – developed in the beginning of the Middle Ages and

In the Alsnö Statute King Magnus Ladulås grants exemption from taxation to "all those men who serve with their horses, whomever they may serve." Shown here is the text in a manuscript from the 1280s. It is the oldest preserved book in the Swedish language and is found in the Royal Library in Stockholm.

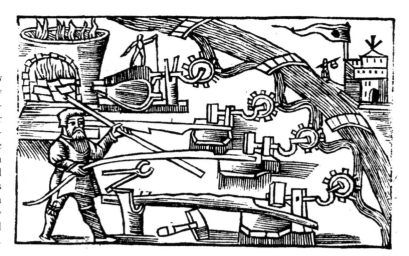

*Historia de gentibus septentrionalibus* by Olaus Magnus describes how the men from the mining and manufacturing regions used water power to run their bellows and their hammers for producing bar iron. These men were peasants who, in addition to cultivating the land, produced iron. In the area today referred to as Bergslagen they constituted a wealthy stratum of the peasantry and gained significant political power.

came to reflect Sweden socially, economically and politically. These four groups together, alongside the King, represented "power" in Sweden. The Estates, however, were not equal; the Nobility and the Clergy long dominated completely the decisions concerning taxes, war and peace. The men from the mining districts became an independent power factor during the fourteenth century, a fact attested to by Engelbrekt's appearance.

The peasants found themselves at a disadvantage, but during the fourteenth and fifteenth centuries became more prominent. Peasant bands were not only significant in domestic struggles, but also played a role in wars with foreign powers, especially after 1460.

International contacts were primarily between members of the same Estate. The upper nobility often owned property in several Nordic countries and sometimes sent their sons to universities outside Sweden. Priests might also receive some of their education at universities or seminaries abroad. The Church and the monasteries had direct contacts, not only with Rome or their respective mother monasteries, but also with other churches, especially in the German states and France. The burghers in the various ports had business contacts with merchants in the Baltic, the German areas and the Netherlands.

## The Emergence of Representation

Sweden became more united during the second half of the thirteenth century. One reason was the sweeping changes made in the military field. Armed fortresses were built and cavalry units designed to serve the King in war. This organization placed different demands on the economy from the earlier one based on peasant forces.

At the same time the King strengthened his position. In the mid-thirteenth century Birger Jarl subjugated the local chieftains by military force. Law-making, earlier in the hands of the provincial

This stone house at Torpa in the province of Västergötland was built in the fifteenth century and is one of the few relatively unchanged medieval fortresses which remain in Sweden.

assemblies, the tings, was taken over by the King. He was granted more power, but at the same time became dependent on the populace for support in maintaining fortresses and cavalry troops. This explains the rise of various kinds of representative bodies where the King sought approval of his decisions and his demands.

During the Middle Ages there were different types of assemblies which may be regarded as predecessors of the Swedish Riksdag. These included everything from committees for the election of the King and meetings of lords (noblemen and bishops) to gatherings at fairs and meetings with the army. Some of the assemblies will be presented below. One important reservation should be made, however. Knowledge about how they functioned varies greatly, and there were also significant changes over time.

A recurring question is which Estates were represented in the various assemblies. What role did each Estate have? Did it dominate, participate or was it merely a passive observer? The sources available for the study of Swedish medieval history are much sparser and of poorer quality than in many other European countries, partly due to the destruction of the documents of the churches and the monasteries in conjunction with the Reformation.

## Royal Elections

During the Early Middle Ages Sweden was a monarchy, but the power of the King was far from unlimited. The King did not inherit his position, but was elected. In the Law of the Land proclaimed by Magnus Eriksson, which was in effect from the 1350s and replaced the old laws of the Swedish provinces, a section of the Royal Code reads as follows:

> A King shall henceforth be elected for the Kingdom of Sweden in the following manner, and that shall not be inherited if the King has been lost: the previously mentioned lawmen shall, each from his own jurisdiction, with the consent of

The Royal Code in Magnus Eriksson's Law of the Land is illustrated here in a manuscript from the 1450s.

all living within that jurisdiction, select twelve wise and hearty men and with them on the appointed day and at the proper time come to Mora ting to elect the King.

The first vote to select the King shall be cast by the lawman from Uppland and those appointed to accompany him; thereafter each and every one of the lawmen from the other provinces ... They shall admonish him to bear the crown and be King, to rule over the land and govern the kingdom, to uphold the law and preserve the peace.

Among other things the King had to assure the Estates that he would not infringe on their rights.

Attempts were made by the Crown to convert Sweden into an hereditary kingdom. But when young Magnus Eriksson was elected King at Mora Meadow outside Uppsala in 1319, the process of electing the King was definitely established, as well as the position of the nobility and the Church. Nor was the King allowed to levy taxes on his own; he had to seek the advice of the Council and the people.

The King was also supposed to make a traditional tour of the realm (*eriksgata*), during which his election was to be verified. The forms of this tour were clearly specified, first in the provincial laws and then from the 1350s in the general Law of the Land. The journey began in Uppsala and followed a special route. Specific ceremonies were conducted in each province. The King had to promise to observe the laws. The people gave assurances that they would help him to defend the realm and that in accordance with the Law of the Land they would "give and carry out their annual and legal obligations to their King with good will without any refractoriness."

The role played by the election of the King and by this traditional tour varied over time and has been discussed among historians. Some interpret the election ceremony at Mora Meadow as a

The newly elected King was to make a traditional tour of the realm, starting from Uppsala and continuing throughout the key areas of Sweden, to be approved as King at various assemblies.

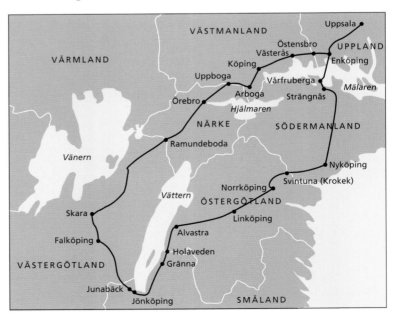

The royal election at the Mora Stone outside Uppsala as depicted in the work by Olaus Magnus. The woodcuts which illustrate Olaus Magnus' descriptions of the Nordic peoples and their life and customs were made in Rome in the middle of the sixteenth century, but still provide some knowledge of life in Sweden during the Middle Ages.

precursor of the Riksdag. Representatives of various groups determined the country's leadership. The power of the King was limited, and the people accepted certain obligations.

On the other hand, little is known about who was present at the election of the King and what power these people had. Often "the people" were present merely to confirm a decision that had already been made. There was no discussion of the merits and shortcomings of the various candidates. Those who assembled at Mora Meadow did not do so in order to determine who could best lead the country. Even if the election had not been decided in advance, there were most often only two candidates to choose from.

In spite of this, the election of the King certainly was important in the development toward a modern riksdag. Although the number participating in the election was small and although the election often assumed the character of an agreement between the most powerful men in the realm and the presumptive King, there were rules and formalities which had to be observed. The King was forced to consider opinion, even if it was limited.

## The Council and the Meetings of the Lords

During the thirteenth century a secular nobility developed in Sweden, an elite with special privileges that owned much of the land of the realm. The growth of a nobility is closely related to the previously described military developments and the creation of a special council which can most aptly be likened to a kind of government. As early as the beginning of the thirteenth century the King had special *consiliarii*.

The Seal of the Realm depicts Saint Erik, Sweden's patron saint, and a shield with three crowns. The seal was in use between 1439 and 1520 and, during long periods when the Swedish throne was vacant, it was used to legitimate the decisions of the Council.

- The Council has been regarded by some as descended from the *hird*, the group of men close to the Germanic kings. A Viking chieftain usually had such a group, which comprised his private guard. Its members were formally initiated and were required to swear an oath of loyalty to the chieftain or King. In return they were granted some influence or fiefs in the form of land.

- Others have regarded the Council as having arisen when a number of locally powerful, independent estate owners banded together and forced the King to share decision-making power, especially regarding the size of the tax levies.
- A third view is that the King's need for support was decisive for the development of the Council. The King needed to be surrounded by people who could shoulder the responsibility for financing horses and equipment. In return they received certain privileges, including freedom from taxation.

In the Skänninge Edict of 1284 Magnus Ladulås set down the rules to be followed when the King convened a *parlamentum*. If a person had not been summoned, he should be present only with good cause and at his own expense. The size of each person's retinue was also specified. Duke Bengt of Finland was allowed forty horses, the bishops thirty horses each and the other members of the Council twelve horses, while the knights, squires and canons were allowed four horses and all other persons two. It is apparent that the Council had established a position which the King had to take into account and that he was apprehensive about the possibility of being "voted down" by nobles who were too strong.

The Council strengthened its position during the fourteenth century, when the kings were involved in incessant kinship feuds. During long periods the Council actually ruled Sweden. At the election of Magnus Eriksson as King in 1319, the Council acted as a Council of the Realm and claimed to represent the entire nation. In the Royal Code of 1335, which is part of Magnus Eriksson's Law of the Land, it was declared that the King had to appoint twelve secular councilors plus as many bishops and priests as were needed. The Council came to form the core of the medieval meetings of the lords. On these occasions the King or the Council took the initiative in calling representatives of the burghers and the peasants to the meetings. Such meetings were first held during the reign of Magnus Ladulås and continued later, more or less regularly, throughout the Middle Ages.

Magnus Ladulås in a mural from the 1440s in Riddarholmen Church in Stockholm. Magnus is buried in the church, as are many Swedish kings who followed.

## The Ting

During the Middle Ages a system developed for electing the King and for appointing the Council of the Realm and the representatives to the meetings of the lords. The King needed help in equipping the army and supporting his own court. But he also needed to build another kind of power base.

After the King was elected at Mora Meadow, he traveled around the country and was hailed by the various *tings* (local courts or

assemblies). These organs, the provincial ting and the ting in the hundred (the basic administrative and legal district), have been traditionally regarded as one of the origins of the Swedish Riksdag. There are many accounts, often romanticized, of how freemen gathered at the site of the ting and made decisions on matters of common concern. They sometimes even reprimanded the chieftain or King.

One of the most renowned and oft-cited speeches in Swedish history is reputed to have been given by Torgny, lawman at the Uppsala ting in the beginning of the eleventh century. The speech is known from a text which was first written down two hundred years later by Snorre Sturlasson, an Icelandic scald whose poems eventually were read throughout the Nordic countries. It probably reveals more about the relationship between the King and the peasantry in the thirteenth century than in the eleventh. No one knows whether the speech was actually delivered or whether it was a product of Snorre Sturlasson's fantasy. However, that is not to say that the document lacks interest. Torgny is supposed to have appealed directly to King Olof Skötkonung:

> It is now our will, we peasants, that you should make peace with Norway's King Olav Digre and marry off your daughter Ingegerd to him. If you then wish to win back under your rule the kingdoms which your kin and ancestors have possessed in the east, we will all support you in that enterprise. But if you do not heed what we say, then we will attack you and kill you and will tolerate neither discord nor violations of the law.

Torgny the Lawman presented himself as a peasant and as a representative of other peasants. In Swedish history he has become a symbol of the "power of the people" resisting the "power of the Crown." However, not even in the poem is Torgny portrayed as an ordinary peasant. He was a lawman and therefore one of the leading men in Uppland, the province which was most important to the King. He represented the powerful men of the province.

Torgny the Lawman's speech to King Olof Skötkonung at the ting in Uppsala. Axel Törneman selected this scene as a motif for one of his murals in the building erected for the Riksdag in 1904.

But, he spoke well, at least in Snorre's version, and he represented those who wanted to assert their power alongside that of the King.

It is uncertain what authority the ting actually had. It varied at different times and in the different provinces. During the pre-Christian era the ting may have had religious responsibilities, but by the beginning of the Middle Ages, it was above all a court. The decisions which were reached at the ting were often of significance for other courts; they provided precedents.

The ting was the highest instance in the province, but its role in development toward national representation should not be exaggerated. It had no interest in anything outside its own province, and, when the ting met with the King, it was in its capacity of spokesman for its own area. The ting also served as a place for negotiations between the King and the people in a defined region.

## Markets and Fairs

During the Middle Ages markets and fairs were of utmost importance for trade. Fairs were held regularly, some of them in conjunction with religious holidays, and were regulated by law. Enköping, Skänninge, Strängnäs, Uppsala, Vadstena and Västerås were well-known market towns. Markets and fairs were the year's high points for people during the Middle Ages.

Markets were announced according to set rules, and they were formally opened with a ceremony at the town hall. In some towns there were permanent stands that were rented by local officials. Both goods from the local area (for example, the Västerås market sold iron from the neighboring mining regions of Västmanland and Dalarna) and goods imported from foreign lands were sold at the markets.

Various people visited markets, which were not limited to the province in the same way as the ting. The King and the members

In the Middle Ages fairs were often held in winter. Snow and ice-covered waterways made it easy to transport goods over great distances. The frozen lakes also offered excellent meeting places. This illustration is from Olaus Magnus.

of the Council were often present at markets and could thus spread their own propaganda, but they could also get a feeling for the prevailing mood of the populace. There is evidence from as early as the mid-thirteenth century that the King and the Council met at markets and made decisions there. These decisions could be announced directly to the visitors, who then passed the news along. Markets served as important centers for the dispersion of news and information.

During the latter part of the Middle Ages a form of dialogue between the King and the people developed at the markets. Royal elections could also be confirmed on these occasions.

Markets, however, could also be dangerous to those in power. Discontent could be expressed in various forms there; rebels could conspire against the King, the Council or the sheriff. During his reign Gustav Vasa made several attempts to forbid markets. These attempts failed, however, as the markets were too important to the economic life of the country.

Beer was a much appreciated drink during the Middle Ages. This fifteenth century mural shows a man rolling a barrel of beer. Tensta Church in the province of Uppland.

Markets thus functioned as meeting places for people from different regions and from various social groups. They therefore were of greater significance for the development of the Riksdag than was the ting. Negotiations between the King and the people became more regulated. They took place on the first day of the market in the square in front of the town hall. Either the monarch himself or one of his official representatives presided. If a representative was sent, he read a document at the beginning of the discussions.

There was no formal division into Estates during these debates. The participants formed a single large assembly, although the members of the Council had special positions.

The negotiations at the market were important both to the ruler and to the people. It was necessary to use the right arguments and to find the right responses. Sometimes special means were adopted to win over those gathered. At the assembly in Arboga in 1471, when Sten Sture the Elder was to be hailed as regent, he supposedly treated the peasants to beer. Olaus Petri related the following in his Swedish Chronicle:

And there were twelve barrels of German beer opened for the peasants. Therefore they voted as he requested.

There are those who question whether beer was actually given to the peasants. Olaus Petri wrote his story sixty years after the event, and it may have been part of the criticism of Sten Sture which is found in other parts of the chronicle. But documentation from other meetings also indicates that beer was sometimes provided for the peasants and the burghers to gain their support.

In other cases the King had to promise the peasants hops or salt. In the struggles between the Danish King Kristian II and the

The clothing of medieval times is visible in church paintings, as here in Tensta Church. The painting is from the fifteenth century.

Swedish King Gustav Vasa salt played an important role as a weapon in the negotiations. The one who could supply the peasants with salt gained their favor.

Rulers were also said to have used other means. Members of the king's retinue, sheriffs or military men might dress up as peasants. These camouflaged king's men mixed with the crowds in front of the King and loudly voiced their agreement. The question is how often this actually occurred. Such stories may be wandering tales or anecdotes spread for propaganda purposes. Although many peasants attended a market and not all knew one another, they most certainly would have recognized "infiltrators." Yet the information says a great deal about the importance of the people at the markets; it was essential to the ruler to have the public on his side.

Until the end of the sixteenth century the meetings at the markets were very informal. Anyone could express his opinion by raising his hand or not. It is hard to imagine that there were any real discussions. Rather, there are a number of examples where public action was limited to declaring loyalty to the King.

## The Path to a Riksdag

Various kinds of gatherings where the King secured support for his decisions or could legitimate his power have been regarded as forerunners of the Riksdag. During the course of the years many such assemblies have come to be considered the "birth" of the Riksdag or, at least, as important stages in the history of popular representation in Sweden.

In 1319, when Magnus Eriksson was elected King at Mora Meadow, the persons representing the King, who was three years old at the time, appealed to all free groups. Instead of turning to the provinces as before, they turned to *communitas*, the community. The representatives of the King promised to accept its privileges and not levy new taxes without its consent. The question is then who was included in *communitas*. Although representatives of the peasantry were present at Mora Meadow, they probably did not actively participate in the decision-making process.

The fourteenth century Chronicle of Duke Erik shows how clear roles were assigned to each group at the meeting. The lords, the nobility, were praised for their loyalty to the dead King in electing a kinsman as successor, while the peasants were given the task of spreading the news of the election of the King when they returned home.

In 1359 a famous open letter was issued in Lund by Magnus Eriksson. He requested a national assembly in Kalmar "for the maintenance of the Crown, the realm and all men of Sweden," and called representatives of the various Estates to the meeting: "Four men from each district, selected men for each market town, two

canons from each cathedral, and all the rest of our men and those of the realm."

History was long dominated by the interpretation that the meeting actually took place, and that it was a riksdag. A critical look shows that the evidence is weak. Nor is it known whether the peasantry was intended to take part in any way other than as observers or disseminators of information. However, the summons does indicate that the idea of representation by Estates did exist at that time.

The 1435 Arboga Meeting was discussed in the preceding chapter in connection with the account of the quincentennial celebration of the Riksdag. The historian Sven Tunberg then assured the assembled guests that the meeting in 1435 really was a riksdag. One of Sweden's most well-known historians, Erik Gustaf Geijer (1783–1847), as did many who followed after, shared the same conviction. They based their interpretation on the fact that the invitation to the meeting was addressed to "the community."

Later scholars, however, have cited reasons for not considering the Arboga Meeting a riksdag. The nobility at that time represented "the community." Although burghers and peasants were present at the meeting, it did not mean that they were allowed to participate in making decisions. Furthermore, the time that elapsed between the summons and the actual meeting was so short that it was practically impossible for representatives to come other than those who lived in the province of Östergötland, the mining district of Bergslagen and the valley around Lake Mälaren.

One copy of King Magnus' summons to a meeting in Kalmar in 1359 has been preserved. We know nothing beyond what is found in the document, not even whether the meeting actually took place.

1464 has also been suggested as the year when the first Swedish Riksdag was held. Karl Knutsson was hailed as King by a large and varied public at the main square (*Stortorget*) in Stockholm, but the participants in that meeting scarcely represented the entire country or all groups of importance. Even less may they be said to have acted independently.

During the 1460s the encounters between the King and the people became more complex. This development was associated with political unrest and the struggles over the post of regent. An underlying cause was the economic progress of the men in Bergslagen and of the artisans and merchants in Stockholm. Iron mining grew, and Stockholm became more prominent as a trade center.

Uncertainty still remains as to whether the delegates to these assemblies could be considered representatives of "all social groups regarded as free." The men who met during this period of unrest belonged primarily to the host, the armed retinue of the king. Local representation became unbalanced, and the valley around Lake Mälaren and the Bergslagen–Dalarna area were overrepresented. The forms of negotiation were simple, and one question was totally dominant: who should rule the kingdom?

Throughout the Middle Ages more regulated popular representation gradually developed. At the end of the fifteenth century and the beginning of the sixteenth rival groups of nobles tended increasingly to seek support from statements of the peasants and the burghers.

In November 1517 a national assembly in Stockholm dealt with the conflict between Sten Sture the Younger, who was regent, and Archbishop Gustav Trolle, who not only represented the Church but also the members of the ancient nobility in the Council who

The Stures dominated Swedish politics for half a century. Sten Sture the Younger, who was a member of the noble family Natt och Dag, is seen here on an altarpiece from 1516, which he commissioned in Antwerp and donated to Västerås Cathedral.

Peasants equipped with crossbows, bows, spears and swords. According to provincial law each man who had reached majority was required to maintain weapons that could be used for defense. The illustration is from Olaus Magnus.

had long dominated Sweden. Sten Sture presented his views to the Council of the Realm, "the privileged classes, merchants, men from Bergslagen and Dalarna and other commoners," and he received approval for the continued siege of the Archbishop's seat at Almarestäket near Stockholm.

Was there any kind of popular representation worth calling a riksdag during the Middle Ages? We have seen how different assemblies met to provide the regent with a mandate and to make important decisions. Summons were issued to and heeded by representatives of various social groups. The sovereign met the people at the election of kings, the meetings of the lords, the ting in the provinces and in the hundreds, and at the markets.

The assemblies of the Middle Ages show that the monarchs could not rule without some form of support from their subjects. In important questions concerning who should rule the country and how large taxes should be, as in questions of war and peace, various groups of people could make their voices heard. This is perhaps more important than the question of whether there was a riksdag which fits a formal definition. What is essential is that Sweden has a long tradition of assemblies with representation from various groups and various regions.

Nor should the importance of the Church be forgotten. Church leaders participated in the meetings of the lords and other assemblies. They also held their own meetings, which played an important role in events.

Armed uprisings were also a power factor during the Late Middle Ages. Following the example of Dalarna, peasant armies from various parts of the country joined forces with or were mobilized by groups of powerful men. These peasant bands have certainly been romanticized, even during the Middle Ages. Yet it is evident that the "tradition of rebellions" must be regarded as a power outside the representative assemblies. Sometimes an uprising supported the decision of an assembly; at other times it was the voice of the opposition.

## Gustav Vasa and the Riksdag

In 1518 Sten Sture the Younger appeared to be on his way to winning the war he was waging against the King of the Nordic Union, Kristian II, representatives of the Church and part of the Council. Kristian, however, mobilized a strong army and attacked Sweden. In a battle on the ice of Lake Åsunden in the province of Västergötland in 1520 Sten Sture was wounded so severely that he later perished during the sleigh journey across Lake Mälaren. Like Engelbrekt, he became a hero in historical writings, and the chronicles glorified his short but illustrious reign. One thing is certain: his demise left a vacuum. Following his death the peasants, the men from Bergslagen and the nobles who had supported Sten Sture in his struggle against the Archbishop and the Council were without a leader.

Kristian II has been called Kristian the Tyrant in Swedish history. He cooperated not only with the Church, but also with members of the Swedish Council who shared his interests. These nobles had estates in various Nordic countries. They may have supported him because it gave them greater power and freedom to have a King whose seat was located in distant Copenhagen, rather than in the center of the kingdom.

The battle for Sweden was won by Kristian II, who in November 1520 was crowned by Archbishop Gustav Trolle. Prior to the coronation the new King promised general amnesty; no one would be punished for crimes committed previously. Yet immedi-

The death of Sten Sture the Younger in 1520 on the ice of Lake Mälaren was portrayed in 1880 by Carl Gustaf Hellqvist in one of the country's most well-known historical paintings. The painting reflects the national romanticism of the nineteenth century and depicts the Stures as fighting for national freedom against foreign sovereignty.

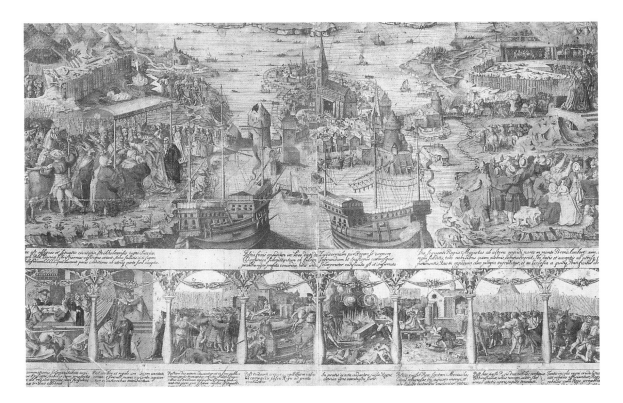

ately following the coronation ceremonies the event occurred which would go down in history as the Stockholm Bloodbath. By declaring Sten Sture and his followers "heretics" (claiming they had broken ecclesiastical law), Kristian did not need to abide by the declared amnesty. Eighty-three persons who had supported Sten Sture were beheaded, including both secular and ecclesiastical notables.

Thus one might believe that Kristian and the Nordic Union had finally won the struggle. With the victory of the King and the old Council, it might also be assumed that the representative assemblies which had played an important role during the reign of the Stures would no longer have the same significance.

The development, however, was not what might be expected. Gustav Eriksson Vasa, who belonged to one of the leading noble families and who was close to the Stures, entered the political scene. He had fled Danish captivity, managed to escape the Stockholm Bloodbath, and was eventually able to seize power with the help of the instruments which had been developed during the fifteenth and the beginning of the sixteenth centuries: bands of peasants and various representative assemblies.

What Gustav Vasa actually did when he returned to Sweden is less well-known. As King, however, he was eager to spread thrilling tales which gave prominence to his popularity. Support from the men of Dalarna and other groups was emphasized, as was the heroic struggle against the Danish "invader."

The Stockholm Bloodbath is shown here on a copper engraving which was a copy of a woodcut commissioned by Gustav Vasa in Antwerp in 1524. It gives an idea of how the King wanted the events to be interpreted. The picture above shows King Kristian's entry into Stockholm. The series below portrays the reception of the Swedish nobles at the coronation banquet, the accusation and condemnation of the guests as heretics, the disposal of their heads in barrels and, finally, the bodies being dragged away to be burned.

This detail from a herald's cope shows a sheaf, the crest of the Vasa dynasty.

Carl Larsson's monumental painting of Gustav Vasa's entry into the Swedish capital has decorated the stairwell in the National Art Gallery in Stockholm since 1907.

Gustav Vasa skillfully utilized the dissatisfaction with Kristian II. He received help from peasant armies and economic support from Lübeck, which preferred Gustav Vasa to Kristian II as King of Sweden. In the domestic power struggle not only were weapons important; Gustav Vasa also used the assemblies, the markets and the tings. In the spring of 1523 a meeting of the lords was assembled in Strängnäs at which, on June 6, Gustav Vasa was elected King according to the old regulations of the Royal Code. At midsummer the same year he rode into Stockholm "through the southern gate."

The royal election did not mean the end of the foreign and domestic conflicts, however. Gustav Vasa met with opposition when he attempted to fortify his kingdom. His ambition was to convert Sweden into what that age considered a "modern" nation state with strong central power and with a military organization loyal to the King.

To a greater extent than earlier the Church formed a state within the state. It was a significant economic and political power factor, owner of more than one fifth of the country's land, and its bishops set the tone in the Council.

Various secular groups of powerful men watched with fear as the power of the Vasa family increased at their own expense. In different parts of the country other groups were dissatisfied with the actions of the King. The old tradition of rebellions survived, and Gustav Vasa had to accept the fact that the men from Dalarna who once helped him gain power turned against him.

In 1527 Gustav Vasa convened a meeting in Västerås, a meeting which history would later call the Reformation Riksdag. The term *riksdag* was not yet used, but to a greater extent than earlier this assembly met the criteria for a true riksdag.

## Gustav Vasa before the Riksdag in Västerås in 1527

GUSTAV VASA'S ORATION before the Riksdag in Västerås in 1527 was long one of the most frequently cited Swedish speeches. It is found in Peder Swart's Chronicle, which was compiled toward the end of the King's life with the obvious goal of glorifying his deeds and legitimating his position as King.

Peder Swart, who wrote at the behest of the King, related how the bishops intrigued against the King and how they had amassed large fortunes which they refused to relinquish. Bishop Brask from the town of Linköping informed the King that the bishops did not need to obey him and that they could not give away property which legally belonged to them. Bishop Brask was supported by one of the most powerful nobles, Ture Jönsson Three Roses. This caused the King to polemicize:

> If this is so, I have no desire to be your King. I had expected another answer of you. I should not now be surprised that the people are wild and show their disobedience, vexation and wrath, as I assume that they have fine instigators. If it does not rain, they blame me; if the sun does not shine, it is the same; if there are difficult years, hunger, pestilence or whatever it may be, then I must bear the blame, as if they did not know that I am human and not God.
>
> That is the thanks that I, with such great distress and concern in my heart, receive for acquiring so much grain for this country, rye and malt from foreign lands, so that this poor Swedish folk does not suffer the misery of wretchedly starving to death. But may I work for your welfare to the best of my ability, in spiritual and worldly affairs, I have nothing more to await in payment than that you would gladly see an axe put to my head, but of which you do not want to hold the handle.
>
> Such payment and such distress I could well do without, just as you could. And all that I must bear, more work and difficulties than any of you could know or understand, both in domestic and foreign affairs, so that I may be called your head.
>
> It is now your will to place both monks and priests and all creatures of the Pope over my head, although we have little to do with his high bishops and others. All in all, it is your will to judge me and to criticize me. And yet you have crowned me here your King. But who can be your King under such conditions? I believe that the most miserable creature in Hell would not wish to be that, let alone any person.
>
> So now you clearly know that I do not wish to be your head and your King. I will relinquish my post and be satisfied that you crown any good man you choose. If you are able to get a person who in every measure and always is able to please you, I would be happy to see it. Be prepared to buy my way out of the country and to first compensate me fairly for every inch of land that I own, and for what I have spent on the realm from my own means. Then I promise you that I will leave the realm, and never again return to this, my depraved and ungrateful fatherland.

The young Gustav Vasa shown speaking to the people of the province of Dalarna. The statue, made by Anders Zorn, was unveiled on the church grounds in Mora in 1903.

The Gripsholm Suite, completed during the 1540s, consisted of a number of paintings on canvas which are known from the watercolor copies made in the eighteenth century. The suite has been interpreted as an allegorical presentation of certain events during the reign of Gustav Vasa. For example, the woman who is being taken before the King in the pictures is supposed to symbolize the subjugation of the Catholic Church.

- The summons had been sent out in plenty of time, and representation was broad: 16 members of the Council and 130 "free-born nobles" participated; some twenty towns and seven areas of Bergslagen were represented; and 105 peasants were present from all regions in the realm except Finland.
- The meeting was inaugurated with an "oration," a political speech, where the state of the nation was painted in colorful terms. The assembly learned of the poor conditions that existed. The country's economy was in disarray, while the Church thrived. On top of all that, the King threatened to resign.
- After negotiations among the representatives of the Nobility, the Burghers and the Peasantry, replies were given to the oration. These responses encouraged the King to move against the Church and the monasteries. The Nobility argued that it should regain the property which had been donated to the Church and the monasteries during the last generations.
- The meeting decided that a number of measures should be taken against the Church. The decisions were spread across the country by decrees which were read aloud wherever people assembled.

The meeting in Västerås had far-reaching consequences. The Catholic Church in Sweden was replaced by a Lutheran State Church. Popular representation also gained a totally different role. After discussions representatives of three Estates, the Nobility, the Burghers and the Peasantry, were allowed to voice their opinions about the King's proposals.

The "Riksdag" in Västerås was the result of royal, rather than popular, initiative, and Gustav Vasa was prepared to pay at least some of those who heeded the call to the meeting. The nobles who had been ordered to bring an armed retinue received special compensation. Even the peasant representatives received payments. On the other hand, the burghers in the various towns and cities probably had to pay the journeys and costs for their representatives.

The King needed support from a strong assembly to break the power of the Church in Sweden. It was essential to him that the Västerås meeting observed certain formalities, and he therefore adopted the pattern of working parliaments in Europe. Swedish representation, however, deviated in one way: the peasants were included. The King also understood that it was necessary to continue this tradition which had developed during the preceding centuries; the peasantry was a power factor which was not to be underestimated.

REX GVSTAVS WLTVQVE H
ROSQVE TEREBAT
IX IMPERIO SVECIA MAGNA
1542

# CHAPTER 3

# The Riksdag during the Vasa Era
## – a Royal Tool

S WEDEN became a nation state and an hereditary monarchy on a European model during the reign of Gustav Vasa. It was the end of a process which started in the beginning of the Middle Ages. Yet, it was far from clear that Gustav Vasa would succeed where other capable men had failed.

Nor was it given that Sweden would become a state with the borders which it acquired in the sixteenth century. One alternative was a union of Denmark, Norway and the combined Sweden–Finland. Such a union would have been a geographically well-defined area and a strong economic competitor with the northern European trade alliance, the Hanseatic League. It would also have been advantageous for many economically and politically powerful individuals; the nobility and the Church had interests in several of the countries.

Instead a strong monarchy developed, while the ecclesiastical nobility disappeared and the secular nobility was weakened. Administration became centered around the King, and the Council's position became less independent than before. The King appointed a large number of sheriffs who not only assumed the responsibilities of their predecessors, but also took over functions which had earlier been carried out by noblemen and the Church.

Kalmar Castle has its origins in a thirteenth century fortress. As Sweden became a state under the Vasa kings, the castle attained its present appearance with its ramparts and round cannon towers.

*On the opposite page:* The Riksdag became an important instrument for Gustav Vasa in his attempt to consolidate his own position of power and give stability to the Swedish nation state. This portrait of the King is considered a copy of an original from 1542 by the German artist Jakob Binck.

Laurentius Andreae's notes in preparation for a meeting between Gustav Vasa and the Council of the Realm in 1524. Laurentius Andreae was the King's secretary and his most important adviser at the time of the Reformation.

Gustav Vasa
on a *daler* from 1534.

## Gustav Vasa and the People

The shift to Protestantism, which was proclaimed by the meeting in Västerås in 1527, did not mean the end of internal struggles. Until his death in 1560 Gustav Vasa cleverly and ruthlessly beat back the blocs which opposed the central power he represented. He subdued the men from Dalarna, who had once helped him seize power, and he revoked the special role which the burghers of Stockholm had earlier played in governing the realm. The king's sheriffs became dominant in different parts of the country and effectively collected taxes. Local gatherings such as the tings and the markets became less important.

The development in Sweden during the reign of Gustav Vasa had its counterparts in other areas of Europe, although far from all countries were strongly centralized. One important reason for the success of Gustav Vasa was certainly his personality. He was the right man at the right time. As do most successful people, he also had good luck. Kristian II had killed most of his potential opponents in the Stockholm Bloodbath, and both the Hanseatic League and the Danish King – major rivals – struggled with domestic and foreign problems.

If Gustav Vasa had lived today, he would have been called a good politician. He was continually faced with large and difficult problems but managed to solve them. He brought order into state finances and was supported by soldiers who became completely dependent on him. He was also able to find the backing for his decisions among the powerful, and he knew that it was important to make his opinions known to the people.

The King often spoke directly to the populace at markets and other gatherings, but he also wrote letters which were read by his sheriffs and by the clergy wherever people assembled. Gustav Vasa pointed out the advantages of the changes which he had made. Above all, he stressed the importance of peace, which now reigned in the country. He claimed the credit for having freed Sweden both from the Danes and from the Hanseatic League, the Germans. Although he had been dependent on the Hanseatic League at the beginning of his rule, he later opposed the trade alliance both militarily and economically.

During Gustav Vasa's first twenty years on the throne, radical changes occurred in almost all sectors. Sweden was "modernized"; it was transformed from a decentralized society into a country with a centralized power which could deal with both domestic and foreign enemies. The transformation of the Church was the most obvious. The old Roman Catholic bishops and priests fled the country. The power once possessed by the churches and monas-

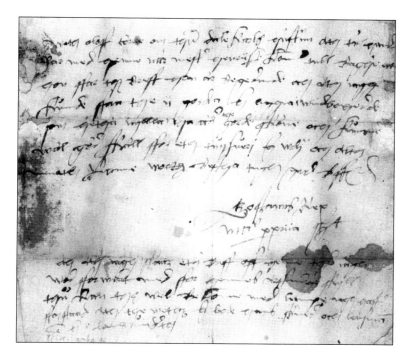

A letter from Gustav Vasa to the sheriff Olof Törne concerning the purchase of a couple of farms. The King had a comprehensive correspondence, but this is one of the few letters in the King's own hand which have been preserved. It was found in an attic by a schoolboy in the 1880s.

teries disappeared. This had a number of negative effects: opportunities for international contacts declined, as did good medical care and quality education. For Gustav Vasa these defects were counterbalanced by the transfer of church property to the state, which gave good income, and by the limitation of the power of the bishops.

The reforms under the first Vasa King were opposed by those for whom the new political order meant economic and political losses. Gustav Vasa was viewed by these forces as a despot who had seized power high-handedly and ruled the country as if it were his own property. A number of rebellions broke out. Most renowned is the Dacke Rebellion, 1542–1543. Nils Dacke was a local peasant leader from the province of Småland who revolted against central power and thus followed in the footsteps of Engelbrekt and others. He had the support not only of the peasants, but also of a number of dissatisfied groups of clergymen and nobles. The people of Småland could not tolerate the King's policy, which reduced their power, gave them higher taxes and obstructed their trade with the neighboring Danish provinces. Dacke accused the King of abolishing and forbidding everything that was "old and ancient."

Dacke is probably the rebel in Swedish history who most powerfully and effectively challenged the central power personified by the King and his civil servants. The outcome of the rebellion was far from obvious. At times Gustav Vasa himself was deeply discouraged. However, in the end he emerged victorious and consolidated his power. The Estates came to play an important role in this process.

In his sixteenth century Swedish chronicle the vicar Joen Klint tells about the death of Nils Dacke, and in the margin he has drawn a picture of Dacke's head set on a "tall enough tree stump."

## Sweden Becomes an Hereditary Monarchy

Erik XIV had the Swedish regalia made for his coronation: the crown, the orb, the scepter and the key. It was important to him to consolidate the hereditary monarchy through magnificent ceremonies.

Erik XIV's medal in gilded silver from about 1560.

In 1544 the Estates met for the first time in fifteen years. The summons to the meeting in Västerås was issued to the members of the Council, the nobility and representatives of the towns and cities and the hundreds. Representatives of the reformed church also received the summons, but the men of the cloth played a different role than they had earlier. The bishops and the clergymen were no longer the owners of large landed estates or members of the Council. They were subordinate to royal power and were granted a position as a special Estate beneath the Nobility and alongside the Burghers and the Peasantry.

The national assembly was opened with an oration. In this speech, delivered in the name of the Council, the demand was made that Sweden should become an hereditary monarchy and that Gustav Vasa's oldest son, Erik, should inherit the throne. Demands were also made for the King's right to levy new taxes. The response from the Estates was positive, and at the meeting in Strängnäs in the winter of 1547, the hereditary monarchy was acknowledged. Erik's brothers were granted titles: Johan became Duke of Finland; Karl, Duke of Södermanland, Närke and Värmland; and Magnus was made Duke of Östergötland and Dalsland.

Gustav Vasa strengthened his power, but he was not able to carry out any far-reaching reforms without the support of representatives of the different Estates. At the same time as Sweden became an hereditary monarchy, the King had to accept the Estates as a power factor. However, the King no longer had to pay the peasants for their costs and lodging in conjunction with the Riksdag. Instead the summons to the Riksdag included the admonition to bring sufficient food for a week.

Erik XIV was thus able to succeed his father on the throne in 1560 without any election being held. His more than eight years as King were characterized by political unrest, which, in turn, caused him to summon the Estates frequently. The reasons varied: the King needed the support of the Riksdag for levying taxes and for making decisions on war and peace; he discussed his marriage plans with the Estates; and he tried to gain their support in his struggles against his brothers Johan and Karl. The Estates also acted as a court on some occasions.

The new position of the Riksdag meant that it could participate in the decision-making process in a way not known in previous decades. It might be thought that the Estates, which thus became more involved in politics, would have been satisfied with their increased influence. This was hardly the case. One of the accusations made against Erik XIV when he was forced from the throne in 1568 was that he convened the Estates too often. Many regarded attending the Riksdag as a burden.

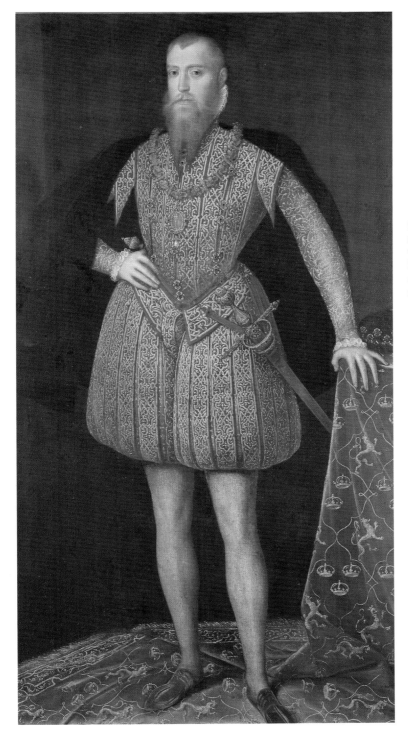

Steven van der Meulen painted this splendid portrait of Erik XIV which was sent to Queen Elizabeth of England. Erik XIV unsuccessfully courted the English Queen in the beginning of the 1560s.

In spite of the fact that the King had tried to gain support for his decisions at various meetings of the Estates, he was not able to retain his position. His psychological state was crucial. He was suspicious and insecure and at the same time felt the need to play the role of a Renaissance prince. He tried to create a court patterned after those on the continent. There was a great difference between him and his father, who had largely ruled the country like a wealthy farmer, the head of the national household directly in touch with his people.

## Gustav Vasa Bids the Estates Farewell

This was how the artist Johan Gustaf Sandberg imagined Gustav Vasa's farewell to the Estates when he painted his frescoes around the King's tomb in Uppsala Cathedral in the 1830s.

A FAMOUS SPEECH of Gustav Vasa is the one which he is said to have given before the Riksdag in 1560, the same year he died. It is probably a reconstruction based on material from Peder Swart. It is interesting, however, because it has influenced the view of Gustav Vasa held by later generations. From the middle of the nineteenth century and far into the twentieth, it was found in a common reader for the elementary school (*Läsebok för folkskolan*). The speech says more about the historical interpretation dominant at that time than about the actual situation when Gustav Vasa bid the Estates farewell.

When they [the Estates] were assembled, the King entered, followed by his sons. He walked up and sat on the throne. The three oldest sons stood one after another on his left side; the youngest, ten-year-old Karl was at his father's feet. Then the King spoke, as follows:

"I honor the power of God, who has in me elevated to Sweden's ancient throne, Sweden's ancient royal line from Magnus Ladulås and Karl Knutsson. Those among you, who are older, have undoubtedly learned how our dear fatherland has for many hundreds of years been subject to the misery and oppression of foreign gentlemen and kings, especially the harsh tyrant, King Kristian, and how God, through me, has freed us from that tyranny. Thus we, well-born or lowly, master or servant, old or young, should never forget this Godly help.

Who was I to expel such a powerful man, who not only reigned over three kingdoms, but was also allied to the Emperor and the mightiest princes? That I could not imagine, when I had to flee to the forest and the deserted mountains from the enemy's bloodthirsty sword. But God did His work and made me His subject on whom His almighty power should be bestowed; and may I compare myself with David, whom God transformed from a mere shepherd to King of his people."

Tears poured from his eyes here.

"I thank you, loyal subjects, that you have elevated me to royal heights and to progenitor of your royal house. No less I thank you for the loyalty and support, which you have shown me during my rule. That during this time God has allowed His pure and clear word to come, and that He has given His blessings to the realm, as it now appears, therefore we, goodmen and subjects, should all with the greatest thankfulness and humility give glory to God.

It is known to me that in the eyes of many I have been a harsh King. But a time shall come, when Sweden's children will wish to tear me up out of my grave, if it were in their power to do so. However, I must admit human weakness and frailty, as no one is perfect. Therefore I beg of you as loyal subjects, for the sake of Christ, to forgive and have understanding for any deficiencies of my government. The intention has always been to do what was best for the realm and its subjects. My gray hair and my wrinkled brow bear witness to the many dangers, horrors and worries I have borne during my forty-year reign.

I know that the Swedes are quick to agree, slower to examine. I can also predict that many restless souls will arise in the future. Therefore I pray and admonish you: keep close to the word of God, and abandon what is not in agreement. May you listen to your superiors, and be yourselves united. My time is soon at an end. There is no need to turn to the stars or other predictions. I feel the signs in my own body, that my time is soon come, and that I shall lay down at the feet of the Greatest King and account for the Swedish realm's heavenly but transient crown. Follow me then with your loyal prayers, and when I have closed my eyes, let me rest in peace."

Erik XIV also had other problems. He was defeated abroad, and there was popular discontent with many of the changes which had come about under his father. In addition, dukedoms had been given to Johan, Karl and Magnus. Magnus was sickly, but Johan and Karl were striving for independent power within their respective regions and became threats to the King.

## The Estates Show Their Power

Johan III was formally hailed as King by the Riksdag of 1569. This gathering has been variously referred to as a meeting of the lords and a riksdag, but it also had the character of the earlier royal elections. Negotiations were carried out with the many representatives of the Estates, and on the fourth day two gentlemen left to announce to those assembled at the Disting Market in Uppsala that the old King had been deposed and his younger brother Johan hailed as the new King. The repeal of a number of decisions made under Erik XIV was also announced.

A casting of Johan III's great seal from 1571. The King's motto: God our Protector.

The Estates supported Johan III, but they demanded something in return. The play for power was obvious. When Johan was crowned, he swore an oath in which he promised not to wage war without the consent of the Council and the Estates. Nor was he to summon foreign men and place them over nobles. At this Riksdag the nobility received its first charter of importance, in which its position as the first Estate was confirmed.

As his brother and his father before him, Johan was faced with numerous conflicts with foreign and domestic enemies, including his brother Karl. Money was essential. Johan was forced to plead his cause at markets and other gatherings and also convened the Riksdag in 1582 and 1587. The meeting places for the Estates were set, and a system of representation was worked out for the various Estates. The Riksdag acted as a cohesive unit, and also as four different assemblies which could individually report their decisions to the King.

- The Nobility probably met in the Royal Palace. It consisted of the aristocracy, the counts, barons and knights, and the gentry. In principle all members of the Nobility were required to attend.
- The Clergy met in the Great Church (*Storkyrkan*) in Stockholm. In addition to the bishops there were also other representatives for the various dioceses.
- The Burghers held their meetings in Stockholm's Town Hall. Their representatives were appointed from among the mayors and councils of the towns and cities of the realm.
- The Peasantry had no obvious location for its meetings. The Estate met, assembled by province, in various churches in the capital. Nor were the representatives selected by free elections.

Until 1834 the Clergy met in the Choir of the Souls in *Storkyrkan* in Stockholm while the Riksdag was in session. The choir was rebuilt in the 1650s, when it received its present appearance.

The room where Erik XIV was confined in Gripsholm Castle in the beginning of the 1570s after he was deposed. He was imprisoned in several different castles after the decision of the Riksdag that he should be held "incarcerated, but in proper and princely custody."

A soldier drawn by Erik XIV in the margin of a book during his imprisonment in Örbyhus Castle. He died there in 1577.

The king's sheriffs in the different provinces were responsible for insuring that the three lower Estates attended the Riksdag. It is difficult to say how representative the Estates were. The sheriffs certainly had an interest in seeing that those who attended the Riksdag were not too critical, but the participants also had to be of acceptable rank in the groups to which they belonged.

In addition to the meetings of the Estates during the reign of Johan III a number of gatherings took place where the King made appeals for his views and announced his decisions, which concerned conditions in the Church and various domestic and foreign problems. In contrast to his brother, Duke Karl, the King took a conciliatory stance in regard to Catholicism. He also had a son, Sigismund, who was Catholic and who was elected King of Poland in 1587. The religious problem came to a head after the death of Johan III in 1592.

Stockholm during the time of Johan III on an engraving by Franz Hogenberg. Among other things we can see the fortifications around the city and the pilings which formed the defense on the side facing the sea.

Sigismund swearing the King's oath at the coronation Riksdag in Uppsala Castle in 1594. The oath was administered by Erik Sparre, one of the leading Swedish noblemen and a diligent fighter for the limitation of the King's power.

The Estates reacted forcefully when faced with the coronation of Sigismund in 1594. The Church was uneasy about having a King who was a Roman Catholic. A large number of clergymen gathered at a church meeting in Uppsala in 1593 and declared the primacy of the Evangelical Lutheran faith. The changes which Johan III had made during his reconciliation with Catholicism were abolished.

It was not only the Clergy that wanted concessions before the coronation, and Sigismund soon understood that there was no room for an "absolute" monarchy. The Estates demanded "a mild and Christian rule according to the laws of the land." The King tried to strengthen his position but met with opposition which was spearheaded by his uncle, Duke Karl. The Riksdag played an important role in the struggle for royal power which took place between Sigismund and Karl. Once again this body alone could legitimate a new king.

The King had to return to Poland and leave Duke Karl and the Council to exercise power in Sweden. However, he tried to establish a number of restrictions; for example, the Riksdag was not to be summoned in his absence. This illustrates a consciousness of the importance of the Riksdag at the time. The Riksdag could play a decisive role in fundamental questions, and Sigismund understood that it could be used against him.

The King had reason to be pessimistic. As soon as he had left, various power blocs in Sweden began to conspire against him. The Riksdag which met in Söderköping in 1595 was summoned contrary to the King's instructions and with considerable skepticism on the part of the Nobility. It brought to the fore clear conflicts between the Nobility and Duke Karl. Faced with this situation the Duke, just as he did later, sought support from the other Estates,

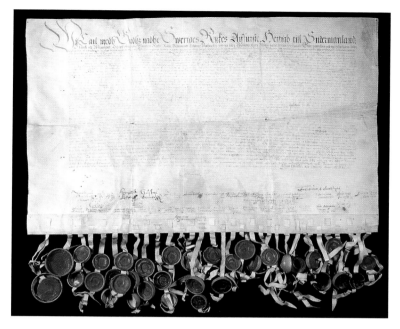

The edict of the church meeting in Uppsala in 1593 with seals from 47 of the country's highest-ranking gentlemen and bishops. The proclamation was made in opposition to the King, and it was therefore copied and distributed throughout the kingdom in order to be approved by as many of the country's noblemen and clergy, towns and hundreds as possible.

especially from the Peasantry. He was a skilled agitator and criticized the King and the Nobility at markets and other gatherings.

Karl also summoned a Riksdag in Arboga in 1597, where only one member of the Council was present. One of the participants in the meeting, who is not known by name, but who was probably a clergyman, kept a journal which contained the following observation:

> February 17 we arrived at Arboga. On February 20 between nine and ten o'clock the Prince [Duke Karl] had the drums roll, so that all the members of the Riksdag would assemble in the town church between one and two and there let their names be noted. This was done by the secretary Mickel Olofsson and the other secretaries, in the presence of some of the members of the Prince's court, but no other nobility had come to Arboga. Only Count Axel was there from the Council.

– – –

Östergötland's copy of the proclamation from the Riksdag of Söderköping in 1595. Because the Riksdag was held against the King's instructions, it was important that as many parts of the country as possible supported and placed a seal of approval on the Riksdag's decision.

On February 22 between eleven and twelve o'clock the Prince appeared on the rampart, which was built by the stone house on the main square. The Prince was together with Count Axel and some servants. The Archbishop and the other bishops, with the exception of the bishop of Åbo, were also there. The Prince spoke to the people and summarized what he wanted to say in seven points.

These points dealt with some important current questions: religion and what stand should be taken in regard to the King in Poland and to the Constable of the Realm (*riksmarsken*) Claes Fleming, who supported the King and openly opposed the Duke. But they also dealt with ordinary items, such as road and stage fees. Furthermore, the notes in the journal tell how the Estates, individually and together, discussed the various points, how they responded to the Duke, and how he, in turn, replied.

Karl negotiated with the Estates and tried both to scare and to appease them. On one occasion two selected peasants called on the Duke, and later one of them talked to the people. Thereafter came Karl:

> The Prince said: Will you support me? The peasants replied yes, yes, yes, and raised their hands. The Duke said thereafter: Because you, my good men, wait here for my sake, I'll give you a food allowance, which will last until tomorrow. And he showed them the way to the treasurer, who gave each of them 6 *öre*.

The meetings at this Riksdag, as at the others which Duke Karl (who eventually became Karl IX) summoned, took different forms. The Duke spoke to the people as at the markets, but he also negotiated with the Estates, and proposals and counterproposals were made. The Estates held discussions both within each Estate and collectively. A decision was also reached at this time that some of the Duke's opponents would be tried. Part of the Riksdag members formed a court and judged the accused.

Duke Karl actively tried to use the Riksdag, particularly the Peasantry, in his struggle with the nobility and the King. At a meeting where a nobleman contradicted him, Duke Karl said: "You don't know what you are talking about, you and the likes of you." It was said that the public in the hall laughed and called out: "Did you get an answer?"

At the Riksdag in Linköping in 1600 four leading noblemen were accused of "perjury, slander and high treason." An "extraordinary court of the Estates" convened with 155 members, and Karl acted as prosecutor. It was a summary political trial. In spite of appeals from their families, who were allowed to be with the accused up to the last minute, the prisoners were ordered beheaded. This event has gone down in history as the Linköping Bloodbath.

With the Linköping Bloodbath and other liquidations Karl had gotten rid of the opposition within the nobility and was feared by those who remained. Eventually he was able to assume the title of

According to tradition, this was the sword used to behead four Council members, Gustaf and Sten Banér, Ture Bielke and Erik Sparre, in the market square in the town of Linköping in March 1600. Some of the most important opponents of strong royal power were thus eliminated.

King and wage successful struggles both within and outside the country. He had a number of foreign enemies to the east and south: Russia, Poland and Denmark. The wars he fought meant more taxes, and that made him at least partly dependent on the Riksdag, which could demand something in return for supporting the ruler.

## The King and the Riksdag – Mutual Dependence

The strong monarchy which developed in Sweden during the sixteenth century in spite of a number of domestic struggles, did not prevent the Riksdag from remaining an important instrument of power. This is unusual, when comparisons are made with other countries. In Germany, Spain and France the monarchs became strong, as the representative bodies lost ground. After 1536 no parliamentary meeting was summoned in Denmark until the beginning of the seventeenth century.

Sweden was one of the few countries during this era which were able to retain a powerful parliament at the same time that royal power was not weakened. There were well-organized, economically powerful groups both in the towns and cities and in the countryside which were accustomed to having influence. And the monarch needed the Riksdag, above all, for economic reasons; the Riksdag retained the power to tax.

The Riksdag did not develop because of deeply rooted popular demand. It was common for the Estates to complain about being summoned too often. Instead popular representation was an instrument of royal power in its struggle against the nobility. This shows that it actually had power; otherwise it would have been of no help to the King. The peasants representing the provinces and the hundreds were important, as were the burghers from the various commercial towns. Together with the clergy they were powerful elements from whom the King could gain support.

However, changes occurred continually. The Riksdag changed its character in the same way as the individual Estates did. The role of the Estates varied with the different kings and according to the domestic and foreign political situations. Well into the seventeenth century there were no written rules for the Estates and their work.

After many struggles, Duke Karl became King of Sweden, Rex Sueciae (R. S.). This portrait of Karl (Carolus) IX is by an unknown artist.

During much of the Age of Greatness the Riksdag was very influential, but toward the end of the seventeenth century power was almost entirely transferred to the King.

This famed tapestry portrays the four Estates taking their oaths. The tapestry is from the 1680s and embroidered in cross-stitch and petit point.

# CHAPTER 4

# The Parliament of the Age of Greatness

D URING THE SEVENTEENTH CENTURY Sweden conquered an extensive area around the Baltic Sea and became one of the great powers of northern Europe. Who held the reins of power during this epoch?

Strong kings ruled in Europe, while parliaments and other representative assemblies often had little influence. The numerous wars cost large sums of money, as the troops consisted mainly of hired mercenaries. These soldiers were paid primarily from the resources of the areas through which the armies marched, but that was not enough. The homeland also had to contribute both money and supplies. The question was where to find these resources.

During Sweden's Age of Greatness there was a long line of strong monarchs: Gustav II Adolf, Kristina, Karl X Gustav, Karl XI and Karl XII. However, in addition to the King, there were different groups that had positions of power. Members of the nobility occupied nearly all the highest offices, were found in the Council and constituted the leading Estate in the Riksdag. Yet, the other Estates – the Clergy, the Burghers and the Peasantry – were also important. When absolutism was introduced under Karl XI, it was with the help of the Riksdag.

There were three important centers of power during the seventeenth century. The first was the King and his court; the second the Council and the central government departments, which were established in the era of Gustav II Adolf; and the third was the Riksdag.

The Riksdag as it had evolved during the sixteenth century had no clear procedures. There was no written document regulating the position of the Riksdag in relation to the Council and the King. The leading nobleman in the first part of the seventeenth century, Axel Oxenstierna, declared that conditions had been insufferable when "upper and lower Estates convene like a bunch of cattle or drunken peasants." Now there would be order.

During the reign of Karl IX the nobility was strongly opposed to the King and his exercise of power. Just as his brothers had done, he surrounded himself with advisers who were not of noble birth. When Karl IX died, his oldest son, Gustav Adolf, was only sixteen. It might be expected that the nobility would try to regain power at

Axel Oxenstierna. A portrait by David Beck, ca. 1650.

Gustav Adolf's Accession Charter was drawn up by Axel Oxenstierna. The power of the King was restricted in important areas, for example taxes and questions of war and peace. The nobility wanted a guarantee that the strong monarchy which developed under Karl IX would be limited.

Gustav II Adolf,
age 18 and new King,
on a gold medal from 1612.

Gustav II Adolf painted ca. 1629 by Jacob Elbfas. The King was then about 35 years old. Sweden's borders were extended under Gustav II Adolf, at the same time that the state and its administration were modernized.

the King's expense, especially as the country was in a precarious position; Karl IX had been at war with Denmark, Russia and Poland.

Gustav Adolf was supposed to be under the care of guardians until he came of age, seven years after the death of his father. But at the age of seventeen he was declared King and accepted an Accession Charter before the Riksdag in the year 1611. This charter designated that no new laws or changes in the old laws would take place without the consent of the Council of the Realm and the Estates. The King also promised not to declare war without the knowledge of the Council and the Estates. Nor would he levy taxes "without the Council's knowledge and advice and the consent of those concerned."

A division of power between the King, the Council and the Riksdag was established. The Council and the Riksdag were dominated by the noble families, and Axel Oxenstierna, 28 years old at the time, made his appearance as the leader of the aristocracy in conjunction with the accession of Gustav Adolf to the throne. It is interesting that he allowed the King to retain much of his influence. There were certainly several reasons why the old families of the aristocracy did not choose to threaten the position of the Vasa dynasty.

Royal power had become firmly established under the first Vasa kings. The Vasa dynasty was no longer merely one of the noble families, but rather was accepted as royalty. Gustav II Adolf and Axel Oxenstierna were two exceptionally gifted and capable leaders who understood that they both had something to gain by cooperation rather than conflict. They certainly personally deserve much of the credit for the domestic political reforms and the success in foreign political affairs which the country experienced instead of being torn to shreds by internal conflicts.

## The Organization of the Riksdag

In 1617 the Riksdag passed its first Riksdag Act, which provided written regulations for its organization and work. The act established how the Riksdag should be opened, and how proposals should be introduced and dealt with. If the Estates made different decisions concerning an issue, attempts should be made to reach a compromise, and if that failed, the King should select the decision which he considered best.

In the year 1626 a new ordinance for the House of the Nobility was authored by Axel Oxenstierna. The Nobility was divided into three classes, the leader of which, the Speaker of the Estate of the Nobility *(lantmarskalken)*, was appointed by the King. The first class consisted of counts and barons, the second of knights, descendants of Council members who did not bear the titles of count or baron, and the third of squires. The Nobility voted on propositions by class. As the members of the aristocracy, who were few in number, were divided among the first two classes and the gentry comprised only one class, the upper Nobility could easily dominate.

Gustav Vasa had given the country a centralized, functioning government. However, in comparison with many other European countries Sweden was still a primitive agrarian society. A number of towns and cities were engaged in international trade, but more than 90 percent of the population lived in the countryside.

This order of things underwent a gradual transformation during the first half of the seventeenth century. Sweden became a modern "bureaucracy," the uppermost level of which consisted of members of the nobility. The system, introduced by Gustav II Adolf and Axel Oxenstierna, was of great consequence for the future, and there are still remnants left today.

The castle *Tre kronor* (Three Crowns) in Stockholm depicted in a painting by Govert Camphuysen about 1660. The castle, the oldest parts of which dated from the thirteenth century, was destroyed by fire in 1697. Many of the government departments which were created during the first half of the seventeenth century were housed there, including the National Archives, which preserved old books and documents. Many of these were consumed in the fire, and thus important sources of Swedish history were lost.

Gustav II Adolf as defender of the Faith, riding on a lion. His Catholic opponent is riding on a wolf in sheep's clothing. A Protestant broadsheet from Germany printed about 1630.

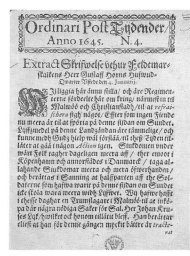

Sweden's oldest newspaper, today's *Post- och Inrikes Tidningar*, was first published in 1645. Here is the earliest preserved copy, no. 4, 1645, which is filled with news on the current war. Through the newspaper the Swedish military leadership could spread propaganda about the course of events.

The Council formed the focus of the government, and five government departments or *collegia* were established, which at least in part correspond to current ministries or central agencies. The heads of these departments, the five high officials of the realm, were the Steward of the Realm (*riksdrotsen*), the Constable of the Realm (*riksmarsken*), the Admiral of the Realm (*riksamiralen*), the Chancellor of the Realm (*rikskanslern*) and the Treasurer of the Realm (*riksskattmästaren*). The structure of the Council became more firmly fixed, and the minutes of the meetings were recorded. The country was divided into counties (*län*) with a governor (*landshövding*) at the head of each.

Important military developments also took place. In Sweden a system was introduced whereby special commissioners raised able troops. Each military unit was made up of men from the same province or hundred. In this way Sweden obtained a cheap, competent, effective army of the kind necessary for success in war.

For a number of reasons Sweden became involved in the European wars, the most comprehensive of which was the Thirty Years' War, which began in 1618 and ended in 1648. One motive was to secure the nation's borders and another to protect "the pure evangelical faith." During the wars with Poland and Denmark Gustav II Adolf and Axel Oxenstierna realized that the country could compete in the international arena. They saw the opportunity of obtaining territory, and, especially, future control of the Baltic Sea trade.

It was not sufficient, however, for the King and the Nobility to agree to the advantages of getting involved in international power politics. It was also necessary to get the other Estates to go along with this policy. The war was difficult business, but the government was able to get the support of the remaining Estates for the expansive project. At one decisive moment in the Estate of the Peasantry it was said that it was better to "hitch our horses to the enemy's fences than his to ours." There was, however, always strong discontent among the peasants, and Gustav Adolf was afraid of losing at home what he had won abroad.

The peasants grumbled, and dissatisfaction was expressed by the Peasantry during the sessions of the Estates and in rebellions in the countryside, which the King and the nobility were able to quell, however. One of the reasons was, of course, the successes on the battlefield. But the clergy also stood behind the King. They supported him, not only in the Riksdag, but also spread pro-war propaganda from the pulpit. It was a religious war against the "papists"; the Catholics would not regain power. The clergy also preached obedience to superiors. For those who did not obey, only Hell remained.

Sweden also had support from beyond its borders. Capital came from France and the Netherlands, but more important was perhaps that the country received assistance in developing mining and manufacturing. Sweden could thus produce weapons for its own use and for export.

After winning the Battle of Breitenfeld in 1631, Gustav II Adolf was regarded as an equal by the great German princes of the era. The King undoubtedly was an extraordinarily talented general, and many regarded the country's successes, both in domestic and foreign affairs, as attributable to him.

Although the Council ruled the country during the King's absence, the Riksdag was by no means powerless. It also played a role in the power struggle after the death of Gustav II Adolf in the Battle of Lützen on November 6, 1632. The heir, the future Queen

Cannon production as seen on an engraving from the late seventeenth century. During the Age of Greatness a number of cannon foundries were established, including one which still produces weapons today, Bofors.

The clothing which Gustav II Adolf wore at his death in the Battle of Lützen is found in the Royal Armory in Stockholm. Here the King's protective moosehide coat with a bullet hole in the back is mounted on his horse Streiff.

Kristina as a child in a portrait by Jacob Elbfas. She was barely six years old when her father died, and she reached her majority and became Queen at 18. She was brought up like a male heir and trained in various sports. This took place under the watchful eye of Axel Oxenstierna and in accordance with her father's wishes.

As the standard of living increased, the habits of nobles changed, and in many places they constructed magnificent palaces and manor houses. Axel Oxenstierna's Tidö in the province of Västmanland was built mainly according to plans by the French architect Simon de la Vallée and was finished about 1645.

Kristina, was not yet six years old, and a regency was appointed consisting of the five high officials of the realm. Axel Oxenstierna managed to see that persons close to him dominated.

Oxenstierna was also behind the Instrument of Government which was proposed to the Riksdag in Nyköping in 1634. It confirmed the position of the regency and the Council, but contained nothing about the authority of the Riksdag. The Riksdag would not need to meet other than on special occasions, such as a coronation. The Instrument of Government of 1634 in practice concentrated power in the hands of the five high officials, and this meant that the aristocracy, with Axel Oxenstierna and his kinsmen in the lead, gained a firm grip on the administration of the state. The economic and political position of the noblemen had been enhanced by the military successes and the comprehensive donations that they had received from the King. Many of their stately castles still survive in all their splendor or stand as remarkable ruins: Carl Gustaf Wrangel's Skokloster, Axel Oxenstierna's Tidö and Per Brahe's Visingsborg.

## Grievances and Petitions

It is easy to regard the Riksdag during the sixteenth and seventeenth centuries as merely an instrument of royal power or of the prominent members of the aristocracy, as meetings to confirm the wishes of the leading circles in society. The lower Estates were often reluctant to heed the summons to a Riksdag; the voters, who had to bear the costs, complained. Yet, during most of the Age of Greatness the Riksdag actually did possess power and made decisions which clearly concerned all citizens.

During the regency of Queen Kristina the Riksdag had to take a stand on a number of important questions. It retained its right to levy taxes and did not make its levies for a longer period than two years. Thereafter the Riksdag had to be summoned anew.

The King's proposals were not always accepted by the Estates as a matter of course. The regent or the Chancellor of the Realm gave a speech to the assembled Estates at the opening of the Riksdag. This speech dealt with the state of the realm and contained proposals for the solution of various problems. Financial questions were paramount, but other issues were also taken up.

The four Estates appointed committees which prepared responses to the various proposals and which negotiated with the representatives of the government and of the other Estates. There were also joint committees. Compromises were made and the various points of view were considered. In the negotiations, as in all the work of the Riksdag, the Nobility set the pace, but the influence of the other Estates should not be underestimated. The nonnoble Estates could clearly make their voices heard to a much greater extent than in many other countries at that time.

The various Estates had possessed the right to submit petitions since the sixteenth century. This procedure meant that the Riksdag members had the right to propose social changes. The petition might concern a conflict between two towns or the border between two hundreds. Such documents were called private petitions, as they concerned local conditions or even personal matters. Grievances could also be general, however. An issue might be considered of such importance that the entire Estate supported the petition and thus gave it greater weight.

At the same time that the representatives to the Riksdag were appointed, decisions were made as to the issues that should be taken up at the Riksdag, that is, which grievances should be presented. This was not always a simple procedure. In the towns and dioceses opinion was often divided. The magistrates, the royally appointed town officials, often had interests which differed from those of the burghers. The same was true of the bishops and the rest of the clergy. Petitions from the peasants were written in consultation with the judge of the hundred court (*häradshövding*).

The county governor, the King's representative in each county, was also important in the preparation of petitions, especially those for the peasants. It was the governor's duty to check all petitions, and some were rejected either on the basis of content or of formalities. The grievances often dealt with different forms of taxation: taxes on the brewing of beer or contributions to the military. But they could also be of a more general political nature with demands for changes in the law.

The way in which grievances were dealt with in the Riksdag changed during the course of the seventeenth century. What was common for the entire period was that the process was long and formal from the initial approval of a petition by the local elective body to the point when it was accepted by the entire Riksdag and became the basis for a royal decree. The question was first discussed in the Estate into which it was introduced, before perhaps being sent to the other Estates for negotiation. Petitions might also be referred to different government departments and county governors before the King in Council reached a decision.

It is not known how often petitions resulted in a decision. Sometimes conflicts were resolved within the Estate. For example, a conflict between two towns might be negotiated with the help of mediators during the Riksdag. The importance of the right to petition is evidenced by the hard work which many people put into giving the petition its initial appearance and then seeing it through the entire decision-making process.

The petitions naturally gave the government much work. But the system also meant that the country's leadership could be kept informed about dissatisfaction in the country at an early stage and in organized forms. The various Estates had the opportunity to lodge complaints and propose changes in a way that must have dispersed a great deal of malcontent. The right to petition meant that the Riksdag was not solely an instrument of the central government.

## The Riksdag during the Reign of Queen Kristina

This portrait of Queen Kristina was painted by her court artist Sébastien Bourdon shortly before her abdication.

Karl Gustav's hat with crown which he wore as heir. Both were made for the coronation of Queen Kristina.

After she came of age in 1644 Kristina proved her skill. Although the Oxenstierna group exerted power, royal power was still strong. One of the explanations why Kristina was able to maintain her position was, without a doubt, her intelligence and talent. She also knew how to utilize the splits within and among the Estates. The growing power of the nobility and the increased donations of royal lands, with the subsequent reduction of the class of free peasants, caused unrest. Although the Peace of Westphalia (1648) was advantageous for Sweden, a number of foreign policy problems remained. The large military apparatus which had been built up during the war also needed to be dismantled.

There was one dominant problem for Queen Kristina at the meetings of the Estates in 1649 and 1650. The Queen wanted her cousin Karl Gustav acknowledged as her heir. One reason for this was that the Estates wanted the Queen to marry as soon as possible, which she definitely refused to do. At the 1650 Riksdag she managed to get her demand concerning succession to the throne accepted by playing the Nobility against the nonnoble Estates.

Discontent was widespread in the lower Estates, as it was felt that only the nobility had benefited directly from the war. A statement from the lower Clergy (the bishops did not concur) questioned why few people enjoyed the fruits of the peace that had been concluded. The war had cost everyone a great deal, but only a limited number had received compensation for their contributions, both material and spiritual. A statement from the Peasantry also bears witness to

Queen Kristina abdicates from the throne before the assembled Estates at Uppsala Castle. She relinquishes the regalia of the realm to her cousin Karl Gustav. Erik Dahlbergh's drawing from June 6, 1654 is one of the oldest known contemporary pictures of an event which took place in the Swedish Riksdag.

unrest: "We have heard that in other countries the peasants are in bondage and fear that the same will happen to us."

Demands were made for a "resumption," that is, the noblemen should be forced to return to the Crown part of the lands which they had received as thanks for their contributions to the war. The Queen kindled this discontent and scared the Nobility, who reluctantly accepted Karl Gustav as Sweden's heir to the throne. The lower Estates, however, continued to demand withdrawal of lands, and this discontent was later used by Karl Gustav when he became King, and by his son, Karl XI.

Four years after the Riksdag agreed to her succession demand, Queen Kristina stepped down from the throne. Her abdication took place at Uppsala Castle in the presence of the Riksdag assembled there in 1654.

The question arose as to how much power Karl X Gustav should have. He had obtained a princely education including foreign travel, and he had studied at various universities, both in Sweden and outside the country. For a while he studied in Uppsala, where the university had been rejuvenated by generous donations from Gustav II Adolf. He had better knowledge of administration and economy than his cousin, Queen Kristina.

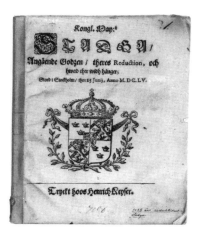

In 1655 an act was passed which formed the basis for the land reform referred to in Swedish history as the one-quarter resumption. About one fourth of the lands which had been granted to noblemen after 1632 were to be returned to the Crown.

## New Land – New Representatives

During the 1655 Riksdag Karl X Gustav intrigued against the Nobility with the help of the nonnoble Estates, as Kristina had previously. He managed to gain their support for a limited resumption of the landed possessions of the nobility. It was, however, only partly carried out and did not bring order into the country's economy. The fundamental problem remained: far too much of the land belonged to the nobility and was thus totally exempt from taxation. The King needed to enlarge those areas from which he could obtain income.

By a daring march across the frozen Danish sounds in February 1658 Karl X Gustav surprised the Danish King on the island of Zealand and forced him to make peace in Roskilde. The painting is by Johan Philip Lemke.

Karl X Gustav on a commemorative medal cast in Amsterdam after his death in 1660.

No Riksdag was summoned between 1655 and 1659, partly because Karl X Gustav was outside the country at the head of the Swedish army. On the other hand there were provincial meetings on various occasions under the leadership of a county governor or some members of the Council. Resolutions were passed at these meetings concerning certain taxes and other appropriations necessary for the war.

Karl X Gustav was very successful during his campaigns, and by his death at age 37, the Swedish kingdom had reached its greatest geographical boundaries. The stories about his death, which occurred in conjunction with the Riksdag that was summoned to Göteborg in 1659, were dramatic. The King had been administered a number of cures which the doctors thought would help him, but which probably caused his health to deteriorate. In spite of his illness, he made a will in which he appointed a regency for his son.

As Sweden had conquered new areas, the composition of the Riksdag had to be broadened. In the Peace of Brömsebro in 1645, Gotland, Halland, Jämtland and Härjedalen became part of Sweden. With the exception of Halland, these provinces immediately received the right to representation. Halland was a special case, because the province became a Swedish possession only for a limited time.

After the Peace of Roskilde in 1658, Halland became a permanent part of Sweden, as did Skåne, Blekinge and Bohuslän. One condition of the peace agreement was that the former Danish nobility in the conquered provinces would become members of the Swedish House of the Nobility: "If they were excluded now, it would be like starting with a cold heart." The gentry protested against the newcomers, however. There was also some discussion in the Council about the standing of the peasants of Skåne, because they did not have as many rights as peasants in the other provinces. However, they were to be represented in the Riksdag, and by 1664 there were representatives from the conquered territories in all the Estates.

The Crown House in Göteborg, where the Riksdag met 1659–60.

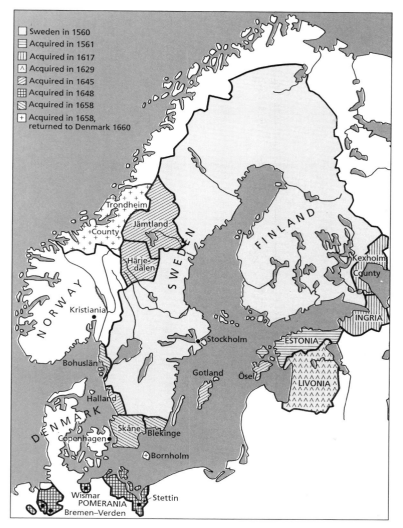

Sweden in 1560
Acquired in 1561
Acquired in 1617
Acquired in 1629
Acquired in 1645
Acquired in 1648
Acquired in 1658
Acquired in 1658, returned to Denmark 1660

The Swedish realm reached its greatest extent after the Peace of Roskilde in 1658. Thereafter followed a new war, the Second Danish War, which did not go as well for the Swedes. In 1660 Sweden made peace with Denmark–Norway in Copenhagen and was forced to return the island of Bornholm and Trondheim County.

**65**

## A Regency under the Riksdag

The Riksdag which was summoned to Stockholm in the autumn of 1660 revealed how opinion was split on the issue of how the realm should be governed until Karl XI came of age. Not only were there differences between the Nobility and the lower Estates, but also within the individual Estates. In the House of the Nobility there were conflicts between the aristocracy and the gentry.

There were complicated negotiations in the Riksdag among the Estates and between the individual Estates and the Council. The most pressing issue was what the government would look like during the regency. In his will Karl X Gustav had given detailed instructions about the composition of the regency. It was to consist of the Queen Mother and the five high officials of the realm; the King's brother, Duke Adolf Johan, was to be given the post of Constable of the Realm.

The decisions in the Riksdag resulted in a regency with a different composition from that prescribed by Karl X Gustav. His brother and others sympathetic to the dead King's policies were

The 1660 Additament, or supplement, to the 1634 Instrument of Government. In his will Karl X Gustav gave instructions concerning his son's regency. The additament, which together with the Instrument of Government replaced his instructions, meant that the regency would be responsible to both the Council and the Riksdag. It was accepted by the Riksdag which met in Stockholm in the autumn after the King's death.

In the 1680s the Bank of the Estates of the Realm moved into this structure designed by Nicodemus Tessin the Elder. It is located in the Old Town in Stockholm and remained the main building of the Bank of Sweden until 1906. The Bank of Sweden is the world's oldest national bank still in existence and one of the few headed by a parliament. Engraving by Erik Dahlbergh.

not given the positions designated in the will. It was not, however, a recurrence of the regency of the aristocracy which ruled during Kristina's minority. One reason was that the Nobility was not as unified as it had been under Axel Oxenstierna. Because of the extensive recent ennoblement, the House of the Nobility had a somewhat different composition.

The Estates strengthened their position at the autumn Riksdag of 1660. They were able to influence the composition of the regency, which would "stand before God, His Majesty and all the Estates of the Realm." Provincial meetings of the kind which had taken place during the reign of Karl X Gustav were forbidden. A bank was established by the Estates in 1668, making the country's monetary policy a concern of the Riksdag and not just of the government or the Council. The Council was not able to get its proposal for increased taxes accepted. Because the country was not at war, the Riksdag did not consider any large expenditures for the army necessary. If they were to pay high taxes, the members of the nonnoble Estates demanded that in return the nobility should relinquish part of the lands which they had been granted. The 1655 withdrawal of lands to the Crown would become a reality.

The significance of the nonnoble Estates was also evident in 1672. Before declaring the King of age, the Nobility made a number of demands that their privileges should be confirmed and the power of the King restricted. The other Estates were opposed. They countered with a demand for a review of the decisions of the regency and for a real resumption of land of the nobility. According to the Accession Charter, Karl XI was to rule the country with the help of the Council, and questions which implied changes in the realm "for its defense, security, development and needs" should not be made without the knowledge and consent of the Estates. Karl XI's charter was nearly identical to that of his father.

## Absolute Monarchy

The absolute monarch Karl XI, here in a marble statue by Caspar Schröder.

There was a great deal of discontent during the coronation Riksdag in Uppsala in 1675. Conditions were poor throughout the country, the economy was in a terrible state and the military forces a shambles. In spite of these circumstances the leadership had been enticed into a war on France's side against Brandenburg, the Netherlands, Austria and Denmark. The King and the Riksdag were not held responsible for the situation, while the regency sat in the docks. The Riksdag decided to investigate the administration of the regency. This investigation was followed by a comprehensive resumption of lands that had been granted to the nobles.

The first years of Karl XI's reign were dominated by war. Sweden had to defend what it had conquered earlier, especially the provinces previously belonging to Denmark. Although Sweden suffered defeats, especially at sea, the Swedish army was not completely out of the fight. Karl XI led the troops in the Battle of Lund in 1676 and showed that the Swedes could hold their own against the enemy. In 1679 Sweden concluded a peace with Denmark which meant not only that the Danish territories captured earlier were kept, but also that the two countries entered an alliance.

The Riksdag of 1680 introduced a period in Swedish history referred to as the Absolute Monarchy. The economic, social and political conflicts were skillfully used by the King. The aristocracy opposed the gentry; the landowning nobility was in conflict with the holders of military and civil offices. The three lower Estates – the Clergy, the Burghers and the Peasantry – also supported the King due to their dissatisfaction with the strong position of the nobility, the economic situation and the lack of order in the country.

The Battle of Lund in 1676, when about 9,000 men, more than half of the combatants, were killed. This battle was probably the bloodiest ever fought on Swedish soil. Painting by Johan Philip Lemke.

Karl XI and his family on a painting by David Klöcker Ehrenstrahl from the 1680s. The King's mother, Hedvig Eleonora, dominates the picture. Karl XI's wife, Queen Ulrika Eleonora, is to the far right of the painting. The children are the future Karl XII and his sister Hedvig Sofia, and behind them is seen Karl XI's aunt. The portrait in the background depicts Karl X Gustav.

Within the Riksdag the idea became popular that the situation demanded a strong leader. The concept was not unique to Sweden, but was found in a number of countries in Europe. The 1680 Riksdag became increasingly sympathetic to the King and more critical of the Council, which had held most of the power during the regency. At the conclusion of the Riksdag the King posed a number of crucial questions to the Estates about the governing of the country. The replies were unequivocal and sensational: they implied that the King was bound by neither the Instrument of Government nor the Council. He was furthermore not to be held legally responsible. A court of the Estates was appointed to carry out an investigation of the regency and the Council. The Estates also decided on a withdrawal of lands to the Crown that was more far-reaching than that which had been initiated in 1655.

The Council was for all practical purposes eliminated by the Riksdag. Its members were not allowed to take any initiative, and the King needed to present his proposals to the Council only when he so wished.

One of the main tasks of the Riksdag from the beginning had been to take part in general legislation. In 1682, however, the Estates declared that they could not "dictate" anything to the King, but rather that the King had the right to make laws without consulting the Estates. In addition the King would be allowed to carry out the resumption of lands as he wished. He asked the

## Johan Gyllenstierna – a Nobleman Loyal to the King

Johan Gyllenstierna's portrait in the Riksdag Building is based on a painting by D.K. Ehrenstrahl.

JOHAN GYLLENSTIERNA (1635–1680) was the son of a baron and thus a member of the aristocracy. More important, however, was that he was the grandson of Johan Skytte – Gustav II Adolf's teacher – and that he did not join the ranks of those who made fortunes or received large estates during the successful wars.

At the age of 19 Johan Gyllenstierna defended a dissertation at the University of Uppsala on the topic of what a prince should observe at his succession to the throne. It was an issue of current interest as Queen Kristina had abdicated the same year in favor of her cousin Karl Gustav. After defending his dissertation Gyllenstierna made a long peregrination throughout Europe together with Olaus Svebilius, the future Archbishop. On his return he was employed as chamberlain by Karl X Gustav and was given a post in the chancery.

In the Estate of the Nobility Johan Gyllenstierna took a stand against the aristocracy and for the gentry. He made numerous enemies among the leading members of the aristocracy on account of both his views and his brusque manner. There were campaigns against him, and he was considered a traitor to the interests of the aristocracy.

At the 1664 Riksdag Gyllenstierna was one of the more prominent critics of the aristocracy and the government. He was regarded as dangerous, and at the 1668 Riksdag the Council tried to lull him into passivity by naming him Speaker of the Estate of the Nobility. He led the proceedings at the meetings with great authority and restrained the opposition of the gentry. As a reward for his services, he was made a member of the Council.

Gyllenstierna, however, did not abandon his fundamental ideas. He worked against rule by noblemen and for strong royal power. Gyllenstierna wanted order in the administration and the completion of the resumption of noble estates by the Crown. He was cautious in questions of foreign policy and skeptical to some of the actions advocated by the phalanx within the Council led by Magnus Gabriel De la Gardie.

The Riksdag was important to Gyllenstierna because it gave him a platform from which he could exert power. His actions in the Estate of the Nobility meant that he had to be taken into account. However, his greatest contributions were made as close adviser to Karl XI and by virtue of the power the King developed.

Johan Gyllenstierna died at the age of 45. He was then the King's representative in Skåne, where he worked for the "Swedification" of the earlier Danish provinces of Skåne, Halland and Blekinge. The King mourned his most loyal and effective aid, but many members of the aristocracy heaved a sigh of relief.

Riksdag if he had the right to grant and withdraw fiefs according to the law of the land. The reply was positive. A comprehensive redistribution of the economic power within the country followed, to the detriment of the nobility and to the advantage of the Crown.

During the regency the Riksdag had gained significant power. It had a clear position in legislation and in economic policy. In spite of this, at the end of the seventeenth century the King was able to legally assume all this authority.

In 1693 the Estates declared Karl XI "an absolute, almighty and reigning sovereign King, who is responsible to no one on Earth for his actions, but who has the power and might to guide and govern his Realm according to his desires and as a Christian King." The Riksdag declared that it relinquished all its power to the King. The Danish ambassador to Stockholm wrote to the King of Denmark about the inscriptions on the milestones that were placed along the highway and met the representatives on their way to the Riksdag:

A soldier's cottage. The military allotment system created by Karl XI was the basis of Swedish defense until 1901.

> What shall be done is done,
> Ye men who shall assemble, do not travel so fast!

There were a number of circumstances behind the development toward absolutism. As we have seen there had been a great deal of discontent among leading groups in the Riksdag, who felt that the regency had mismanaged the country. The landowning nobility had taken possession of much of the land at the expense of the tax-paying peasants. Simultaneously the country's finances and defense had been allowed to deteriorate. Opposition grew, not only among the peasants, but also among the burghers, the clergy and many of those noblemen who did not have large landed estates. Because of the poor finances of the state, the noblemen did not receive their salaries as military or civilian officials.

How did Karl XI use his position of power? In the beginning of his reign he had to defend the newly conquered territory in southern Sweden, and he had seen the deficiencies in the Swedish military organization. The army was now given permanent support through the military allotment system. The farms were grouped together, and within each group the peasants agreed to supply a soldier or a seaman who was provided with a cottage and a small amount of land. The King also managed to put the state finances on a sound basis. One of the reasons why Karl XI could have the absolute monarchy confirmed was his success in domestic politics. He also gave the country peace for two decades.

Did the absolute monarchy mean that the King could make any decision he wanted? He certainly had the right to make laws and wage war, and he brought about many changes in Sweden during the twenty years that he ruled. He accomplished this, not together with the old aristocracy, but rather with a group of officials loyal to him, many of whom had recently received titles of nobility. Yet,

When families were matriculated into the House of the Nobility their coats of arms were mounted in the assembly hall. During Karl XI's reign many new titles were awarded to officers and officials. This was significant for the outcome of the power struggle between the King and the old hereditary nobility.

The gray cape which belonged to Karl XI is preserved in the Royal Armory in Stockholm. The King traveled a great deal throughout the country, and the tales are many about how he intervened when he found negligent officials. It is said that he often appeared anonymously dressed in his gray cape and mixed with the people to get an impression of prevailing conditions and opinions.

there were significant limitations on royal power. Karl XI was aware of his need for support from various social groups. Nor did he believe that he stood above the law.

Karl XI traveled a great deal within the country, and life at his court was relatively simple. He was later called "Gray Cape" for the garment which he wore when he was out and inspected his officials. When he found that they neglected their duties, he intervened immediately.

Many of the stories about the King's travels are anecdotes of later origin. He was, however, conscious of the need to have contact with the people, to argue for his proposals, and to win support for the various reforms. There were always groups prepared to resist. He had experienced the rebellion of the 1670s, when peasants, tradesmen and brigands in the province of Skåne revolted against Swedish authority. To travel among common people and visit markets was a way of keeping informed.

Karl XI died in 1697 and was succeeded by the young Karl XII. During the rule of Karl XII the Riksdag played practically no role at all. It was summoned once by the Council and met in 1713–14 when the King was in Bender in the realm of the Turks after being defeated in the war against the Russians. The Riksdag displayed the ability to act, but the representatives who were assembled had to return home when the King ordered the dissolution of the Riksdag in a letter. It was only after the death of Karl XII that they assembled again.

This portrait of Karl XII was painted by his general Axel Sparre during the time the King was in Bender. He let himself be portrayed with his small-pox scars and dressed as an ordinary soldier, which was uncommon for monarchs of that era.

Karl XII, aged 15, is hailed by the Riksdag before his coronation in December 1697. This was the only occasion on which he met the Riksdag. At the coronation ceremony he placed the crown on his own head. The drawing is by Nicodemus Tessin the Younger.

## The Nobility, the Clergy, the Burghers and the Peasantry

In the beginning of the seventeenth century the Estate of the Nobility was totally dominated by the landowning aristocracy, but new groups came to be included as a result of large-scale granting of new titles. The most common way of being ennobled and introduced into the House of the Nobility was to become an officer or to reach a leading position in the bureaucracy, either at the national or regional level. With the new noble families the Estate of the Nobility became an increasingly diversified assembly during the seventeenth century. It represented many varied interests, but reflected well the new ruling class in Swedish society.

Noblemen in a drawing from the Italian diplomat Lorenzo Magalotti's account of his journey to Sweden in 1674.

At the 1693 Riksdag there were about 500 nobles in attendance – five times as many as at the beginning of the century.

- No fewer than 75 counts and barons participated in the meetings of the House of the Nobility. Many had received their titles from Karl X Gustav and Karl XI.
- The knights numbered only ten or so; most of the descendants of members of the Council were counts or barons.
- 407 persons who belonged to the gentry, the squires, were registered.

The Estate of the Clergy was more clearly defined and more uniform than the first Estate. The bishops were ex officio members, but otherwise the regulations concerning who should be representatives in the spiritual Estate were ambiguous, and practice varied from one diocese to the other. Sometimes the representatives were chosen in free elections among the clergymen; sometimes they were in reality appointed by the bishops. Vicars made up the majority of the clerical Estate, but there were also members from the gymnasia and from the universities in Uppsala and Åbo. The bishops, the higher clergy and some of the theology professors formed the upper stratum of this Estate which consisted of a total of about 60 persons.

Swedish clergymen in an illustration from Magalotti's account of his travels.

The Clergy prepared the election of new bishops, and nominations were thereafter presented to the King. The Estate also dealt with a number of other ecclesiastical issues which were not directly concerned with the work of the Riksdag. The political role of the vicars was significant during the seventeenth century. They spread information from the King and the Council to the people from the pulpit and were thus important for the formation of opinion in the country.

The Estate of the Burghers represented the towns and cities of the realm. At the beginning of the seventeenth century towns were still small and insignificant. Gustav II Adolf described them as "without trade, rotten and dilapidated." He worked hard to establish new towns and create better conditions for the old. Göteborg

Gustav II Adolf founded Göteborg as a combined fortress and port on the Dutch model. L. van Anses' engraving shows the city on a maritime chart from 1694.

The picture shows a detail from a guild's savings chest from 1652. The man's clothing was common among burghers at that time.

This peasant and his wife are found as a vignette on a 1689 land and maritime chart of Lake Mälaren.

and Sundsvall were among the many places which were granted town charters by Gustav Adolf. In conjunction with wars and increased trade, especially in arms, the towns grew in importance.

During the reign of Queen Kristina the governing of towns and cities changed. Earlier, the mayor held an honorary post and was elected from among the councilmen, who were ordinary burghers. In the middle of the seventeenth century local government became more professionalized, which meant that, at least in the larger towns, there was a royal mayor and a town council, the members of which were not elected among the burghers but appointed by the King or by his representative, the county governor.

Each town or city had the right to send two representatives to the Riksdag, but many did not avail themselves of the opportunity. Instead smaller towns often got together and chose one representative. There was no election in the modern sense of the word; the appointment of representatives varied from one place to another and changed over time. Usually, the town council made a nomination and the citizens or the elders in the town then chose the candidate. The mayor or a member of the council was often selected to represent the town in the Estate of the Burghers.

By the end of the seventeenth century there were more than one hundred burghers present at the Riksdag. Stockholm held a special position, as it had three to five representatives and its mayor served as Speaker of the Estate, while one of its city clerks served as secretary.

The Estate of the Peasantry consisted of approximately 200 persons. Each hundred was allowed to send a representative. Two or more hundreds often banded together and chose one representative. Election took place at the ting in the hundred, and only the "permanently settled peasants of means" were eligible. We know little about how freely the peasants were able to elect their representatives. Some of the officials, who represented the King, the county governors, the judges of the hundred courts and the sheriffs, were involved in the election process and could interfere in the election for or against a candidate.

At the end of the seventeenth century the Riksdag was thus a large and varied assembly with nearly a thousand participants. Some were members because of their birth, others due to their office, and some because they had been elected.

## Reluctant Attendance

To be a member of the Riksdag during the seventeenth century was for many a burden rather than a privilege. Nobles often tried to avoid attending. Strict attendance rules were therefore set up, and those who did not observe these rules could be fined. Severe illness was accepted as a legitimate reason for absence, but a certificate was required. Lack of means was no excuse for not attending.

Within the Clergy the member who did not appear on the third day after the opening of the session could be fined, and the regulations of the Burghers from 1632 state: "He who neglects some hour and is not present at a whole meeting, shall be fined one *daler* for each hour."

The King and the Council were anxious to see that as many as possible were present at the Riksdag. It gave greater authority to the decisions, but also greater opportunities to manipulate the various groups. Still attendance was not always good. Burghers and peasants often went home when their allotted funds ran out.

A 1654 decision of the Riksdag. The resolutions of the Riksdag summarized the results of its work. They were signed by the members and printed. This handwritten original document is found in the National Archives.

The court artist Ehrenstrahl made this portrait of Per Olsson, the Speaker of the Estate of the Peasantry during the 1686 Riksdag.

The relations that existed between the Estates are illustrated by the diary of the Västervik vicar Olaus Bodinus from the opening of the Riksdag in 1686. Bodinus tells how the three upper Estates gathered in *Slottskyrkan* (the Palace Church) at eight o'clock in the morning for a service. First came the Burghers "in order" and then the Clergy "by rank." A while later the Nobility began to take its seats, and "crowding, occupied all the chairs." At last the Marshal of the Realm (*riksmarskalken*), the Council and the King himself entered the church. After the service they walked in procession up to the Hall of the Realm, where the "peasants stood on raised stands and benches."

The Marshal of the Realm took the floor, after which the Chancery President (*kanslipresidenten*) gave his speech and "hailed the King and the Estates, but spoke very slowly." During this time the King stood with his head bared. After a while a secretary was asked to read the King's proposals. "Then the King sat and covered his head."

After the reading, a sign was given to the Speakers of the four Estates to come forth and give their speeches, during which the King again sat with his head bared. Bodinus thought that the speech of the Speaker of the Nobility was "precious," while the Archbishop was "very humble" and the Speaker of the Burghers expressed himself "beautifully." For the Peasantry "a gray-bearded peasant from Uppland, dressed in gray woolen clothes," spoke. The act concluded with the Speakers bowing three times before they took leave of the King. The peasant was so humble that he touched the King's shoe. It was all over by half past one.

When these entries were written in 1686, the Riksdag had lost nearly all its power. They tell us more about the absolute monarchy than about the significance of the Riksdag. The vicar who made the notes was apparently not as impressed by the King as were the representatives of the Estates who were presented to the King at the opening ceremony.

## Compensation for the Members of the Riksdag – a Matter for Negotiation

During the seventeenth century the Crown was not responsible for paying the travel costs and the board and room of the members of the Riksdag. Instead, the participants in the Riksdag and those who elected them had to pay. Members of the Nobility were expected to pay their own expenses, and the other Estates often appointed the person who was "cheapest." If a burgher had to go to the capital on business anyway, he could also take responsibility for the Riksdag assignment. Among the peasants men were often chosen who could bear some of the costs themselves.

Such were the wagons which Maga-lotti met on Swedish roads in the 1670s. The roads were poor and dangerous, but a journey could be worth some hardships. The participants in the Riksdag could return to their regions and relate what legislation had been passed. They also learned about people and places which few others in the town or parish had experienced. Below is a set of eating utensils for traveling.

About the year 1600 rules began to come into being as to how the peasants should pay their representatives. In the hundreds some money was to be taken from the chest where fines were kept, while the farmers were to make a contribution as well. A regulation from 1618 set the Riksdag compensation at 2 *öre* for each farm liable to pay taxes to the Crown and at half that amount for those farms leased from noblemen. The question of which peasants were liable to pay caused repeated conflicts, debates and decisions during the seventeenth century.

Compensation for the burghers did not cause as much discussion as did that for the peasants. It was usually established in conjunction with the election at the town hall. The burghers often tried to get the sum reduced, but an increase could also be offered as an inducement to "speak out about the many problems of the town."

The clergy developed different rules within the various dioceses. In several cases the parishes paid according to their means. The collection of the contributions for the Riksdag occurred through the deans, and the money was later distributed so that the bishops received twice as much as the vicars. Many representatives were required to keep detailed accounts of their expenses at the Riksdag. Everyone was suspicious of waste.

# Wij ULRICA ELEONORA

## med Guds nåde, Sweriges Göthes och Wendes utkorade Drottning,

Stor Furstinna til Finland, Hertiginna uti Skåne, Estland, Eifland, Carelen, Brehmen, Verden, Stettin, Pommeren, Cassuben och Wenden, Furstinna til Rügen, Frÿ uti Wÿrnarmarland och Wÿdhmaren, Pfaltz Grefwinna wid Rein i Bajeren, til Gülich Cleven och Bergen Hertiginna, Landtgrefwinna uti Hessen, Furstinna til Hersfeldt, Grefwinna til Cathen Ollenbogen, Decke, Zingenheim Nidda och Schauenburg. Giöre witterligit, att såsom förmedelst Den stora Gudens milda försÿn, skickelse och ÿtrande, samt sedan Sweriges Rÿkets Ständers samtÿcke, Wÿ nu den nÿtÿande, föllnande och warigare att wara en Regerande Drottning öfwer Swea Rÿke och det underliggande Länder; Så hafwa Wÿ icke mindre Radelsa Wåre Konungsliga macht och mÿndighet, att til Rÿkets tiänst, skydda och

# CHAPTER 5

# The Age of Liberty
## – the Great Era of the Riksdag?

**D**IFFERING JUDGEMENTS have been rendered, and still are, about the Age of Greatness and Karl XII, the foremost figure of the later part of this era. The period which followed the absolute rule of Karl XII, and which as early as the mid-eighteenth century was called the Age of Liberty, has also been evaluated in different ways.

The Riksdag of the Age of Liberty has been regarded by some historians as a precursor of a more modern form of government. Liberty in this context means that the influence of the national representative body was extensive for that time and unique in an international perspective. Science and commercial life flourished. Others have emphasized the negative aspects of the eighteenth century Riksdag. Bribes from foreign sources were common, and the leadership involved the country in two devastating wars.

Historical interpretations are always colored by the values of contemporary society. This is especially true of the Age of Liberty, which received widely varying interpretations even in its own day. There were several "modern" elements in the government, which have made the period a useful example in later political discussions. Parties, the Hats and the Caps, were formed within the Riksdag, and the Council became dependent on the Estates. A kind of parliamentary government developed. But the eighteenth century parties were of another character than those of today. The Council's dependence on the Estates was different from the government's dependency on the Riksdag after the breakthrough of modern parliamentarism.

The Age of Liberty stretches from the death of Karl XII in 1718 to Gustav III's assumption of power in 1772. It was a period which changed in character over time. The party system was not established definitely until the end of the 1730s.

Johan Peter Molin's statue of Karl XII was raised in the King's Garden in Stockholm in 1868 on the 150th anniversary of the King's death.

*On the opposite page:* The Instrument of Government of 1719 was a settlement with the earlier absolute rule and laid the foundation for government during the Age of Liberty. The Riksdag came into focus instead of the King.

## The Estates Assume Power

The Riksdag which the Council called in 1713 was ignominiously dissolved the following year by a simple letter sent from Karl XII in Bender. Adversaries of the absolute monarchy both within and outside the Riksdag were neither sufficiently strong nor unified to be able to make their voices heard. The King's word still ruled.

After the death of Karl XII everything looked different. Absolute monarchy had outlived itself, and the Council and the Riksdag took over. Eventually most power passed to the Estates, and the King became nearly powerless. The pendulum had swung, but why was the change that complete and dramatic?

The failure of Karl XII's policies was fundamental. He had lost the wars, both in the east and in the west. His father, Karl XI, had developed absolute monarchy during a period of peace. Numerous and highly appreciated reforms in military and civil organization had been carried out and order brought to the economy. The reign of Karl XI was still a model during the first half of the Age of Liberty.

"Emergency coins" which were minted in Sweden 1716–1719. They were made of copper and were valued at one *daler* in silver, regardless of the metallic content. They did not have a likeness of the King, but rather figures from antiquity and various heraldic signs. These emergency coins came to symbolize the economic decadence at the end of Karl XII's rule and are associated with his "minister of finance" von Görtz.

It is remarkable that Karl XII was able to remain in power so long. The extended wars burdened the country with great hardships, and many of the King's closest men were extremely unpopular. Baron Georg Heinrich von Görtz from Holstein was the King's right hand in both domestic and foreign affairs during the last phase of the war. He was the King's chief minister and head of the deputation which was responsible for the Crown's income and expenses.

Görtz came to symbolize all that was bad during the later part of the rule of Karl XII, and a commission of the Estates condemned him to death. Absolutism was at an end, and its leading official had to pay with his life.

Developments might have been different if Karl XII had had an heir who could have assumed power immediately. Lack of clarity concerning a successor was one of the reasons why absolutism could be rescinded in only a couple of months. There were two people with claims to the throne: the King's sister Ulrika Eleonora and Karl Fredrik of Holstein-Gottorp, the son of the King's deceased older sister. There were, however, no laws which clearly gave one or the other precedence. This meant that the Estates were able to place demands upon the successor; it was possible to play off the rivals against one another.

One half *daler* from 1720. The value was given in silver, although the coin was copper.

Immediately after the King's death Fredrik of Hessen, who was married to Ulrika Eleonora, tried to gain the support of the leading military officers by allowing them part of the war chest at the front. The generals took the money but were not ready to accept a new absolute monarchy. To become Queen, Ulrika Eleonora had to promise to submit to a radical reduction of the power of the monarch in relation to the Council and the Estates. She pledged "always to acknowledge the Estates as sovereign and in the future to render such decisions, to issue such statutes and decrees ... as would serve the common good and happiness."

After only a year the Queen abdicated in favor of her husband, Fredrik I, and thus further reduced the power of the Crown to the advantage of the Estates. The Instrument of Government, which the Riksdag passed in 1720 and which was based on what had already been approved in 1719, was decisive for the entire Age of Liberty. The Riksdag Act of 1723 regulated conditions in the Riksdag in detail.

This medal was minted in December 1718 to commemorate the announcement of Ulrika Eleonora's accession to the throne in 1719. At the foot of the throne are representatives of the four Estates.

- The King would rule the realm, but all important questions would be decided in the Council, where he had only two votes. In case of a tie, the King would cast the decisive vote. This was far from the absolute monarchy, when the King dominated the Council and was not even required to summon the Estates.
- The Council came in principle to be led by the Chancery President, who was the head of the most important government department; the heads of the other departments did not have seats on the Council. The Chancery President may best be compared to today's Prime Minister. There were sixteen members of the Council, and they were increasingly dependent on the Estates. They were appointed by the King, but for each member his choice was restricted to three candidates proposed by a committee of the Estates.
- The Riksdag Act established who was eligible for election, and the criteria for those who could be accepted as members of the various Estates were regulated. The class division in the House of the Nobility disappeared, and as the gentry was greater in number than the aristocracy, the power of the former increased. The Estates were granted the right to review the work of the Council.
- Detailed regulations determined the working order of the Riksdag, for example, that it should convene every third year. Work routines for the Riksdag were also formalized.
- The committees were to have decisive significance. They had already played a role during the Absolute Monarchy, but during the Age of Liberty they would be central to the work of the Riksdag. The so-called Secret Committee became especially important because it dealt with foreign policy, defense, and budgetary and banking matters. The Nobility dominated the committee. The Peasantry was not represented and repeatedly demanded the right to participate. The Speaker of the Estate of the Nobility served as chairman.

## Representatives of the People

In the 1760s the Marieberg factory in Stockholm produced a series of figures in faience which depicted the four Estates.

Nobleman.

Clergyman.

The Nobility dominated the Riksdag during the Age of Liberty just as it did during the Age of Greatness. There was no election to the Estate of the Nobility, but rather a representative from each matriculated family had the right to be present at the Riksdag. The number was limited by the fact that all families were not financially able to send a member to Stockholm.

The parties, however, had recruiters who traveled around the country to assure that people who were sympathetic to their opinions attended the Riksdag and to purchase proxies from nobles who for one reason or another could not participate. According to contemporary critics, lies, threats, money and promises were among the methods used by the parties to gain supporters.

At the opening sessions of the Estate of the Nobility, when the important elections took place, more than a thousand nobles could be present. Four to five hundred persons usually attended the normal sessions. The minutes and documents reveal lively and intensive debates. They also show the blend of important and trivial matters. A member of the Nobility could bring up practically anything for discussion. A person who was dissatisfied with an appointment or with some government authority could ask that the matter be taken up by the Estate. The meetings were frequent, long and sometimes also chaotic.

In the Estate of the Clergy the bishops held the positions of leadership, but just as in the previous century this Estate represented not only the Church, but also the learned professions within the universities. In the work of the Riksdag the Clergy assumed the role of mediator between the Nobility and the Peasantry. The vicars in the countryside lived close to the peasants. The most important source of income for the clergymen in the parishes was the tithe, which was a tax which the peasants paid to the Church.

Eligibility for election to the Clergy was extended during the Age of Liberty, and limits were set on the opportunities for the bishops to intervene in the election procedures in the deaneries. The upper echelons of the Clergy were not as dominant during the Age of Liberty as they had been earlier.

The composition of the Estate of the Burghers also grew more varied than it had been during the seventeenth century, and it contained a number of important political figures. There were town officials, artisans and merchants. The opinions voiced among the Burghers were especially important in the formation of economic policy.

Interest in the elections to this Estate increased from the 1730s onward, which led to an attempt to establish more standard procedures for the elections. The burghers took part in the election, which was held either directly, in the town hall, as a rule supervised by the county governor, or indirectly by electors chosen by the magistrates and the burghers. As in the Age of Greatness, deals were made concerning compensation for those sent to the Riksdag, sums which had to be paid by the towns themselves. Thus small towns sometimes came to an agreement concerning a common representative. If a representative was not sent in some way, the town could be fined.

The fourth Estate, the Peasantry, had the least influence, which was emphasized by the fact that it had no seats on the Secret Committee. One of the reasons was certainly that many of the peasants could not write. Several of Finland's representatives in the Estate did not understand Swedish and needed interpreters to be able to follow the debates. The Peasantry, however, was not lacking in significance, as voting on decisions in the Riksdag was done by Estates. It came to play an important role in the rivalry between the parties and in the struggle between the Estates and the King. The questions they were most interested in concerned taxation and the right to distill alcohol.

Burgher.

Election to the Peasantry usually took place at the traditional meeting of the ting, where the various parishes in the hundred were represented by electors chosen at parish meetings. According to the Riksdag Act of 1723 several hundreds could get together and select a representative to the Riksdag. In the beginning of the Age of Liberty the elections followed nearly the same pattern as during the Age of Greatness. The judge of the hundred court had considerable influence on the election, and in general there was consensus as to who should be elected. Gradually the election meetings became livelier, and the power of the judges declined. The discussion concerned not just who should be elected but also which hundreds should join together to send a representative to the Riksdag, how much he should be paid, and what petitions should be submitted.

How well did the four Estates represent the people? It is certain that only a small part of the population, a very small percentage, had the right to a seat and a voice in the Riksdag. The four Estates, however, reflected the power blocs in the country at that time. Furthermore, it was often in their interest to look out for the groups which were not represented.

Peasant.

The more power the Riksdag acquired, the more important the election of its members became. In the Estate of the Nobility the member represented his family. But what was the relationship between the voter and the person elected in the remaining Estates? Were the representatives supposed to vote according to their own opinions, or were they to reflect the wishes of the voters?

The problem came to a head in the 1740s. A number of burghers in Stockholm felt that the voters should have control over the way their representatives voted. If the representative did not heed the opinions of the voters, he should be removed from office. The

## Disruptions in the Estate of the Peasantry

FEELINGS could sometimes run high in the Estate of the Peasantry. The minutes of November 29, 1755 record a heated discussion between the Speaker, Olof Håkansson, and some members of the Estate. The question was whether the Speaker himself should appoint the delegates who together with him would hand the decisions of the Estate over to the King in Council or whether the matter should be voted upon. The controversy was not merely a matter of form; the protests were a way for the royalists in the Estate to try to get rid of the anti-royalist Speaker. The following is a summary of the minutes:

> Whereupon there was even more noise than before, when Lars Larsson stepped down from his bench and came to the front and, energetically and making a big fuss, shouted that the Speaker did not allow them their rights and that he should no longer be Speaker.
>
> Erik Persson from Stockholm County began to hit the railing again and harder than earlier and in addition to several scornful statements about the Speaker, which it was not possible to understand clearly, burst out with bitterness: "The King complains and is not heeded, we complain and are not heeded; that's your fault, you rogue, and you shouldn't be our Speaker any longer."
>
> It was possible to discern during the frightful noise that followed that Erik Månsson with a loud voice, fists clenched and stamping declared that there should be a vote as to whether the Speaker should continue as the Speaker of the Estate. For his part he screamed and hollered that the Speaker should leave the Estate today, and that he should never more be allowed to rule the Estate as he had done.

The question was eventually settled in the Speaker's favor, but only after the intervention of the Speaker of the Nobility and a bishop who seriously admonished the recalcitrants.

In this allegorical painting from 1734 Engelhardt Schröder let four women represent the four Estates. Clergy has her head covered and casts a pious glance toward the heavens; Nobility sits regally in the center, her hand on the handle of a sword; the Burgher, engaged in crafts and trade, holds a pair of compasses in her hand; while the Peasant, with a fruit basket on her head, stands subservient in the background.

Riksdag, however, did not give its approval. According to the decision reached by the Riksdag, its members were not bound to the decrees of their principals, but rather had the right to present their own views and vote according to what they felt was right. One of those who had pressed for the rights of the principals was even sentenced to life imprisonment.

The structure and organization of the Riksdag of the Estates made it slow and bureaucratic. One way of reaching decisions more quickly was to increase the authority of the joint committees. During some periods the Secret Committee was regarded as a miniature Riksdag, but the representation there was unbalanced. It consisted of 50 representatives from the Nobility and 25 each from the Burghers and the Clergy.

In addition to the Secret Committee and its subcommittees, which prepared various items, there were more than ten specialized or investigative deputations. These included the general deputation for petitions, the trade and manufacturing deputation and the treasury, finance and commerce deputation.

Although the various Estates were represented in joint committees and deputations, the members often had to call upon the other Estates to deliver messages concerning the decisions made in the respective Estates. During a Riksdag in Stockholm it was common to see a deputation from one Estate on its way to another to render relevant information about decisions on a particular issue.

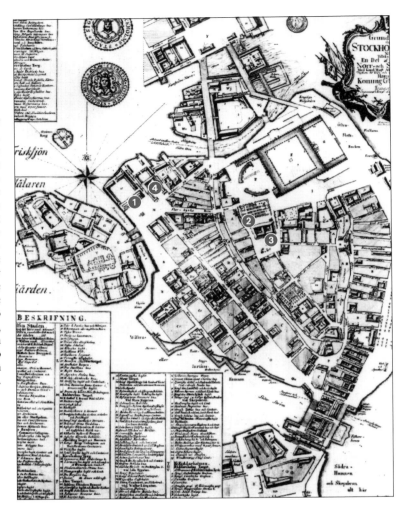

Central Stockholm during the Age of Liberty from a 1771 map by Jonas Brolin. The distance between the meeting places of the four Estates was not especially great. However, with the thought that deputations were sent between them constantly, the members of these groups covered a good many kilometers during a Riksdag. All Riksdag documents, committee reports, minutes and memos were carried between the Estates. Usually such a document was sent from the House of the Nobility (1) to the Clergy in *Storkyrkan* (2), thereafter to the Burghers in the old Town Hall, later the Stock Exchange Building, on *Stortorget* (3), and finally back to *Riddarhustorget* and the Peasants in the new Town Hall (4).

## Petitions – a Way of Making Changes

The members of the three lower Estates had a number of different duties. They were to take part in the decisions made for the good of the country, to further the interests of their Estate and to represent the local voters. When it came to this last task, grievances and petitions played a decisive role, as they had done in the seventeenth century.

The issues to be taken up in a petition were determined in conjunction with elections and could vary greatly in character. Petitions could deal with small grievances such as the one from Uppsala which questioned the quality of nails and which registered complaints concerning the removal of a table from the town hall that the county governor had sanctioned. But the petitions could also deal with questions of principle, such as the role birth should play in appointments or how the law allowing freedom of the press should be interpreted.

The petitions from the peasants were written in stages. At the time the electors were chosen to select their representative to the Riksdag, the decision was made as to which grievances the parish would present. Thereafter the grievances of the parishes were collected, and when the electors, under the leadership of the judge of the hundred court, met to appoint the representative, it was decided which grievances the hundred would support.

Historians have discussed the reliability of petitions as sources. Do they reflect conditions in the Swedish countryside in the eighteenth century, and do they say anything about popular opinion at that time? The judges of the hundred courts edited the petitions and could even remove items from the texts, but their interference should not be exaggerated. In the petitions which have been preserved there is a considerable range of both problems and solutions, which indicates that they were not subjected to any rigorous censorship.

The most common grievances concerned alcohol and the right to distill alcoholic beverages. The motivation as a rule was not the need for drink, but rather that the waste products from distillation were needed as cattle fodder. The peasants often claimed that only the worst grain which was not fit for human consumption was used for distilling. Thus, distillation could be defended during crop failures and times when access to grain was poor.

The petitions were not only a way for the members of the Estates to bring about changes; they also provided an opportunity for those in power to find out what the people wanted.

On July 19, 1755 the farmers of Oland hundred in the province of Uppland agreed to present a number of grievances to the Riksdag. The peasants met at the inn at Österbybruk together with the judge of the hundred court, who signed the petitions and placed his own seal and that of the court on the document. The peasant they elected to the Riksdag thus had written orders to take with him and, when he returned, he had to account for how well he had succeeded. The petitions allowed local grievances to reach the national level.

The decisions of the Riksdag from 1756. At that time such a document usually contained twelve clauses or so. Today the Riksdag passes so many resolutions that it is not possible to summarize them in a similar manner. This document corresponds to today's parliamentary papers which formally notify the government of a decision.

## The Dominance of Arvid Horn

Arvid Horn wearing the robes of a member of the Council of the Realm, an ermine trimmed, crimson mantle with wide arms. The portrait was painted by Engelhardt Schröder in 1727, when Horn was 63 years old.

One person left his mark on the first part of the Age of Liberty: Arvid Horn. He had served Karl XII, both as an officer and as a member of the Council. He became Chancery President under Ulrika Eleonora and served during several meetings of the Estates as Speaker of the Nobility and chairman of the Secret Committee. Horn was very successful in both domestic and foreign policy. The country's economy recovered quickly after many years of war.

After the death of Karl XII peace was made with conditions that were acceptable to Sweden. However, there lay a danger in the fact that Russia attempted to further solidify its position in the Baltic area. Great Britain was opposed to this policy, and Horn tried to approach England without antagonizing Russia. During his first years Horn had to struggle against the Holstein sympathizers, who wanted both closer ties to Russia and a stronger King.

Arvid Horn ruled, not because the King wanted him to, but because he was able to manipulate the Estates. During the entire period there were groups or parties in the Riksdag that either supported or opposed him, but until 1738 he had the situation under control. Horn knew how to win a majority; he could give and take. One example of his skill was when, in 1726, he won the vote of the Clergy in a number of questions by accepting the so-called Conventicle Act. This ban on religious gatherings was aimed at those who did not accept the "pure, correct" faith. Private religious meetings other than family prayers were forbidden.

The politician and cultural personality Carl Gustaf Tessin was not a friend of Horn but described him as follows:

> Count Arvid Horn had most qualities which make a great minister: beautiful appearance, gift of speech, congeniality, courage, ability to make an impression, experience, assiduousness and an incomparable memory. Persistent in his designs, resourceful in finding ways out, sharp in the choice of workers; somewhat more pious than a Chancery President should be; a God-fearing heart, but perhaps with too much of an exterior glow; never did the clock strike ten but what he rose from his chair in the Council or chancery and prayed.

The period of Arvid Horn's rule may be seen as a transition from absolute monarchy to the era of political parties. During the entire time he was in power there were indications of the coming party rivalries: political clubs, party meetings and contacts with foreign ambassadors. But it was not until the end of the 1730s that the parties fully flourished.

The Conventicle Act of 1726 was aimed at the revivalist movements which had gained increasing numbers of followers in Sweden in the 1720s. According to the act people were forbidden to hold religious services at home without the presence of a clergyman. Regular prayers and family devotions were excepted. The act against religious assemblies remained in force until the middle of the nineteenth century.

## The Hats Take the Initiative

The opposition to Horn was referred to as the Hats: the hat was a symbol of freedom and manhood. Nobody knows exactly when the word was first used in this context and where it came from. Many members of the party were officers who wore conspicuous hats. An observer wrote in 1738 about "our heroes with the hats," and the year after he spoke about "our hat heroes." Horn and his supporters received the derogatory name "nightcaps," because they were considered old and tired and too passive in their policies. "Hats" and "Caps" were thus not official names.

The Hats advocated expansive measures in both domestic and foreign policy. They dreamed of Sweden again becoming a great power. The most active Hat politicians were young civil servants who belonged to the Nobility, but merchants and other members of the Estate of the Burghers were also found in their ranks.

Before the opening of the 1738 Riksdag the Hats agreed on a common political program. First of all, they had to organize their supporters so that they won the post of Speaker of the Nobility and thereby the position as chairman of the Secret Committee. Furthermore, it was necessary to control the so-called benchmen elections. In the House of the Nobility there were no chairs, only long benches. The person who was elected benchman voted for all

A sketch of a commemorative medal for the victory of the Hat party in 1738. While the hat on the top of the obelisk gets a crown of laurels, the "nightcap" lies thrown beneath the table. The symbols of the four Estates are found on the table: a sword (Nobility), a book (Clergy), a rod (Burghers) and a sickle (Peasantry).

those who had their seats on the bench, and it was essential for the parties to see that the right man was elected.

The leading Hats appointed persons who could influence those sharing their bench. One of the Hat leaders, Admiral Carl Tersmeden, tells in his memoirs how he was given the task of finding out who would sit on the same bench and of trying to win their confidence. Of the fifteen who sat on the bench, nine "were of a similar frame of mind" as he. The benchmen in turn appointed electors, who chose the members of the committees.

In 1738 the opposition was successful, not only in the Nobility but also in the Estate of the Burghers. Arvid Horn's power was broken, and a party with a majority in several Estates arose in the Riksdag. The party organization was most developed in the Nobility and in the Estate of the Burghers, but it was also found in the Clergy and the Peasantry.

This drawing from the Riksdag in 1738–39 is rather difficult to interpret. Sweden has been thrown upside down (1), the Nobleman says that he wants it this way (2), the Clergyman does not think that it will hurt him (3), the Burgher hopes to gain something by it (4), and the Peasant says he is used to it (5). Who or what the fox represents (6), who is clearly behind all this, is difficult to say.

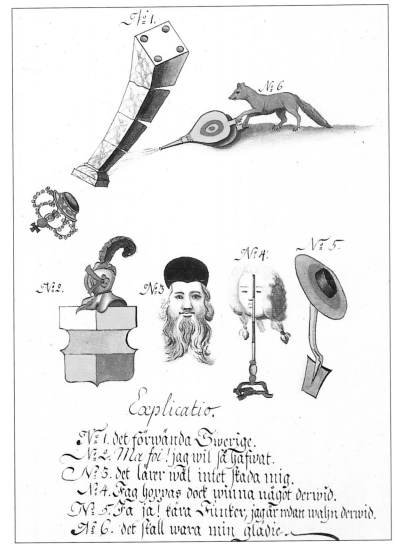

The Hats deposed not only Arvid Horn but also his supporters in the Council. The members of the Council could not actually be removed from office, but the Hats devised a system whereby members who belonged to the opposing camp held their titles and pensions but lost their political power. When the Estates reviewed the minutes of the Council, these members were accused of not having carried out the decisions of the Estates. They were dismissed and replaced by Hat supporters. For each new Council member the Estates proposed three Hats, after which the King was to appoint one of them.

The Council became politicized along party lines, and political, not bureaucratic merits determined who was to be a member of the Council. One of the most outstanding Hats, Carl Gyllenborg, succeeded Horn as the Chancery President. The system, which was introduced at the 1738–39 Riksdag, meant that the composition of the Council became dependent on the majority in the Riksdag; a type of parliamentary government was thus introduced. The new men in power had entirely different policies from those of Arvid Horn.

The chair of the Speaker of the House of the Nobility, a German seventeenth century piece in ebony and ivory. The chair was sold during the reign of Gustav III, but it was returned to the House of the Nobility as a gift in 1823.

In domestic policy, economic questions were important to the Hats. There was an intense economic debate going on both within and outside the Estates. The goal was to gain wealth through an active economic policy which favored trade and domestic industries. Holland and England were regarded as models. The Hats favored Swedish "manufactories" and levied high tariffs on foreign goods.

The Hats also hoped that scientific advances would make Sweden stronger. The Academy of Sciences was established in 1739 with the primary task of supporting the natural sciences and mathematics. The work of the academy was very pragmatic, and it became largely an agricultural society. By collecting and publishing useful "science and observations" the academy encouraged more effective utilization of the country's resources and development of the economy.

Carl von Linné undertook far-ranging journeys throughout the country at the request of the Estates. His assignment was to look for natural resources in the form of plants and minerals which could be used in factories and for improving agriculture.

In spite of the great interest in manufacturing, trade and shipping, agriculture was still entirely dominant. However, agriculture was little developed, and it was, if anything, less rational than earlier, as the land had been divided into increasingly smaller parcels every time it was inherited. Each farm as a rule had strips of arable land in a number of different locations. The Hats were also leaders of change in this area. Jacob Faggot, who was a surveyor and a Hat supporter, convinced the Estates and the Council of the

In 1723 Jonas Alström (who was later ennobled with the name Alströmer) founded a manufactory in the town of Alingsås with the support of the Riksdag. During the entire Age of Liberty the venture was dependent on substantial government subsidies. The book above is a document from the 1734 Riksdag and contains cloth samples which were submitted with an application for government support for the manufactory.

The most important question dealt with by the Riksdag of 1740–41, the war with Russia, was presented in this unpretentious manner. In this document the Secret Committee requests the authority to make all necessary decisions if "the realm's safety, welfare, honor and development demand *wärckeligheter*," a word that has the double meaning of "realities" and "action." When some members of the Clergy asked what was meant by "*wärckeligheter*" the Speaker replied: "Thereby should be understood the declaration and waging of war against the enemies of the country." The Secret Committee's request for this authority was granted, and war was declared on Russia a week later.

necessity of a reform. In 1757 the first enclosure was decreed, which meant that strips of land should be exchanged among landowners to consolidate holdings in larger units of cultivation.

In one area after the other reforms occurred under the Hats which were intended to improve economic conditions in the country. However, during their first years they concentrated on foreign policy. With the shift in power they received not only the post of chairman of the Secret Committee, but also the majority in the body. A new foreign policy was introduced which opposed Russia and favored France. In the party propaganda it was said that the areas lost under Karl XII would be reconquered; Sweden would once again be a great power in northern Europe.

The shift in power meant that an activist party interested in war replaced a regime which had worked to keep Sweden outside European conflicts. The young Hats thought that it would be possible to win an easy victory in the east, as Russia appeared to be disrupted in a struggle over succession to the throne. Under pressure from France, Sweden declared war on Russia in 1741. The Swedish troops were poorly prepared, and order was restored in Russia sooner than the Swedes anticipated. The Swedes were defeated, and Finland was occupied by Russia. Peace was not made until 1743. It was milder than expected, but in Sweden discontent with the military failure had already given rise to violence.

A soldier from the Hats' war with Russia 1741–1743. An ink drawing by Jean Eric Rehn.

## The Dalarna Rebellion

Sweden had a long tradition of rebellions stretching back to the Middle Ages. During the reign of Gustav II Adolf, there were minor uprisings against the war and the sacrifices which war meant to the common man. But not even under Karl XII was dissatisfaction expressed in more serious uprisings. In 1743, however, a rebellion occurred in the province of Dalarna which was directed against both the economic and foreign policies of the Hats.

The farmers of Dalarna had suffered crop failures, and heavier tariffs had been levied on the border trade with Norway. In addition, many men from the province had fallen in the war against Russia. When Riksdag representatives for the Peasantry were to be elected in 1742, a provincial ting was summoned in the town of Falun, where discontent proved to be general. The following year a call for an uprising was sent from Mora to all the other parishes of Dalarna.

In the summer of 1743 nearly five thousand primitively armed men left for Stockholm to protest the actions of the Estates. Even the Peasantry with its Speaker in the lead had accepted the declaration of war against the Russians.

The rebellion was well-disciplined. The rules of order for the march on Stockholm included the following:

> In a neighborly fashion please see that no damage is done to fields and meadows, as much as is possible, where the troops approach, neither for friends nor foes, and if food supplies should wane, they should be obtained properly, either through gifts or by purchase for a small sum.

The men from Dalarna went through the countryside without being hindered by any troops, and they did not stop until they came to Norrtull in Stockholm (where tolls were collected at the northern entrance to the city). Negotiations began between the King and the leaders of the rebellion, as well as between the rebels and the Estate of the Peasantry. A number of leading Hats fled the city in fear. Activists among the men from Dalarna at last entered the city, and there was open fighting in the middle of the capital. The rebels were subdued by regular troops, and some of the

The "message stick" was used to send messages from farm to farm and from village to village. It was an effective means of communication far into the nineteenth century. This message stick from the Dalarna Rebellion exhorts the people of Hedemora parish to general mobilization: "Each and every man who can bear a rifle should within twelve hours, armed and supplied with eight days food, be present at the parish's usual meeting place."

A pike from the Dalarna Rebellion.

leaders, at least one of whom was a peasant representative in the Riksdag, were condemned to death, while others were imprisoned.

It is difficult to judge the rebellion from this vantage point in time. The eighteenth century author Olof von Dalin derogatorily referred to it as "the great dance from Dalarna," while others have claimed that there were really deep-rooted causes. At any rate, it frightened the arrogant Hats and showed them that serious discontent with their policies existed among the peasants. This unrest had not been channeled through the Riksdag, where the Peasantry apparently was not sufficiently strong or sufficiently representative.

## The Parties in Focus

The significance of the parties varied during the course of the Age of Liberty, but without a doubt parties played a decisive role in political life from the 1730s until the coup d'état of Gustav III was carried out in 1772. The parties did not emerge from the need to cooperate to reach long-range goals based on a common ideology. Rather the party of the Hats was built up around opposition to Arvid Horn. According to one contemporary account, it was an attempt to "assemble a large party," which had to be done with the help of "money, offices and titles."

Before a new Riksdag met, the party's supporters tried to come to an agreement about a common position in the most important questions. They adopted a plan of action where the party's policy was clarified, and they decided what stance they would take regarding the decisions made by the Council since the previous Riksdag.

The parties were led by party bosses who, in turn, were supported by persons who comprised the real party leadership. The leader of a political party of that day should not be confused with such a role today; nor should the parties be equated with their modern counterparts. There were no formally elected leaders or steering committees responsible to any other body. On the other hand, individual members of the Riksdag or groups of persons assumed leading positions.

The party bosses were responsible for negotiations between the Estates. Subordinate to them were a number of key persons, whose duty it was to report to the party leadership about what was happening in the various Estates and to coordinate and lead the actions of the party sympathizers. They met not only with members of their own Estates, but also with their counterparts in the other Estates. A system also developed which included other party functionaries, who worked both within and outside the Riksdag.

The goal of the party apparatus was, of course, to create unity in policy. This was not easy, considering the structure of the Riksdag of the Estates and the composition of the Estate of the Nobility. There were many varied interests within the Nobility. Attendance at the House of the Nobility varied considerably during a Riksdag, which made it difficult for the parties to evaluate the situation.

An important feature of the life of the political parties was the various forms of entertainment. Usually one of the leaders invited party comrades to dinner, either at home or at some inn. Many critics described these free dinners as a way of buying votes with the help of food and drink, but they also had a serious goal and could be compared to today's working lunches or official dinners. At such events plans were made, and the doubters were convinced of the benefits of the party's programs and views.

The political clubs were also important forums for the parties. They existed before parties came into being and had always served as places where members of the various Estates could meet and discuss politics. The clubs became increasingly important meeting points where decisions were made and where friendships developed. There is a story from the Riksdag of 1738 about a festive evening at Castenhof, where a number of Arvid Horn's supporters drank the "Rhinish wine." As Horn was going to celebrate his birthday the next day, the group ended the evening by going to his home and playing in his honor outside. Horn's sons opened the doors and the group was invited to further entertainment far into the wee hours.

How great then was unity in the parties? There were party whips, and the will existed among party leadership to keep their respective groups together. But it is still difficult to ascertain to what degree the supporters could be controlled. The official minutes of the meetings of the Estates tell us something, but the most important meetings were secret. The members of the Secret Committee were pledged to silence. Differences were also great between the parties. In 1741 the Caps were described as lacking unity, leaders, soul and courage. It took a long time before they had an organization similar to that of the Hats.

In a contemporary brochure the members of the two parties were depicted as crews of two ships. The Hats' crew included "a bunch of timid and inexperienced sailors, who, uncertain as to whether they should go on board this ship or that, follow along in small ships, as long as some food is thrown out to them." The Caps' crew was portrayed as having many who were on board to get food, but they readily crept below deck if it began to blow. They would desert, if the leadership did not keep its promises or give them enough aid, according to the text.

During the Age of Liberty even young ladies were involved in party rivalries according to Carl Snoilsky, who in his poem "Hats and Caps" at the end of the nineteenth century expressed his negative views of the party system. The Finnish artist Albert Edelfelt illustrated a quarrel between two noblewomen.

The House of the Nobility was well attended, but few members took part in the debates. One scholar has studied the minutes of the meetings from the 1760–62 Riksdag and found that, although the number of members exceeded nine hundred, the debates were dominated by little more than ten people from each party. The parties were able to control the political discussions, and the speakers generally followed the party line.

Although the parties were very significant, the majority of the members of the Riksdag were not part of these groups, and it was for their favor that the parties had to compete. The work of politics consisted mainly in getting these "middle-of-the-roaders" on one's own side.

Party activities were also very costly. The journeys of poor nobles and their upkeep in Stockholm often became party matters. Entertainment in the clubs and party meetings in various places also cost large sums.

Much "party support" for both the Hats and the Caps came from outside the country. In the struggles which took place in Europe, Sweden was an interesting country to have on "the right side." France contributed actively with advice and money when the Hat party was established, and Russia supported the Caps. The ambassadors of Denmark and England gave money to the parties. The foreign representatives became significant actors in the political game. Diplomatic reports from Stockholm reveal how members of the Riksdag could be influenced and how foreign ambassadors steered the parties. There were even regular negotiations between the party bosses and diplomats where the size of party support and the per diem of the Riksdag members were determined.

Both contemporary and modern commentators have argued that this dependency on foreign diplomats was such an abomination that it is sufficient cause to consider the government of the entire period a failure. Those who had been designated to look out for the best interests of the country accepted foreign contributions to their own personal incomes. Others have argued that the importance of bribes has been exaggerated. The Riksdag members were not that easy to control. They certainly accepted money and allowed themselves to be entertained, but they followed their own minds and acted mainly in the best interests of the country. They were forced to accept foreign gifts to be able to live in Stockholm, but that did not mean that their opinions could be bought. The Hats were not more sympathetic to the French due to bribes, but rather because of their convictions.

The foreign subsidies were not the only means of finance for the parties. The ruling party always had posts and privileges to distribute. Even more important were the somewhat regular contribu-

Later critics of the Age of Liberty have often condemned the bribery system as one of the greatest weaknesses of the period's political life. Contemporaries were also critical. This caricature depicts the Cap party as a donkey weighted down by Russian orders and medals. The Hat party is represented as a frisky steed.

tions which individual politicians made to their party's chest. This support was perhaps a more serious threat to the independence of the Riksdag members than that of the foreign ambassadors.

## Political Crises and Attempted Coup d'État

The Hats were in power from 1738 until 1765, a period characterized by political problems. The party barely managed to survive the war with Russia, and the Dalarna Rebellion was evidence of the unrest in the country. The Council and the Estates were forced by the Russian Empress Elizabeth to accept Duke Adolf Fredrik of Holstein as successor to the childless Fredrik I. The Estate of the Peasantry would have preferred another candidate, the Danish Crown Prince Frederick, but there were stronger powers backing the Holstein Duke.

Before embarking for Sweden Adolf Fredrik gave the assurance that he would obey the Swedish constitution and not demand more power than the law allowed or than the Estates could be expected to legislate. Shortly thereafter the King married Lovisa Ulrika, sister of Prussia's regent, Frederick the Great. The new royal couple would soon launch an intensive campaign to strengthen royal power at the cost of the Estates.

Strangely enough, the Hats were able to retain power during the 1746–47 Riksdag in spite of the unsuccessful war and the domestic unrest. They also received a great deal of help from the Russian ambassador, who used methods that were entirely too crude in supporting the Caps. The Hats exploited the dependency of the Caps on the Russians in their propaganda. The Caps were discredited, and this contributed to the fact that the Hats were again able to gain support for their anti-Russian policy.

Lovisa Ulrika is painted here by Antoine Pesne. As Queen she fought an intensive battle to strengthen the power of the monarchy. During an attempted coup d'état in 1756 the Estates proved strong enough to retain their power.

Bishop Johan Browallius from Åbo, here in a portrait by M. Capsia, adhered to the Hats and was an eager spokesman for the rule of the Estates. He was also an outstanding natural scientist in the spirit of the times.

Adolf Fredrik's Accession Charter of 1751 did not imply any formal reductions of royal power, but after a conflict concerning the appointment of the Chancery President, the three upper Estates decided that the post would be filled directly by the Estates without consultation with the King. The Council was empowered to represent the Estates of the Realm, and the King in reality lacked all power. In a famous statement the Åbo bishop Johan Browallius declared that "the idea that the Estates could be wrong is against the fundamental law of the land."

In the beginning of the 1750s the King and Queen allied themselves with the Caps, especially the younger officers and the royalist sympathizers among the peasants. The alliance was so obvious that the Caps were often called the party of the Court. During the 1755–56 Riksdag an acute conflict arose between those who wanted to strengthen the power of the Crown and those who wanted to preserve the existing system.

The Hats held the majority in the Estate of the Nobility and in the Secret Committee. The King tried to maintain his position of power and prevent appointments which were less desirable from his point of view. But the Estates and the Council won the day. The

Riksdag decided to introduce a seal with the King's own signature. It was to be used if the King did not sign an official document after twice being requested by the Council to do so. The Estates thus rendered the King's person totally superfluous in law-making and administration.

There was, however, dissatisfaction in the country with the Hat regime and its autocratic attitude. The Prussian-born Queen and those loyal to her thought that they had sufficient support to be able to bring about fundamental changes in the constitution which would give the King more power. The Queen pawned some of the crown jewels, and the money was distributed to various groups, especially military officers. A coup d'état was supposed to take place at the end of June in 1756, but the plans leaked out to the Hats, and instead of a coup there were investigations and court proceedings. The leaders of the coup were tried and eight of them condemned to death after a short trial.

The royal couple had not officially given their support to the coup, but it was apparent that they had acted in opposition to the ruling Hats. The Queen was reprimanded, and a sharp protest was read to her by Bishop Samuel Troilius from Västerås. It was later disclosed that the King also knew about the coup and helped those who were behind it. There was cause enough to depose the ruler, but the Estates let compassion go before justice. The story ended in a victory for the Hats, who strengthened their position, while the Court was in disgrace.

In Europe 1756 marked the beginning of the Seven Years' War with Prussia and England on one side and Austria, France and Russia on the other. From the various warring nations came proposals for Sweden's involvement, and references were made to Sweden's role in the Thirty Years' War. In Sweden some groups had territorial ambitions and wanted war, just as ten years earlier such ambitions had led to the war with Russia. This time the goal was to regain parts of Pomerania. Sweden again went to war, in spite of the fact that the country was as poorly prepared as in 1741.

The war in Pomerania, 1757–1762, was a failure for Sweden. Although the Swedish troops were not without success, prestige was lost, as the goals which had been set were in no way attained. The Swedish army was in poor condition, and morale was low among both the officers and the soldiers. Noble officers left the war to take part in the Riksdag of 1760–62. Peace was finally made without any changes in the country's borders. The result, however, was that the Hats were weakened, the economy was in a catastrophic state and the royal family and the Caps gained renewed strength.

The stamp with Adolf Fredrik's signature made by order of the Estates in 1756, a revealing symbol of the weakness of the monarchy during the Age of Liberty. There had also been a stamp with the royal signature during the last year of Fredrik I's reign, when the King was old and ill.

In commemoration of the defeat of the coup d'état in 1756 the Estates had this medal made with the motto "The Preservation of Liberty."

## Olof Håkansson – Speaker of the Estate of the Peasantry

THE ESTATE OF THE PEASANTRY was called the fourth Estate, but should not be underestimated. In the many party struggles during the Age of Liberty it played an important role.

One of the reasons was that for more than twenty-five years the position of Speaker of the Estate was held by Olof Håkansson (1695–1769), a peasant from the parish of Lösen in Blekinge. He first attended the Riksdag of 1726–27, when he represented two hundreds. From 1731 onward he represented all of Blekinge in the Estate, and in 1738 he became the Speaker of the Peasantry.

Håkansson was a typical parliamentarian in a way that makes him seem almost timeless. He often spoke in favor of moderation and caution, but he always pursued the interests of the farmers and participated in political intrigues. It was said that he could get the Estate where he wanted it, and as Speaker he showed more cunning shrewdness than impartiality. He managed to get out of difficult situations, which is evidenced by his actions during the war with Russia.

The Secret Committee met on July 21, 1741 and was complemented then by representatives from the Peasantry. The war with Russia was on the agenda. Olof Håkansson gave an enthusiastic speech in favor of the war and encouraged action rather than negotiations. The speech met with applause. As is known, the war did not go very well for the Swedes, and the Speaker of the Peasantry was called into account. He defended himself with the excuse that he was not given the opportunity to witness the minutes of the meeting, thereby intimating that they were not correct, and also that he thought that "action" meant "caution."

However, Olof Håkansson also demonstrated consistency and firmness on many issues. He was acquainted with the moods of his

Olof Håkansson painted by Lorens Pasch the Younger in 1769.

Estate and among the farmers in the countryside. He sometimes supported the Hats, sometimes the Caps. Håkansson was a skillful mediator and a gifted speaker. In a contemporary brochure it was said that he could "make the most complicated subject understandable to his colleagues who had not had the opportunity to acquaint themselves with the matters."

As Speaker of the Peasantry Olof Håkansson had many contacts with foreign emissaries and numerous times accepted bribes. At the 1746–47 Riksdag, when he supported the Caps, he met in greatest secrecy with the Russian ambassador who was strongly disliked. The latter was impressed by the Swedish peasant and wrote home in a report: "I can well say, that I have never before seen a peasant with such ingenuity, intelligence, insight into and knowledge of general conditions and who speaks in such a fine and natural way."

## A Change in Power

The election to the Riksdag in 1764 was bitter and more politi-cized along party lines than previously. Opposition to the Hats was strong. They had lost a second war, and the country suffered from the expenditures that they had made. On top of that there was an international economic crisis which caused the value of Swedish currency to decline sharply. In the background was increasing rivalry among the Estates.

The granting of titles of nobility had continued unabated during the Age of Liberty. By about 1760 nearly two thousand noble families had been introduced into the House of the Nobility. Many members of the nobility thought that the number was too great, and in 1762 it was decided that no new nobles would be matricu-lated. This caused irritation in the other Estates, where a number of members had looked forward to occupying a place in the House of the Nobility one day. The Estate of the Clergy demonstrated its dissatisfaction by excluding all members who were of noble birth.

The coalition of public officials and entrepreneurs that had supported the Hats had acquired new and powerful opponents, including the increasingly stronger group which represented small and medium-sized businesses. The election results in 1764 meant that the Caps won a majority among both the Clergy and the Burghers. In the Estate of the Peasantry the legendary Speaker Olof Håkansson was defeated by the Cap member Josef Hansson. In the Estate of the Nobility the Caps had control of the appoint-ments of the Speaker and the committees.

The "young" Caps quickly gained power in the 1765–66 Riksdag and revamped Swedish policy in a number of questions. They generally wanted more restraint in economic policy and an orienta-tion in foreign affairs toward Russia and England rather than France. There was also an intensive constitutional debate. The Court wanted the King to have the right to veto constitutional questions, a proposal which was not accepted. On the other hand, the matter was settled concerning what should be considered a fundamental law: only after a decision was approved by two succes-sive meetings of the Estates would such a law be considered valid. Thus the voters would have an opportunity to take a stand on a question, and it would be possible to prevent a temporary majority in the Riksdag from abusing its position. The rule is still in force.

The reforms of the Caps did not lead to any rapid changes, and the Court was disappointed, as the King's position was not strengthened in the way that they had hoped. The Caps were as unwilling to share their power as the Hats earlier had been. But not just the Court was dissatisfied; there were also other groups in society that at least temporarily suffered from the new restrictive economic policy.

Josef Hansson was a wealthy farmer from Mossebo in the province of Västergötland. He owned several manors and was typical of a new kind of self-confident entrepreneur in the Swedish countryside. From 1740 un-til 1772 he represented his area in all sessions of the Estates except that of 1769–70, when the election was not approved. The painting is by Ulrika Pasch.

The 1766 Freedom of the Press Act, the first such act in the world. In England censorship had been abolished in 1695, but the 1766 Swedish law was the first enacted which stated that everything that was not expressly forbidden could be printed and that every intervention against the printed word should be tried in court.

*Folkets Röst*, one of the many newspapers which appeared after the introduction of freedom of the press, was a channel for radical and democratic ideas.

The Estates did something of lasting value in December 1766 when they passed a proposal concerning freedom of the press which had originally come from Anders Chydenius, a member of the Clergy. The Swedish Freedom of the Press Act was unique in an international perspective. It meant that freedom of the press would be unrestricted. Censorship was abolished, and all official documents would be made accessible to the public. In order to gain the support of the Clergy, however, it was still forbidden to criticize or deny the true evangelical doctrine in print, and publications which concerned the Christian faith had to be approved by the Church.

The act guaranteeing freedom of the press had a direct effect on politics. Bitter pamphlets in which opposing sides lashed out at one another became common and an integral part of political life. The debate intensified the rivalries between the centers of power: the Court, the Hats and the young Caps. There were also fundamental differences of opinion within the various parties.

The hard political battle, which continued until Gustav III's coup in 1772, had both social and economic causes. Somewhat simplified, it might be said that the Hats represented the interests of the higher public officials and the aristocracy, while the Caps were spokesmen for the lower Estates and the gentry. During the last part of the Age of Liberty there were far-reaching demands for an equalization of the Estates and for democratization. This was also reflected among the populace. In 1769 the newspaper *Folkets Röst* (the People's Voice) demanded that all mature men should receive the right to vote in elections to either the Estate of the Burghers or the Estate of the Peasantry.

After an acute crisis arose between the King and the Council, the Estates were summoned again in 1769. This time the election led to a victory for the Hats. One of the reasons was the economic crisis, which to a certain extent was the result of Cap policies. The attempt by the Caps to use the discontent with the Hats which existed among the gentry and the lower Estates was to no avail. Among the first measures which the Hats took when they returned to power was to purge the Caps from the Council.

Rivalry between the Estates became even more intense. The three lower Estates increasingly protested the privileges of the nobles, while there were many Hats in the Estate of the Nobility who preferred increased royal power to a continued radicalization of the country's government. There was also dissatisfaction with the Riksdag of the Estates, whose decisions did not lead to anything positive. On top of that, crop failures created dissatisfaction among the peasants, and poor economic conditions in general affected the burghers. The continual shifts in power in the Riksdag (the Caps won the election of 1771) increased the unrest and discontent.

The situation seemed favorable to Crown Prince Gustav, who was in Paris when Adolf Fredrik died in 1771. Gustav III was

## Anders Chydenius – the Man behind Freedom of the Press

ANDERS CHYDENIUS (1729–1803) came from an old clerical family. He studied natural science and theology in Åbo and Uppsala before he served as a clergyman in the 1750s in the Finnish province of Österbotten. He became a member of the Riksdag in 1765–66 as the representative of Österbotten's chaplains and immediately made his presence felt.

Anders Chydenius in an engraving by Johan Fredrik Martin.

In spite of the fact that his background was far from simple (he belonged to what was known as the "clerical aristocracy" in western Finland), he was fundamentally a liberal and spoke for freedom and for those who had difficulties. He voiced his opinions on a number of questions, especially economic matters, where he took a stand for liberal solutions – greater freedom and less regulation. He was obviously a strong opponent of the Bothnian trade embargo, which meant that all towns north of Gävle were forbidden to trade south of Stockholm or Åbo and were not allowed to receive foreign vessels.

At the Riksdag of 1765–66 Chydenius was one of the most active Caps and gave more than a hundred speeches in the Estate of the Clergy. He was an intense party supporter and demanded hard punishments for deposed Hats. He was certainly regarded as difficult by many, and, after he published a brochure which attacked a financial plan already passed by the Riksdag, the Clergy decided that he should lose his seat in the Riksdag during that session and the following.

The Clergy thereby lost one of its most energetic and gifted members. Before Chydenius left Stockholm he wrote the general deputation's report to the committee on freedom of the press. In this question, as in economics, he went further than most people. He was first and foremost opposed to censorship; he had personally experienced its implications with the publication of his debate articles in economic questions. But he also worked for the principle of "the right of access to public documents."

Although the 1766 Freedom of the Press Act was passed after Chydenius had left the Riksdag, his report and his agitation for a radical reform are regarded as having been decisive for this remarkable law which still at the end of the twentieth century influences the Swedish view of freedom of the press and the public's right to information.

Chydenius began as a Cap but left the party and eventually supported Gustav III's coup d'état. He became the vicar and dean in Gamlakarleby in Finland, and, as such, he was conservative and kept good order among the members of his parish.

During recent decades Chydenius has been given increased attention, although it is doubtful whether he had any great importance for economic policy. The economist Eli F. Heckscher wrote in the 1930s that Chydenius was characteristic of the Age of Liberty "but for him, as well as for many others who turned their minds to social problems during that era, his work in a strange way came to naught after the revolution of 1772, at least as far as current research has been able to ascertain."

Carl Gustav Pilo's gigantic, unfin-
ished painting of the coronation of
Gustav III in *Storkyrkan* in Stockholm in 1771. Between the pillars to
the left stands the Speaker of the Nobility Baron Axel Gabriel Leijon-
hufvud and behind the throne are
found the three other Speakers of the
Estates: Chief Magistrate Carl Fredrik
Sebaldt, Bishop Anders Forssenius
and the peasant Josef Hansson.

cautious during the first months of his reign. He immediately
signed the Accession Charter and prior to his coronation promised
the Estates that they would retain their rank. At the Riksdag which
met after the death of Adolf Fredrik it also appeared that everything would be as it had been before. The new King was positively
received when he opened the Riksdag and declared that he wished
to be none other than "the first citizen of a free people." He also
mediated between the parties in the Estate of the Nobility.

Radicalization continued among the nonnoble Estates, and
demands were made that the privileges of the nobility should be
abolished regarding appointments to public office. These developments made many nobles uneasy. The Caps also made themselves
unpopular in the Estate of the Nobility when they reduced the
defense budget, which hurt the military officers.

Thus criticism of the young Caps increased within the nobility,
whose privileges were threatened, and the Estate of the Nobility
no longer held a clear position of leadership. The Court was the
center of the nobles' opposition, which focused on the idea that
their privileges could be retained if they supported the King. The
antagonism between the first Estate and the other three became a
great advantage to Gustav III in the play for power. He planned his
coup with the help of noble officers and other leading groups in the
House of the Nobility.

France also supported Gustav III, and he accepted subsidies
from the French government. None of the countries which had
agreed to protect the constitution of the Age of Liberty reacted;
Russia was occupied with other matters, and Denmark did not
dare to intervene. The situation with regard to foreign affairs was
very advantageous to the King. He, however, could not be com-

"Gustav III leaves the Royal Palace on the day of the revolution." Pehr Hilleström painted the scene only a few months after the royal coup d'état on August 19, 1772.

pletely sure of victory and took a number of measures intended to prevent retaliation. The memory of the failure of the 1756 coup certainly lingered at Court.

The political situation was complicated when Gustav III summoned the Riksdag on August 21, 1772 to the Hall of the Realm in the Royal Palace and gave a speech to confirm the coup d'état which had occurred two days earlier. The King had taken command of the troops, and the army was in place outside the palace. The Council and some of the leading members of the Riksdag had been taken into custody. Decisive was the fact that there was no party which could rally its members against the King, as had been the case in 1756. The King was victorious, and the Age of Liberty came to an ignominious end.

## A Period of Greatness or Deterioration?

The constitution which had developed on the basis of the Instrument of Government of 1720 was for its time a nearly unique experiment in parliamentarism. Royal power was increasingly circumscribed, and the Council of the Realm functioned as a parliamentary government. By politically motivated shifts in members of the Council, the Estates found a way of bringing about changes in government. The Peasantry was certainly in some ways subordinate to the other Estates, but the peasants did have representation, and they could submit their grievances and have them dealt with, which often led to changes in the existing law. The Estate of the Peasantry has been characterized as "a popular corporation without a counterpart in Europe."

In his speech to the Estates after the coup d'état Gustav III painted the form of government of the previous decades in the darkest of colors. Two parties had divided the country into two camps and brought it deepest misery. The King thus created a picture of the Age of Liberty which would long remain in the public consciousness and which would be used by men who fought against democracy and parliamentarism at the end of the following century.

The historian Ludvig Stavenow wrote in 1903:

> A noble military revolt, led by the King himself, all of a sudden repudiated the proud position of power of the Estates. It collapsed with hardly a hand raised in its defense. That best shows how decayed it was, how devoid of real strength and dignity.

But the picture is far from clear. The political scientist Fredrik Lagerroth wrote in 1915:

> The person who looks closely at the last decade of the Age of Liberty, however filled the era may have been of dirt and slag, will see the formation of principles upon which modern Sweden has chosen to base its welfare.

The Age of Liberty encouraged scientists, people interested in public debate and persons engaged in industry and trade. There was the desire to try new forms for developing society, which are attractive to people of our own era. Freedom of the press was introduced, and traditions were established within science, politics and trade.

A commemorative painting of the vicar Gustaf Fredrik Hjortberg and his family in Släp Church in the province of Halland. Hjortberg was a representative of the eighteenth century enlightenment. The various objects around him, the plants, the animals and all the books, bring to mind versatility and scientific progress.

## Gustav III's speech to the Estates after the Coup of 1772

HONORABLE, noble and well-born, revered, venerable, learned, venerated, wise, respected, worthy and honest good gentlemen and Swedish men!

Filled with the utmost distress concerning the condition in which the fatherland now finds itself, and forced to show you the truth in full daylight, when the Kingdom stands on the brink of its downfall, would it not be surprising if I today did not receive you with the happy feelings which always fill my heart when you are assembled before the throne. My heart cannot reproach me for having hidden something from you. I have twice spoken to you, with all the truth which my calling demands, with all the sincerity, which proper honor loves. The same sincerity will now speak, when the past must be repeated, to be able to cure the present.

It is a deplorable, but generally known truth, that hate and dissension have torn the Kingdom asunder. The Nation has, for some time past, been divided into two parties, which have cloven it, so to speak, into two kinds of people, united only in tearing the fatherland apart. You know how this schism has given birth to rancor, rancor to revenge, revenge to persecution, persecution to new revolutions, which at length have become a periodic disease, which has maimed and debased all of Society.

These upheavals have shaken the Kingdom, for the sake of the ambitions of a few persons; rivers of blood have flown, first pouring from one party, then from the other, and the People have always been the victims of the discord, which was of little concern to them, but whose unfortunate consequences they first and foremost were acquainted with. To secure their rule has been the sole goal of the rulers; everything has been adapted to this, often at the expense of the other citizens, always at the expense of the Kingdom; where the law was clear, the letters have been distorted, when it was obviously contrary to the design, it was broken; nothing has been sacred for a crowd aroused by hate and vengeance, and the chaos has finally gone so far that the opinion has been confessed, that plurality is above the law and has no other norm than arbitrariness.

Thus freedom, the noblest of all rights, has been converted into intolerable aristocratic despotism, in the hands of the ruling party, which itself has been repressed and arbitrarily run by a few men within it. One has trembled at the announcement of a Riksdag, and far from thinking about how the affairs of the Kingdom could best be dealt with, the major occupation has been promoting the majority of the party, in order to be protected against the other party's lawless undertakings and violence. Even if the domestic situation of the Kingdom has been dreadful, how horrible has not its foreign predicament been. I am ashamed to mention it. Born Swedish and a Swedish King, it should be impossible for me to believe that foreign intentions could rule a Swedish man, and moreover, that the most lowly means have been used for this purpose. You know what I mean, and from my shame you should understand the ignominy into which your dissension has submerged the Kingdom.

It was in such a state that I found the Kingdom, when, by the Providence of the Almighty, I accepted the Swedish scepter. You are aware that I have not spared any effort in reconciling you, that I have in my speeches to you from the throne called for, as in other situations, unity and obedience to the law; I have sacrificed both that which only concerned me, and that which to me as King was dear; no obligations, no steps have I found difficult and heavy to submit to or to undertake, in order to achieve such a healthy goal for the fatherland. If there are any among you, who can deny this truth, stand up!

### Ridderskapet och Adelen

Wårt stånd af undersåtlig ifwer
Nu kysser på sin Konungs hand
Och ewig trohets löfte gifwer,
Den allas Hjertan lagt i band.

### Präste Ståndet

Hwar redlig Präst sitt hjerta skjäncker
Til den som Swerges wäl beredt,
När Himlens Nåd man rätt betäncker,
Hwar Swensk blir nögd med hwad som skedt.

### Borgare Ståndet

Gustafs Milda Hand oss fägnar,
Gustafs tappra arm oss hägnar,
Swerjom Honom tro och nit,
Bort med afwund, hat och split.

### Bonde Ståndet

Gustaf ingen Swensk föragtar,
Allas wälgång eftertraktar.
Gläds Hwar Bonde wid din plog;
Gud, i Gustaf, gjedt oss nog.

Tryckt i LUND, åhr 1773

# CHAPTER 6

# From No Power to Division of Power

"A glow there was on Gustav's day ..." The poem which the poet Esaias Tegnér wrote several decades after the death of the King contained a strong element of propaganda. Gustav III is portrayed in all his splendor. There have been strong kings in Swedish history and a learned queen, but none of them have been surrounded by such an aura. For many generations the Gustavian Age was regarded as a brilliant epoch, while the Age of Liberty was considered a period of decline.

The King who carried out the coup d'état in 1772 was a tactician who knew how to influence public opinion. But propaganda alone is not sufficient to convince an entire nation. At the end of the Age of Liberty the form of government was criticized by all the Estates, just as there had been discontent with the absolute monarchy in 1718. Many former supporters had become critics.

The coup d'état was the prelude to what Swedish history has called the Gustavian Age, which lasted for nearly four decades and ended in 1809 with a revolution that overthrew Gustav III's son, Gustav IV Adolf.

Johan Tobias Sergel's statue of Gustav III at the foot of the Royal Palace in Stockholm was unveiled in 1808. As does Tegnér's poem from the fiftieth anniversary of the Swedish Academy in 1836, it gives expression to the cult which developed around Gustav III during the first decades of the nineteenth century.

## Autocracy – with Certain Reservations

The young Caps who held power in the Council at the time of the coup d'état were not able to offer the King any resistance. His supporters were stronger, and the Estates had to accept an Instrument of Government entirely different from that of the Age of Liberty. The King could go much further than he had been able to do before the coup, when he had negotiated with the leading Hats for a reinforcement of the power of the monarchy.

Gustav III had studied contemporary political thinkers, and the ideas of Montesquieu had earlier appealed to him. According to Montesquieu, power should be distributed among an executive branch (king/government), a legislative branch (parliament) and a judiciary branch (courts). In the Instrument of Government, which was written during the summer of 1772 and approved by the Estates after the coup, the balance of power was not a prominent feature. The King held a totally dominant position. Nor did Gustav III refer to any contemporary political philosophers when

*On the opposite page:* The four Speakers kissing the hand of Gustav III after having sworn their oath of allegiance in August 1772. The monarchy had again become strong, and the Riksdag retired to the shadows. This print from 1773 was of a kind that was often glued inside the cover of a chest.

The Instrument of Government of 1772 was read aloud before the Estates and accepted without any discussion. The King had taken the initiative from the Riksdag.

Gustav III shows the bust of Gustav II Adolf to his little son. The King was fascinated by his great and strong predecessors, which was also expressed in artistic form. He wrote a draft of an opera on Gustav Vasa and plays on Gustav II Adolf. Drawing by Sergel.

he presented the new constitution. He merely expressed the desire to restore the same order that existed during the reign of his great predecessors to the throne, especially Gustav II Adolf.

The Council became the King's advisers and had no power of its own. The members of the Council who had been appointed just prior to the coup had to leave their posts and were replaced by men on whom the King could rely. With the exception of the part of the Council which served as the Supreme Court, the Council was very weak under Gustav III.

The role of the Estates also changed fundamentally. In the future they would be summoned when the King so wished. The Riksdag retained its power in only a few areas according to the new, somewhat ambiguous Instrument of Government. The King was not allowed to initiate an offensive war without permission from the Estates, and they furthermore reserved the right to levy taxes, as well as to control the Bank of Sweden. There were no directives as far as the committee system was concerned. Only the Secret Committee was specifically named in the new Instrument of Government, and it was to be headed by the King.

The Riksdag was dissolved after the Instrument of Government was passed, and it was not to meet again for six years, in 1778. Until that time decisions were largely made by the King alone after presentation by an official and in the presence of some members of the Council.

The first period of Gustav III's reign was successful. He took measures to alleviate the shortage of grain and the economic crisis in the country, and he made the bureaucracy more effective. The country's defense, which had deteriorated during the Age of Liberty, was reorganized. He abolished torture, which had been introduced in the sixteenth century and had been used in the Age of Liberty during the bitter party struggles.

Many of the reforms in the economy, defense and bureaucracy which Gustav III carried out had been proposed and discussed by the Estates earlier. However, the Estates had not been able to act on these proposals before the King assumed power.

One of the questions which had not been resolved after the coup was the status of the Freedom of the Press Act. It had been passed by the Estates in 1766, but, as the King had declared that no fundamental laws passed after 1680 were valid, its status was uncertain. Gustav III claimed to be in favor of freedom of the press, but in the new act which was passed in 1774 this liberty was no longer protected by fundamental law. The new Freedom of the Press Act also contained a number of restrictions which made it more difficult to publish political tracts. The right of access to public documents, however, was preserved.

The lively political debate in newspapers, magazines and pamphlets now ceased. Criticism was silenced, not only due to the change in the laws, but also due to the change in the political climate. The King and the Court became dominant instead of the Estates. Not all were sorry to see this development. Many people had disliked the unrestrained debates and unbridled criticism at the end of the Age of Liberty. The King could thus count on support for his encroachment on freedom of the press.

The Riksdag which met in Stockholm 1778–79 did not resemble those of the Age of Liberty. There were no longer any parties, and

Gustav III on his way to the opening of the Riksdag. Drawing by Sergel.

Gustav III decorated with the blue ribbon of the Order of the Seraphim in a famous portrait by Lorens Pasch the Younger. The King wore the white armband so that he would be recognized during the coup d'état of 1772. The officers who wished to follow him were admonished to do likewise. Until 1809 the armband remained a part of the uniform of Swedish officers.

This apparatus for distilling alcohol was common in Swedish homes. Distillation for household use was one of the big political questions during the eighteenth century. The struggle concerned the right to distill and the size of the fees to be paid to the Crown.

Gustav III's attempt to make production of distilled alcohol a state monopoly did not succeed. The royal distilleries which he founded never made a profit. Instead they became the focus for great discontent, which was also expressed in the Riksdag. When the monopoly was abolished in 1787, most of the distilleries were closed. This picture is of the old royal distillery in Gävle.

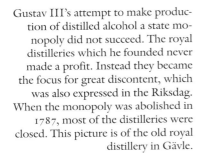

the Estates did not have the right to review the actions of the Council, much less those of the King. The House of the Nobility was again divided into classes with reference to the 1626 Ordinance of the House. Most important was the fact that the King had the initiative. The Speakers of the Estates, who were appointed by the King, had to swear an oath that they promised to work in their respective Estates according to principles which the King had laid down.

There was, of course, dissatisfaction in the various Estates, and attempts were made to form an opposition. Within the Nobility there were many public officials who were subjected to individual investigations, a check of how they carried out their duties. Many members of the Estates also thought that the economic policy, including monetary policy, was a failure. The Burghers opposed the weaker guild law which the King had adopted, and the Peasants were especially critical of the fact that Gustav III had rescinded their right to distill alcohol for household needs and had established royal distilleries.

The Clergy was opposed to the more liberal religious legislation. A proposal for freedom of religion for immigrants was presented in the Estate by Anders Chydenius. Typically, it had come into being only after negotiations with the King. The proposal was passed, and Sweden thus obtained its first law concerning freedom of religion in 1781. Immigrant Catholics and confessors of other faiths were granted the right to practice their religions as they wished; later some Jews were permitted to immigrate to the larger cities. These changes were vehemently opposed, especially by the bishops and the leading Clergy.

The first Riksdag after Gustav III took over was a demonstration of the King's power and influence. The old party men who hoped that the meeting of the Estates would mean a certain return to the Age of Liberty went home disappointed. The reason why the

King could control the Riksdag was undoubtedly the fact that, in spite of everything, he had broad support. Although there were certain oppositional groups, they had no real base; they were not even able to gain a majority in their own Estates.

But times changed. In the years that passed until the next Riksdag in 1786, the King's position was weakened. Crops had failed again, and there were also other reasons for discontent. In the Estate of the Peasantry criticism of the government monopoly on distillation became stronger. Dissatisfaction with the King grew in the other Estates as well.

The mood of the 1786 Riksdag was very different from that which had prevailed in 1778–79. The King could no longer tame the Estates. The committees appeared again, as did the party system to some extent. The Riksdag disapproved of some of the King's proposals and acted more independently than during the first Gustavian Riksdag. The session did not bring about any revolutionary changes, but there was a change in the political climate.

The King had reason for concern and, after the Riksdag ended, he immediately began to take measures to alleviate the discontent, but, above all, to pit the interests of the Estates against one another.

## Royalism in spite of War and Autocracy

During the Age of Liberty the leading members of the Riksdag had ushered Sweden into two wars. Behind this policy had been the desire of the former great power to regain some of its losses. Sweden tried once again to play a role in international politics and recoup its position as a power to be reckoned with. The results were nearly disastrous both times. The country's defense was in poorer shape than was thought, and the Swedes misjudged the strength of the enemy.

Gustav III was driven by the same desire as the Hats during the Age of Liberty: to reconquer territory and return to Sweden its old position of power. He also thought that a successful war against Russia would strengthen his political position at home. This is a classical strategy which has often been repeated throughout history: to attempt to unite the people by fighting against a common enemy.

The King tried to disguise the war as defensive after claims of Russian provocation, but in reality he started an offensive war against Russia (1788) in defiance of the 1772 Instrument of Government. His plan was to make a surprise attack on St. Petersburg and thus create an advantageous position for negotiations while the Russian Empress Catherine II was occupied by war with the Turks.

The soldiers of Gustav III's poorly prepared army went away to war in uniforms with hats that had blue and yellow plumes.

During Gustav III's Russian war two sea battles were fought at Svensksund in the Finnish archipelago. After repeated defeats the Swedes won their first great victory in 1790, and the war could be concluded without loss of territory for any of the parties. Painting by J.T. Schoultz.

The war did not turn out as was hoped this time either. It did not go well for the Swedes on land or at sea. Discontent spread among the officers and resulted in what became known as the Anjala League. A number of officers protested against the illegal war and took direct contact with the enemy, the Russian Empress, who, however, remained indifferent.

The King was hard pressed, especially when Denmark attacked from the south. He had to fight a war on three fronts: against Russia, against Denmark and against the domestic revolt. In this situation Gustav III returned to Sweden from Finland and energetically sought support by traveling around the country. As Gustav Vasa had done, he turned directly to the men of Dalarna in Mora and spoke about the treachery of the nobility, and how the Danes had taken unfair advantage of the situation and attacked the country at a difficult time. According to the King's version the noble officers had committed treason, risking the country's security, and Denmark, as earlier in history, had acted as the traditional foe.

In reality Gustav III was on the way to losing the war which he had started. The Danes had attacked because of a treaty with Russia which obligated them to join the Russian side. The Danish actions were thus foreseeable, but the King had believed in a quick victory which would deliver the enemy a fait accompli. This proved to be a misjudgement.

Gustav III summoned a new Riksdag in 1789, where the atmosphere was significantly more favorable to the King than it had been earlier. Gustav III was clearly popular among the lower Estates, not only because of his good speeches, but also because of the aura which he created about his person and his court.

"Royalists" dominated the three lower Estates, while the "patriots" were found in the Estate of the Nobility. The opposition was split and was not able to get any proposals accepted due to the King. Gustav III ordered the appointment of a Secret Committee consisting of twelve members from the Nobility and six from each of the other Estates. The Peasantry was at last represented on the committee.

In spite of strong opposition from the Nobility the King was able to get through his Union and Security Act, which gave him an even stronger position and further weakened the Estates. The Riksdag retained some of its legislative power and control of the Bank of Sweden, as well as the possibility of regulating the public debt through the newly established National Debt Office.

The Council disappeared when the King had the right to determine the number of members: he set the total at zero. Judiciary power was assumed by the Supreme Court. The Union and Security Act was approved by the four Estates at a *plenum plenorum*, which meant that the Estates convened together led by the King.

Gustav III completely dominated the assembly. For the members of the Riksdag there was no other alternative but to say "aye," or "nay," to the King's proposal. A number of representatives of the Nobility called out "nay!," but it did not affect the decision. As thanks for their support, the lower Estates gained access to a number of offices which previously had been reserved for the nobility. Perhaps the peasants won the most, as they gained the right to purchase and take noble estates into their possession.

## The Assassination of a King and a Bloodless Coup d'État

The last Riksdag which Gustav III attended took place in Gävle in the beginning of 1792, three years after the French Revolution, when the French King was divested of nearly all power. The news from Paris also contributed to some of the unrest in Sweden. The development, however, had gone in a direction totally different

The official opening of the Riksdag in 1789 in the Hall of the Realm in the Royal Palace. The members of the Council, dressed in their special robes, sit in front of the King's throne. In the hall are seated the four Estates with the Nobility closest in the picture and the Clergy, Burghers and Peasants on the other side of the aisle. Painting by Pehr Hilleström.

The Union and Security Act of 1789 further decreased the power of the Riksdag and meant a transition to almost complete royal autocracy in Sweden.

A plaster model of the provisional Hall of the Realm which was built in the town of Gävle for the Riksdag of 1792. Gävle wanted to give the Riksdag something of the capital's glamor.

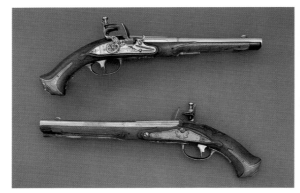

Items associated with the assassination of Gustav III in March 1792: Anckarström's pistols, the blood-spattered chair in which the King was said to have been carried from the Opera House to the Royal Palace after the attack, and the costume and mask which the King wore at the masquerade.

from that in France. The King had become an absolute monarch and the Riksdag nearly powerless.

One of the reasons why the Estates were scheduled to meet outside the capital was that it was thought that the King's safety could be more easily guaranteed in a town far from Stockholm. Gävle has been described as a town under siege during the Riksdag. Another reason for meeting outside Stockholm was that it made it more difficult for the civilian and military nobles to participate. They had their work to attend to in the capital city, and they also had to pay for their own travel and lodging.

The Riksdag did not demonstrate any power; the opposition had gone underground. The stage was dominated by the King. However, the opposition would soon brutally manifest itself. At a masquerade at the Opera on March 16, 1792 Gustav III was shot by one of his enemies within the nobility, Jacob Johan Anckarström. The idea was that assassinating the King would put an end to royal "despotism" and that the power of the nobility could be restored. But the changes which the perpetrators of the coup had hoped for did not come about. The conspirators were poorly prepared, and the assassination was condemned by public opinion. There was no revolution of the nobles. Instead the leveling of the Estates continued.

The son of Gustav III, Gustav Adolf, was only thirteen years old when his father died, two weeks after the shots were fired at the Opera. A regency was appointed under Duke Karl, the dead King's brother. He did not summon the Estates after the murder, and they did not play any significant role during the remainder of the Gustavian Age. A sufficient number supported the monarchy, and the nobility was split and therefore was not able to form a unified opposition.

During the first years of Gustav IV Adolf's reign a number of economic reforms were carried out. The first was enclosure, which began in Skåne under the estate owner Rutger Macklean and which was later carried out in most of the country. Land which before had been divided into a number of tiny strips was concentrated so that every farmer had his lots assembled in a few larger fields. The old villages were split up. Thus the land reform which had been initiated during the Age of Liberty was continued.

The Riksdag had a very small role in the reform work. Crop failures, economic difficulties and foreign policy problems caused the King, however, to summon the Estates to Norrköping in 1800. In spite of the strong opposition to autocracy the King had the situation under control. Nor could criticism appear in newspapers, magazines or brochures, as censorship became increasingly efficient.

Anckarström was subjected to whipping before a crowd in the square in front of the House of the Nobility before he was taken away to be executed for the assassination of Gustav III.

Gustav IV Adolf painted by Per Krafft the Younger shortly before the coup d'état in which the King was deposed in 1809.

The 1800 Riksdag was held in Norr-köping, a town with about 9,000 inhabitants. The official explanation for the selection of Norrköping was that food was cheaper there than in Stockholm. The real reason was probably that the King considered the residents of Stockholm unreliable, and he feared riots in the capital. Engraving by J.P. Cumelin, 1797.

The only contact the King had with the Estates after 1800 was with those committees assigned to inspect the Bank of Sweden and the National Debt Office, which met every other year. Gustav Adolf understood that a new Riksdag could be dangerous, as domestic and foreign problems had weakened his position. The opposition was no longer concentrated in a small group of nobles, but rather had become more widespread.

During the period 1792–1815 there was nearly continual war in Europe. Initially Sweden was able to hold itself outside the conflicts, but eventually the country became involved in the struggles. Gustav IV Adolf felt great antipathy to Napoleon, and in the spring of 1805 Sweden joined England, Russia and Austria in a coalition against France. Swedish troops were sent to Pomerania, which was regarded as an important area for deployment. But the war did not go well, and the coalition was dissolved.

The treaty between Russia and France at Tilsit in 1807 meant that both countries had become enemies of Sweden. Gustav IV Adolf hoped that he could conquer Norway with England's help, but instead found himself at war with his neighbor to the east. Russia attacked, and the Swedish defense did not hold. At the same time Denmark declared war, and Sweden had to fight on two fronts. The help from England which the King had hoped for never arrived.

The Swedes planned a counterattack on the Russians in the spring of 1808, but it failed. Sveaborg, the fortress outside of Helsinki which was the cornerstone of the Swedish defense against Russia, was easily taken by Russian troops, and thus the field was open to the enemy. The Finnish army had some success, but failed on the whole. At the end of 1808 the Swedish troops were forced to retreat from Finland. The Russian army advanced into northern Sweden and attacked the Åland Islands in the Baltic over the ice. For a short time Gotland was also occupied.

The King's failure in foreign affairs and the economic problems which the war created were the basis of the opposition which became organized at the end of 1808. When troops stationed on the Norwegian border began to move toward Stockholm, it was the starting signal for a coup d'état in the capital on March 13, 1809. The King was arrested, and he was later deposed by the Estates. Behind the coup were civilians and military officers led by Adjutant General Carl Johan Adlercreutz.

It is difficult to say how widespread dissatisfaction with the King was. It is clear that Gustav IV Adolf was not as clever a propagandist as his father. He received no help from his closest allies in the military or civilian administration, but he was not without support in the country. According to the nineteenth century author Bernhard von Beskow, most of the burghers were royalists. There is also evidence that other lower social groups supported the King. According to another contemporary source, he was mourned by "housemaids, servants and old women."

On March 14 a summons to a Riksdag was issued, and the meeting began in May.

When six officers came to arrest Gustav IV Adolf on March 13, 1809, he seized the rapier from one of them and fled out to the Palace Yard. Royal Forester Johan Ludvig von Greiff ran after him. He was wounded by the King's rapier but managed to overpower him. The event is recounted here by an unknown artist.

Sveaborg Fortress at the entrance of the harbor of Helsinki was founded by Augustin Ehrensvärd who also made this painting from the construction work. Although Commander C.O. Cronstedt had forces as large as those of the Russians at his disposal when the fort was under siege in 1809, after a short bombardment he chose to capitulate and surrendered with 2,000 cannons and the whole coastal fleet of 110 ships.

## The Instrument of Government of 1809 – a Compromise

Some radical changes have occurred in Sweden's government throughout time. They have varied in character and had different goals. Since the Middle Ages it has generally been possible to bring about these changes without bloodshed. The self-confident party representatives during the Age of Liberty remained silent when Gustav III seized power. It is true that he became the victim of an assassin's bullet, but it was not a question of an organized revolution. Gustav IV Adolf could be deposed in a bloodless coup; it was done quickly, effectively and with no real opposition. His supporters turned their sails to the wind and joined the rebels. Eventually he was allowed to leave the country and the rest of his life traveled around Europe as Colonel Gustafsson.

What happened in the spring of 1809 after the King had been removed from the throne? Did the Riksdag regain its sovereignty? Duke Karl again served as regent. He was both politically and physically weak and lacked heirs, but he was, after all, the uncle of the deposed King. For the perpetrators of the coup it was especially important to maintain legitimacy. Future struggles concerning claims to the throne could not be discounted, as the deposed King lived and had an heir who was a minor.

Plans for a new constitution were not lacking. The nobles had sat in their salons, the writers in the inns and the learned in their libraries pondering over what the ideal constitution should look like. When Gustav III came to power he had used the King's position in the seventeenth century as his point of reference. What prototypes would be chosen in 1809?

The leaders of the coup were well aware of two autocratic regimes: the Estates during the Age of Liberty and Gustavian rule. Just as Gustav III had done, they tried to paint the previous era black, and their interpretation also long left its mark on the history books. Gustav IV Adolf's rule became a dark period in Swedish history.

When the Riksdag assembled in May 1809, a Committee on the Constitution was appointed for the first time to work out a new Instrument of Government. It worked very quickly, as the country was in the midst of an acute crisis in both domestic and foreign affairs. There were numerous earlier proposals which could be used as a basis, and the so-called Håkansson proposal proved of great importance. It had been worked out by the county governor Anders af Håkansson, son of Olof Håkansson, the Speaker of the Peasantry in the Age of Liberty.

For the Riksdag it was important to solve the country's fundamental problems, to give the nation a new government and to make peace with foreign enemies. On June 6, 1809 the Riksdag approved the new Instrument of Government and immediately afterwards hailed Duke Karl as King. In the Instrument of Government the power of the King had not been eliminated.

- The King should "alone govern the realm" in the manner prescribed by the Instrument of Government. The members of the Council of State were responsible to the Riksdag for their counsel, primarily by means of the review of their proceedings by the Committee on the Constitution. It was, however, not a question of "parliamentarism," as no demands could be made for political accountability.
- The legislative power was divided between the King and the Estates in the case of fundamental and general laws. Responsibility for economic and administrative legislation was vested in the King.
- The right to tax belonged to the Riksdag. The Instrument of Government stated: "The ancient right of the Swedish people to tax themselves shall be exercised by the Estates of the Realm at a general Riksdag." The Bank of Sweden and the National Debt Office were also to remain under the jurisdiction of the Estates.
- The judicial power belonged to independent courts with judges appointed for life. The Supreme Court, established during the reign of Gustav III, was retained.
- The office of Ombudsman was created. The Ombudsman was to be appointed by the Riksdag and was to safeguard the interests of the citizens against the authorities.

Lars Augustin Mannerheim, the first Ombudsman of the Riksdag. The office of Ombudsman was created in 1809, and the officer had as his task to safeguard the interests of citizens and to speak on their behalf against authorities. During the course of time this institution has been adopted in many other countries. Engraving by L.H. Roos.

The Instrument of Government of 1809 was a compromise. It gave the King a strong position, but not as strong as in other proposals that had been discussed. The power of the Riksdag increased. The nobles were divested of their special privileges regarding appointments to public office, and they had to accept an equalization of taxation. The members of the Peasantry, however, were not satisfied, as they felt that nobles still had too much influence, and they signed the new Instrument of Government only after a lecture by Karl XIII.

The new Instrument of Government proved to be durable; it was not replaced until 1974. Fundamental changes in the form of government did occur during this period, but the Instrument of Government of 1809 remained valid. Perhaps this indicates that a country is ruled by forces other than the content of the Instrument of Government. Sweden eventually became a parliamentary, democratic state in spite of the fact that the constitution still said that the King "alone" should rule the land.

The origins of the 1809 Instrument of Government have continued to be the subject of lively debate. One of the main questions has been whether it was a domestic product or if it was inspired by foreign models, especially by Montesquieu's concept of the division of power. The debate was especially intense during the period when Sweden was becoming democratized more than one hundred years after the Instrument of Government came into being.

The Instrument of Government provided the principles for governing the country. At the same time certain rights and freedoms were established for its citizens. Each citizen was guaranteed freedom of religion, if he did not disturb "society's peace or create a public nuisance." The fundamental law named freedom of conscience, freedom of speech, freedom of the press and security for persons and property. In 1810 a new Riksdag Act was approved which regulated the work of the Riksdag. A new fundamental law concerning freedom of the press was passed as well, which was based upon the 1766 legislation, but which forbade all censorship, even in theological matters.

The new Riksdag Act also made the Committee on the Constitution permanent, with responsibility for the legal review of the work of the King. The old Riksdag of the Estates was preserved, but the question had already been raised in debates as to whether the Estates had not outlived their usefulness. The French Revolution in 1789 had shown that it was possible to reject an old society based on the Estates. Louis XVI had become a victim of the guillotine, and the French nobility had lost much of its power. Other forces became dominant. The society which the Riksdag of that time reflected had been challenged as early as the eighteenth century, and increasing numbers felt that the Estates no longer represented the Swedish people.

In 1809 there was a proposal which would have given Sweden a more modern representative body. It suggested that the four Estates be replaced by a bicameral Riksdag and was based on models from France and the USA. The supporters were radicals and other groups which did not have seats in the Riksdag in spite of their power in society at large. The foundation was laid for a debate which would go on for the next sixty years concerning the form and status of the Swedish parliament.

## Motivating the 1809 Instrument of Government

THE INSTRUMENT OF GOVERNMENT was adopted by the Riksdag on June 6, 1809. In a memo the secretary of the Committee on the Constitution, Hans Järta, made the following comment:

> The committee has tried to create an executive power, active within a definite framework, with unity in decision-making and full strength in the means to carry out decisions [the King in Council]; a legislative power, slow to act, but solid and strong in the face of opposition [the Riksdag]; a judicial power, independent under law, but not above it. Furthermore, an attempt has been made to direct these powers to internal restraint, without becoming involved with one another, without leaving the restrainer something of the ability to act of the restrained.

— — —

> The members of the committee do not propose great and brilliant changes in our constitution's old and basic forms. They have believed that such forms should not be lightly remolded, especially not immediately after recovering freedom, when ways of thought are bound to go asunder. They have believed in that which the example of Europe's freest state [England] also shows: for a nation's common rights and its citizens' personal freedom and safety, there is no more stable protection than those forms, surrounded by the sanctity of the centuries and fortified by a general national power working within them.

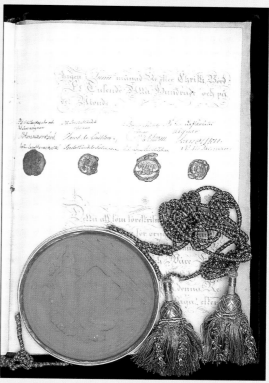

The 1809 Instrument of Government was signed by the Speakers of the four Estates and had Karl XIII's signature, seal and confirmation. The Speaker of the Peasantry, Lars Olsson from Groeröd, did not sign the document on June 6, as did the others, but rather tried in vain to have the paragraph changed which protected prevailing privileges. His signature was added three weeks later.

Influenced by the French Revolution Hans Hierta renounced his title of nobility during the Riksdag in Norrköping in 1800. His signature is seen here when he resigned his membership in the Committee on the Law on April 1, 1800. He still signed his name then as Hans Hierta. But during a tumultuous session at the end of May he also resigned from his seat in the Riksdag, renounced his title and changed the spelling of his name. Nine years later he was one of those who worked out the new Instrument of Government. As secretary of the Committee on the Constitution in 1809 he signed the minutes as Hans Järta.

## The Proceedings of the Riksdag as a Political Weapon

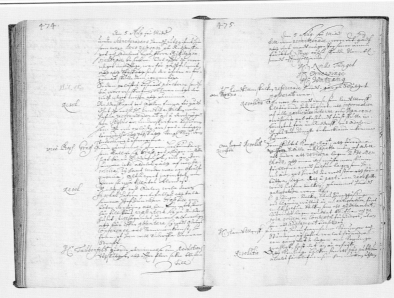

Two pages from the Nobility's minutes in 1668. The style is German Gothic, which many still used in the beginning of the nineteenth century. The handwritten records are preserved in the National Archives. Until 1810 the minutes of the Estates were internal documents. Then the Riksdag Act established that the minutes should be printed and made available to everyone.

The three volumes on the left are the minutes of the Estate of the Burghers from the 1760–62 Riksdag, while the volume on the right contains the minutes of the Burghers from 1786. During the Age of Liberty the meetings were many and long and produced a comprehensive material. The Riksdag at the time was really sovereign. The meetings of the Gustavian Age were few and short, because Gustav III did what he could to restrict the power of the Riksdag.

THE PROCEEDINGS OF THE RIKSDAG are important to all those who are interested in Swedish history. They give us knowledge about all areas of society. In the Estate of the Clergy during the eighteenth century education, culture and social questions were central subjects. The minutes deal with everything from the recreational activities of youth and the salaries of clergymen to religious delusions and the death penalty for infanticide.

As early as the beginning of the seventeenth century the decisions of the Riksdag and the petitions of the various Estates were printed and thus accessible to the general public. On the other hand the minutes of the debates in the Estates were long regarded as confidential. A handwritten version of the minutes was preserved in the archives of the respective Estates, but copies were not distributed.

It had been easy to publicize opinions in newspapers, magazines and pamphlets during the later part of the Age of Liberty. Gustav III, however, introduced considerable restrictions on freedom of the press and thus on the opposition's opportunities to be heard. In this situation all the Estates except the Clergy began to print the minutes of their meetings from 1786 onward. They took advantage of a loophole in the law, as it contained no prohibition of publication of the minutes of the Riksdag. Opinions which otherwise would not be made known could thus be spread to the public.

Until 1810 each Estate itself decided whether or not its minutes should be published. The Clergy chose not to make its proceedings public, as there was the risk that differences of opinion within the Estate in questions of religion might be revealed. In the Riksdag Act of 1810 it was stipulated that the minutes should "as soon as possible, be published in print with their complete contents."

The minutes today are printed, along with government bills, motions, committee reports and other documents, a total of between 60,000 and 80,000 pages per year. The official documents of the Riksdag are published in bound books at the end of each session.

As far as is known, Sweden was the first country to stipulate in its fundamental law that the minutes of the parliamentary debates should be made public. Norway was second (1814), and of the remaining Nordic countries, Iceland began to print its minutes in 1845, Denmark in 1848 and Finland in 1863. Some parliaments in Europe began to publish their proceedings in the middle of the nineteenth century, but in most countries this was not done until the turn of the century, 1900.

The publication of parliamentary proceedings could be used for political purposes, as was illustrated by the Estates in 1786. But the minutes, of course, are also important for general information about the state of political opinion. Not only are the decisions important, but also the arguments for and against these decisions.

For historians and others interested in Sweden's past the minutes of the Riksdag, which are preserved in the National Archives, are of great value. They are, however, handwritten and difficult for any but specialists to read. As early as 1855 the House of the Nobility began to print and publish earlier proceedings. Since 1936 the Riksdag is responsible for publication of all proceedings. Today the entire minutes of the debates of the Nobility and the Peasantry are available in printed form. The minutes of the Burghers and the Clergy have been partially published; other parts are in progress.

In modern times it is considered important that the minutes are published quickly. Today preliminary minutes are available in print the day after the meeting of the Riksdag. The final, approved versions are ready after a few weeks.

# CHAPTER 7

# The Estates out of Step with the Times

PROPOSALS FOR REFORM of the Riksdag of the Estates had been made earlier and received varying degrees of support. At the time of the 1809 governmental reform a bicameral Riksdag was discussed, but it would take nearly sixty years before the Riksdag of the Estates disappeared. Its shortcomings were apparent, however. The structure of the Riksdag made decision-making a lengthy and difficult process. It was a reflection of the dissolution of the old society.

Powerful forces opposed reform. A strong lawmaking body was not favored by the monarchy. Many representatives in the Riksdag of the Estates also feared their exclusion from a new Riksdag. The Nobility and the Clergy had special reason to be apprehensive.

Representation was a central question during Riksdag debates. There were of course other pressing political issues during the first half of the nineteenth century. Sweden was in the midst of a crisis when Gustav IV Adolf was deposed. He was succeeded by Karl XIII who did not have any heirs. Foreign policy was also a problem. Sweden was involved in a complicated game of power politics. Could the men who had toppled the King find solutions to the various problems? What role should the Riksdag play?

## Bernadotte Takes Command

Gustav IV Adolf was blamed for all evil which had befallen the country. The propaganda against him was also very effective. In a short period of time Sweden received a new Instrument of Government which was agreed upon, but the question of a successor to the throne proved to be complicated. Some of the conservative members of the Riksdag wanted a legitimate successor, and Gustav IV Adolf's son Gustav was the one who was closest in line. However, there was considerable opposition to a continuation of rule by the Gustavians. Instead the choice fell upon a Dane, Prince Kristian August, who had been commander of the Norwegian army.

*On the opposite page:* Karl XIV Johan was a child of the French Revolution. As King of Sweden his policy was conservative, and he opposed the liberal demands for a reformation of the Riksdag of the Estates. The King is seen here in a painting from the province of Dalarna by Kers Erik Jönsson dated 1836, which is done in the traditional style typical of the area.

The sudden death of the heir to the throne, Karl August, at Kvidinge Heath in the province of Skåne in May 1810 depicted in a contemporary engraving.

An unknown artist's portrayal of the murder of Axel von Fersen. Von Fersen is pleading for his life as the crowd attacks with sticks and stones.

Much was expected of the new successor. He was regarded as the person who could lead the country out of the crisis. We know little or nothing about what Karl August, as he was called in Sweden, thought about the situation, even less how he would have performed as Swedish King. He fell off his horse while he was inspecting Swedish troops in May 1810, probably as a result of a stroke. The death of the successor to the throne caused dismay and unrest.

The inflamed state of public opinion which reigned after the revolution and after the death of Karl August provided a hotbed for rumors. One of the most popular of these was that the Gustavians, led by the Marshal of the Realm Axel von Fersen, had gotten rid of the Danish prince in order to place the young Gustav on the throne after all. One of the contemporary pamphlets exhorted:

> Swedes! A prince, murdered by poison – may this persuade you to avenge his memory. A few prestigious, sly people are links in this abysmal chain. Swedes! Awake! There is still a glimmer of hope, but that should not be neglected and blood must flow.

People demanded revenge for the crime which they thought had been committed. Axel von Fersen was the person in the carriage nearest that of the deceased in the funeral cortege which followed Karl August's coffin through the streets of Stockholm. The bystanders began to shout derisive remarks as the procession passed, and in the vicinity of the House of the Nobility the Marshal of the Realm was pulled out of his carriage. Neither the guards nor the army intervened. Devested of his medals and his clothing, he was stoned to death. In Sweden, where riots have been rare and where strong obedience to authority has been a distinguishing feature, the murder of von Fersen is nearly without a counterpart.

At an extremely critical time one of the country's leading officials was subjected to the most brutal violence. Hatred of the nobility

Örebro Castle in an engraving by Johan Fredrik Martin at the time of the 1810 Riksdag. Örebro then had only 3,000 inhabitants. The Riksdag was scheduled there as Stockholm was not considered safe after the murder of von Fersen.

was great in Sweden and sympathy for the Danish successor strong, but the murder caused a shift in opinion. There was fear that unrest would continue and that more would meet the same fate as von Fersen.

Who would succeed to the throne? There was another Danish prince who was available, but he aroused little enthusiasm. Someone was needed who could bring order to the country and who could pursue a foreign policy bent on revenge. The field was wide open for an unconventional solution. By chance, a French field marshal was proposed as the Swedish King: Jean Baptiste Bernadotte, a child of the French Revolution.

For Gustav IV Adolf the struggle against Napoleon had been his foremost foreign policy objective, and he had the support of the nobility, who saw revolutionary France as a threat to its own position. But that did not prevent the Estates from electing one of Napoleon's field marshals as successor to the Swedish crown at a Riksdag in Örebro in the summer of 1810. A new fundamental law was also approved, the Act of Succession, which still regulates succession to the throne in Sweden. Bernadotte had a good military reputation, and the Swedes hoped that with Napoleon's

This picture of Field Marshal Bernadotte portrays him as a brave and decisive warrior. It was shown to the 1810 Riksdag in Örebro and is regarded as significant for his election as heir to the throne.

To express his gratitude for his election by the 1810 Riksdag in Örebro, Jean Baptiste Bernadotte had portraits painted of the four Speakers, who had signed the Act of Succession: Baron Claes Fleming, Archbishop Jacob Lindblom, Johan Wegelin, who was a top official on the Board of Commerce and the peasant Lars Olsson. The portraits were painted by Carl Fredric von Breda and now hang in the Riksdag Building.

Tsar Alexander I addresses the Finnish representatives of the Estates in the cathedral in Borgå in 1809. Under Russian rule Finland retained its constitution from the Swedish era. The Riksdag of the four Estates was not abolished there until 1906, while Gustav III's Union and Security Act was valid until 1919. Copy of a work by E. Thelning.

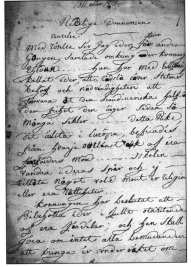

In spite of attempts to do so, Karl Johan never learned Swedish. On the few occasions he gave his speeches in Swedish, as before the Estate of the Peasantry in Örebro in 1812, spelling was adapted to French pronunciation.

help he could recoup some of their losses. Bernadotte had also demonstrated a talent for administration and had been popular as governor of the Hanseatic towns of Hamburg, Bremen and Lübeck.

At the peace concluded in Fredrikshamn in September 1809 Sweden had been forced to relinquish Finland and the Åland Islands and other areas to Russia. Sweden lost one third of its territory and one fourth of its population. With French support and a skillful commander, Sweden hoped to be able to regain Finland. In domestic affairs Bernadotte gave rise to other hopes. The radicals believed that the former revolutionary would support their efforts to change representation in the Riksdag. The conservatives assumed that he would keep the extreme young military officers in check. Hans Järta, one of those responsible for the Instrument of Government, wrote the following: "What captivates me most is the conviction that under him, more than anyone else, lieutenants will remain lieutenants."

In November 1810 Karl Johan, as Jean Baptiste Bernadotte was called in Swedish, came to Stockholm and swore his oath of loyalty before the Riksdag. He was formally Crown Prince, but in reality he became the Swedish ruler, as Karl XIII was very frail. In his first speech to the Riksdag, delivered in French, Karl Johan addressed each of the four Estates:

- The "Most Venerable Knighthood and Nobility" was characterized as "the Crown's and the country's foremost defenders."
- The "Revered Clergy" was declared caretaker of "the sacred teachings of the gospel."

- The "Honorable Burghers" were said to represent "industriousness, trade and business" and to have the task of striving for the development of the kingdom and increasing its welfare.
- The "Worthy Peasants" were told to "with your hands provide sustenance for the kingdom and work for its defense."

The characterization which Karl Johan gave of the four Estates was traditional, but it was important that the statement was made on this occasion. The audience could understand that there would not be a return to either the Age of Liberty or to the preceding period.

The Crown Prince quickly took command of Sweden and in 1812 managed to get two controversial domestic measures through the Riksdag. One concerned universal military service for men between 20 and 25. This reform was accepted by the Riksdag without any great opposition. The other regarded freedom of the press. The Chamberlain of the Court (*hovkanslern*), who was a member of the Council of State, was given the right to confiscate periodicals which were regarded as "dangerous" to general security or which were considered to be of "libelous" character.

There was opposition to this restriction of freedom of the press, but it was not sufficiently strong. Although freedom of the press was protected in the constitution and changes in fundamental laws required the approval of two successive meetings of the Estates, it did not help. The new heir to the throne had demonstrated his power, and the Estates had shown that they were prepared to follow his lead.

In the field of foreign policy Karl Johan made decisions which were surprising, to say the least. In the background lay not only the interests of Sweden, but also his goal of attaining a position from

A satirical drawing from the 1810 Riksdag which shows the Estate of the Peasantry fleeing in fright when threatened with universal military service. The opposition of the Peasantry to universal military service could be partially attributed to the horrible memories of the 1808–1809 war.

The riot at *Södermalmstorg* in central Stockholm on July 19, 1838 was caused by the way in which the Chamberlain of the Court dealt with issues concerning the withdrawal of printed material. The protests were especially directed against the fact that the publicist Magnus Jacob Crusenstolpe had been sentenced to three years imprisonment for lese-majesty because of his writings about Karl XIV Johan. The riots broke out when he was to be transported to the fortress at Vaxholm. Lithograph by Ferdinand Tollin.

A Swedish soldier from the time of the campaign against Norway in the spring of 1814. Sweden has not been involved in a war since. Drawing by C.J. Ljunggren.

Clergymen, nobles and burghers as captured by the pen of an unknown artist during the 1823 Riksdag.

which he might be able to gain control in France after Napoleon. He was not able to accomplish the latter, but he was not without success in his new homeland, where he alone controlled foreign policy.

In August 1812 Karl Johan met Tsar Alexander I in Åbo, Finland. As a result of the meeting, Sweden accepted the existing state of affairs in the east, and the Tsar's control over the Grand Duchy of Finland was recognized. In return Russia supported Swedish ambitions in the west. In the great European war Sweden opposed Napoleon. The country did not have any outstanding place in the struggles, but still managed to force the Danish King to relinquish Norway.

In the Treaty of Kiel in January 1814 Denmark agreed that Norway should "belong to His Majesty the King of Sweden and be a Kingdom united with Sweden." The Treaty of Kiel was not accepted by the Norwegians. They declared Norway an independent kingdom and adopted a radical constitution at Eidsvoll on May 17, 1814. By the use of arms, however, Karl Johan forced the Norwegians to approve the Kiel agreement. One clause was that the two countries would have common diplomatic missions.

Economic questions dominated the meetings of the Estates in 1815 and 1817–18, in which Karl Johan was the leading political power factor. Any kind of opposition irritated him, and he toyed with the idea of a revision of the constitution which would have reduced the power of the Riksdag. No reform was carried out, however, because he understood that he could control the Estates within the framework of the existing laws. Until the death of Karl XIV Johan the Riksdag met regularly once every five years. The Riksdag was summoned to extra meetings, however, on special occasions.

## The Liberal Opposition

In the beginning of the nineteenth century there was rapid economic and social development in Sweden. A middle class grew consisting of officials, large landowners, businessmen, industrialists and writers, who demanded power and influence proportionate to their economic and social positions. Such a goal could not be achieved within the framework of the old Riksdag of the Estates, although some individuals from these groups did have seats in the Estate of the Nobility or in one of the lower Estates.

The government was appointed by the King, but only three of the ministers had specified tasks: the Minister of Justice, the Foreign Minister and the Chamberlain of the Court. This government did not have any prestige to speak of and was dominated by old and powerless men. In reality the King made many decisions together with his favorites, who did not have any formal positions.

In the 1820s a liberal group arose which opposed the King and his conservative policy. In his memoirs Lars Johan Hierta, founder of the newspaper *Aftonbladet*, related how one member of the opposition, Carl Henric Anckarsvärd, brought upon himself vociferous criticism from the conservatives in a debate in the House of the Nobility. They shouted "throw him out," when he raised objections to higher appropriations for the administration of foreign policy. Hierta wrote:

The end of the Riksdag in 1830. The Royal Life Guard Dragoons parade through the streets of Stockholm. Both the opening and closing of the Riksdag long remained formal ceremonious occasions which received a great deal of attention. Lithograph by Adolf Schützercrantz.

> It is impossible to describe the enthusiasm with which I witnessed that and other political scenes – with lively conflicts between the formerly unchallenged all-powerful government and Court party and an opposition which, although as good as newborn, was full of fire and the power of youth. ... The impression of the revelations, which I witnessed, was so overwhelming, that it awakened a burning desire to also try to do something for the cause of the country within public life, which until then had been something alien to me, and would later on be the choice for the main course of my life.

Hierta would soon be disappointed in the Estate of the Nobility. The conservatives were well organized, while the liberal opposition found it difficult to find a common thread. Together with Magnus Jacob Crusenstolpe, a member of the opposition, Hierta published *Riksdags-Tidningar* which contained summaries of what had taken place in the various Estates. The newspaper was a success and made a profit for both publishers. The Riksdag was significant as an opinion-maker, and a large number of people were willing to pay to find out what was said.

Lars Johan Hierta, who began publishing the newspaper *Aftonbladet* in 1830. Drawing by Ferdinand Tollin.

Hierta had learned stenography in Germany and also worked as a clerk and reporter in the Estate of the Nobility. In *Riksdags-Tidningar* he could discard objectivity and allow himself to make comments and reveal his sympathies. He described the cheers and excited stamping and how the Speaker of the Nobility called for order in the assembly. At that point in time there was a spontaneity, audacity and joyful spirit of debate in the House of the Nobility.

Hierta also reported on the Estate of the Peasantry in his paper. He published the speech by one of the leaders of the Estate, Nils Månsson, against the power of the government to confiscate printed matter. This speech, he said, had so much "power and warmth" that most were moved "to tears." He also quoted the

Reform-minded politicians from the
Estate of the Peasantry drawn by
Maria Röhl.

Nils Månsson from Skumparp in the
province of Skåne, "the enlightened
peasant," was a member of the Peasantry between 1810 and 1835 and was
deeply involved in questions concerning public education and freedom of
the press.

Anders Danielsson from Bondarp in
the province of Västergötland was
leader of the opposition in the Peasantry from 1823 onwards, and during
the last Riksdag in which he served,
1834–35, he represented 27 hundreds.

representative Anders Danielsson from Bondarp in the province of
Västergötland, who declared that the peasants had now outgrown
"their state of minority, in which many simple and short-sighted
men still believe that we are found."

The power to confiscate printed material had originally come
into being so that the King could take action against criticism of the
pro-Russian policy of 1812. It was retained, however, and was first
used against the newspaper *Argus*, but later became notorious and
controversial when, via the Chamberlain of the Court, the King
tried to stop the newspaper *Aftonbladet*.

It was scarcely by chance that *Aftonbladet* began to be published in 1830. Liberalism had popular support in Sweden, as in the
rest of Europe. The rules and regulations which restricted trade
and business, as well as spiritual life, were regarded as negative by
increasing numbers. France had experienced a liberal revolution
in 1830, and in 1832 after long debate a parliamentary reform
was carried out in England. Still more important were perhaps
the social and economic changes in Sweden, and the new influential middle class.

People gathered outside the office
of the newspaper *Aftonbladet* to
hear the latest news.
Lithograph by
J.A. Cronstedt dated 1841.

№ 5.
Lördagen
DET TJUGONDESJETTE
**AFTONBLADET**
1851.
den 4 Jan.

*Aftonbladet* has a place in history, not only because it was Sweden's first modern political newspaper, but also because with humor, irony and sarcasm it criticized the King, the ministers and the conservatives in the Riksdag. On the King's behalf the Chamberlain of the Court intervened against the new newspaper with support of his power to withdraw the right of publication. Hierta, however, saved his paper. He found various means of circumventing the King's measures, and *Aftonbladet* became very influential. Within one year it had a circulation of 3,000 copies, far more than any of its competitors.

The King thus failed to stop the liberal organ. This failure was mainly due to Hierta's tactical maneuvers, but *Aftonbladet* would never have been able to win the battle if the liberals had not become strong in Sweden, both economically and socially. The King and the conservatives were simply not able to control the new middle class.

The King and the authorities tried to stop the newspaper *Aftonbladet* with the help of indictments and confiscation of published issues. Lars Johan Hierta won the battle by continually changing the name of the newspaper and appointing new legally responsible publishers. With the publication of *Det Tjugondesjette Aftonbladet* (the Twenty-sixth Evening Paper) the newspaper did not need to change its name again. The battle was over.

## The Representation Debate Renewed

The problem of representation in the Riksdag was long a matter of political concern. One of the more serious proposals for a new Riksdag, and one which received a great deal of attention, was published in 1830 by the judge of the hundred court Johan Gabriel Richert and Carl Henric Anckarsvärd in a pamphlet which contained a proposal for national representation. The authors wanted a Riksdag which would be chosen in a "general election," not according to Estates. Certain criteria of wealth were advocated for voter eligibility, but the sum recommended was low. Those with larger incomes, however, would alone elect a part of the Riksdag. As in the Norwegian parliament the Riksdag would consist of one chamber with two divisions.

The liberals were successful in the election of the 1834–35 Riksdag, which increased the chances of getting some change in the system of representation. The Burghers had been strengthened by a couple of liberal owners of ironworks, Thore Petre from the province of Gästrikland and Jonas Wærn from the province of Värmland. In the Estate of the Peasantry the radical Anders Danielsson gained significant influence, and he also played a role outside his own Estate. Above all, he opposed the rising defense expenditures.

In spite of the growing strength of the opposition, its success was limited. One of the reasons was that it was very difficult to

RIKSDAGEN.
A. T. Sundin & Co.
WESTERÅS.

The struggle for representation reform was not merely a matter for the elite. There is ample evidence of how widespread discontent was in various circles with the Riksdag of the Estates. It could even be found in this caricature from a tobacco case.

The Bernadotte family in 1837 portrayed in a painting by Fredrik Westin. From the left are seen Prince Oscar (II), Queen Desideria, Crown Princess Josefina, Prince August and Princess Eugénie, Crown Prince Oscar (I), Prince Karl (XV), Karl XIV Johan and Prince Gustaf, who died young. The bust is of Karl XIII.

organize a unified opposition in all four Estates. Prior to the 1840 Riksdag an attempt was made to bridge the gap in views and the organizational problems by building a coalition consisting of radical men of the opposition and conservative reform supporters. There was unity in the desire for reforms and for a limitation of royal power. Some wanted Karl XIV Johan to abdicate in favor of his son Oscar, who was regarded as more positive to reform.

The 1840–41 Riksdag was long and stormy. *Aftonbladet*'s role was significant in the debate prior to the session and in the election. The newspaper helped numerous liberals to gain seats in both the Estate of the Burghers and the Estate of the Peasantry. The opposition was also successful in the elections to the standing committees and vigorously attacked the government.

The Committee on the Constitution, which was common for the entire Riksdag, exercised its right to approve a proposal for a constitution which could be presented and approved by the following Riksdag without a hearing before the Estates. According to

The four Estates prepare their common burial in this drawing by A.C. Wetterling from the 1850s. The Speaker of the Nobility and the Archbishop appear to be the least enthusiastic of the four coffin makers.

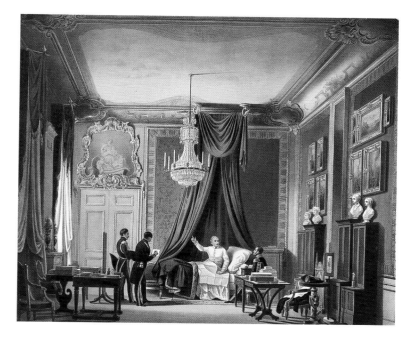

Karl XIV Johan was accustomed to arising about one o'clock in the afternoon and joined the Council of State first about three o'clock. It was thus practical to receive visitors and to carry out certain business of government in his chamber during the morning. Painting by Carl Stefan Bennet.

the committee's proposal the Riksdag should be chosen by universal suffrage, but this right would be restricted by a number of criteria including wealth and the ability to pay taxes. The limitations were defended with the argument that the right to vote should be given only to those who possessed "insight and independence" and, although wealth did not guarantee this, "it brought, however, a strong presumption of both."

When the proposal of the Committee on the Constitution was dealt with by the Estates in 1844, it was defeated by the Nobility and the Clergy.

During the years when representation was discussed enormous economic and social changes took place, both in the countryside and in the towns. Population increased rapidly, and Sweden gained a proletariat, a large group of poor and propertyless people who also often lacked employment. Many experienced them as a threat to the established order; none of the leading liberals wanted this group represented in the Riksdag. There was general agreement that great importance should be placed on the formulation of the rules for voter eligibility and for eligibility for election to the Riksdag.

There was no reform of representation under Karl XIV Johan. On the other hand, there was another constitutional change, the ministerial reform, which was finally approved by the Riksdag in 1840. This change had also been preceded by a long series of studies and proposals. The background was the widespread dissatisfaction with how the Council of State was organized and how the members did their jobs. The members of the Council lacked independence and were powerless in comparison with the King's favorites, who could not be controlled by the Riksdag. These "yes-men" participated in the so-called bedroom cabinet (the King arose late), where many decisions were in reality made.

Although elementary school was made compulsory in 1842, it took many decades before the law was carried out. Many parishes did not feel that they could afford their own school, but rather employed an itinerant teacher who traveled from village to village. Parents could also choose to educate their children at home. In 1859 only 65 percent of the children aged 7–13 years attended public school, and only 7 percent received education above the minimum level. In the picture we see a well-equipped classroom in the 1860s as the artist Frans Lindberg remembered it in the 1930s.

The ministerial reform meant that the four offices of the royal chancery were replaced by seven ministries, each with its own head. Furthermore, three ministers without portfolio were appointed. The office of Chamberlain of the Court, which had become notorious in connection with the confiscation issue, was abolished.

Sweden did get a new government, but it was not a question of parliamentarism. The King still appointed the ministers without consideration of the majorities in the Riksdag. The members of the government were scrutinized by the Committee on the Constitution, but they could not be reprimanded on political grounds, only on juridical. (They had to do something illegal while in office.) No liberal received a post in the new government. The reform was still important, however, for parliamentary development. The ministers acquired a totally different kind of influence in conducting business than they had earlier and thus greater authority in relation both to the King and to the Riksdag.

Other important decisions were also reached by the 1840–41 Riksdag. Public elementary school for everyone was a liberal demand which was accepted by the Estates. In 1842 the Public School Act was passed, which stated that each parish should have "at least one, preferably permanent, school with a properly approved teacher." The state could contribute to the costs, but in principle it was the responsibility of the local authorities to see that there was a schoolhouse and a teacher. The common public school has been considered important for Sweden's development in general and a prerequisite for democracy in the country.

## A New King but the Same Old Riksdag

Karl XIV Johan died in 1844 at the age of 81. He had ruled the country "alone," as it was stated in the Instrument of Government. However, the Riksdag had not been as powerless as during the Gustavian Era; there had been a strong liberal opposition which balanced the King and the conservatives. A number of more liberal reforms had been carried out, especially in the area of economics.

As Crown Prince, Oscar I had been known for his liberal sympathies. He was even called "The Future," and he had actively participated in the political debate and influenced public opinion during the discussions on the public school reform. The moderate liberals had a great deal of faith in the new King. The old organ of the opposition, *Aftonbladet*, suddenly became sympathetic to the monarch. During the first period of the new King's rule a number of reforms were carried out, but the liberals did not consider them sufficient.

Oscar I did not give the representation question high priority. Different proposals saw the light of day, and an investigative committee was appointed by the government, but no unity was achieved. The King was uneasy about what a change might mean for him. The lack of action, however, cannot be explained by the King's unwillingness alone. It was perhaps equally due to the many conflicting interests within the Riksdag.

First, there were differences among the Estates. Should the Nobility relinquish its most precious privilege, the right to constitute its own Estate during the Riksdag, where the families which had been matriculated into the House of the Nobility had the right to be represented? For the Clergy, all the proposals implied a weakening of its power. But both within the Nobility and the nonnoble Estates there were also differences of opinion which caused the members of the Riksdag to prefer varying solutions, to the extent that they wanted any reform at all. These conflicts played into the hands of those who wanted no change in the constitution, and among those was found Oscar I.

At the 1844–45 Riksdag at least one change was made which strengthened the Riksdag: the Riksdag would meet every third year instead of every fifth.

Oscar I
on a coin (*riksdaler*)
from 1844.

The view from the Royal Palace in 1840. The long building on the left is the famed *Bazaren*, which was razed in 1902. In the group which is conversing in the foreground, the man on the left is August Blanche, the newspaperman, author and later member of the Riksdag. The stately man on the sidewalk to the right of the cavalryman is the editor of the newspaper *Aftonbladet*, Lars Johan Hierta. The lithograph is based on a drawing by Ferdinand Tollin.

During 1848, the revolutionary year, there were many revolts against ruling conservative regimes through-out Europe. In March unrest broke out in Stockholm as well and was swiftly quelled by the authorities. Drawing by Fritz von Dardel.

## Revolutionary Spirit

1848 has gone down in the history of Europe as the year of revolutions. No monarch sat safely on his throne. The first revolt occurred in France, but unrest continued in a number of other countries. Sweden was also affected. There were large demonstra-tions, as well as proposals for broader representation.

On March 18, 1848 the Society of the Friends of Reform, which was dominated by liberal burghers, met in De la Croix's salons in Stockholm to discuss representation. Workers and artisans had gathered outside, and a crowd began moving toward the Royal Palace. Windows were smashed, revolutionary slogans were shouted, and the army was forced to intervene. Shots were fired, and 27 wounded or dying were counted; seven bodies were exhibited in the police morgue.

A picture of the prevailing mood is found in the notes made in the diary of the officer and Marshal of the Court (*hovmarskalk*) Erik af Edholm dated March 18, 1848:

> Johanson, the orderly, said this morning that a large number of proclamations against the King had been set up on the walls of buildings. I have one which says:
> King Oscar is a shit, a King unworthy to rule over the land of Svea. He fears for his crown, which is not worthy of one who has the honor of sitting on the throne of the Karls and Gustavs. Therefore, citizens, depose him, the coward, and proclaim the beauteous republic this evening at Brunkeberg. Depose Oscar. He is not fit to be King. Long live the republic! Reforms! Down with the royal family! Long live *Aftonbladet*, death to the King. Republic! Republic!

The King was frightened by the dramatic and bloody events. He called for the resignations of all ministers except one, and the successors were less conservative. To the 1847–48 Riksdag he also submitted a new proposal for broader representation in the Riks-dag, another proposal in a long line. It was largely a tactical move, and Oscar I did not do anything to see that it was passed. The spirit

Gustaf Wahlbom portrayed the burial of the proposal for a representation reform in the radical, nearly socialistic newspaper *Folkets Röst* in 1850. The coffin is borne by representatives of the four Estates, and behind them is seen the tearful Lars Johan Hierta.

of the times would also move in a more conservative direction after 1848, and the pressure for reform receded.

During the 1850s the mood reflected a certain tiredness with ideological conflicts. Few people were concerned with the larger question of the composition of the Riksdag. On the other hand, the Riksdag managed to reach major decisions in several areas, including the economy. The most radical concerned the railways. Between 1850 and 1880 a railway network was constructed which was decisive for the country's industrialization.

Oscar I died in 1859 and was succeeded by his son, Karl XV.

## The Bicameral Riksdag at Last

The question of representation was discussed for more than fifty years in Sweden, more or less intensively. Certain minor reforms were carried out which made the Riksdag more representative. The non-theological faculties of the universities and the Academy of Sciences became represented in the Riksdag in an 1823 decision, the owners of the rural manufactories in the Estate of the Burghers in 1830, the owners of farms formerly owned by noblemen in the Estate of the Peasantry in 1834 and people involved in business and owners of property in the towns in the Estate of the Burghers in 1858. But it stopped there.

People such as Lars Johan Hierta and August Blanche were able to win seats in the Estate of the Burghers (after 1858). Blanche was a great orator and a much appreciated author. He had also participated in the organization of the Sharpshooters' Movement, which was supported by the new middle class. This association was patterned on a Swiss model, and the idea was that people should be educated to defend their country by means of these voluntary organizations. The movement clearly bore a liberal stamp and was regarded with suspicion by the conservatives.

Karl XV with a cigar and a Napoleonic pose. The photograph was taken in the 1860s.

A meeting in the House of the Nobility during the last session of the Riksdag of the Estates, 1865–66. *Ny Illustrerad Tidning.*

The Town Hall in Örebro in a photograph from the 1860s. Local self-government increased in importance with the 1862 municipal reform. The town council, which met in the town hall, became the highest decision-making body in the towns and cities.

In the constitutional area the spirit of liberalism characterized an important change in the beginning of the 1860s, the reform of local self-government in 1862. Each city, town and parish was to become a municipality which would be governed by a council or by elected representatives. On the regional level a county council (*landsting*) was established in each county. The members of these councils were elected indirectly.

In local elections the principle of the Estates was abandoned, and instead elections were held in which voting eligibility was determined in relation to wealth and income. General elections, instead of Estate elections, were also of fundamental importance for the Minister of Justice Louis De Geer, the man behind the representation proposal which was finally adopted by the Riksdag in December of 1865. In 1861 De Geer wrote in a famous memorandum to Karl XV, an opponent of a reform, about the need for a new form of representation:

> Most important in the matter is the acceptance of the fundamental principle of general elections. Limitations and qualifications in its application are certainly necessary, but the drawing up of these is of lesser importance than people in general imagine, because as soon as different interests are not brought forth and placed in opposition to one another, a common way of thinking about a problem most often emerges among the plurality of both the more and less wealthy and the more and less educated.
>
> A bicameral system should, however, be most suitable in order to avoid simple and hasty decisions, but both chambers should be based upon the population in its entirety and not on election corporations, where the one represents the higher in society and the other the lower, through which only the eruption of society's inner struggles is called forth.

Both the Nobility and the Clergy regarded Louis De Geer's proposal with doubt. Pressure from the outside was considerable, however, and the mood in Stockholm was extremely agitated. Troops were on alert around the capital in case riots should break out if De Geer's proposal met with defeat.

Louis De Geer's ministers in the oldest known photograph of a Swedish government, taken in 1859 or 1860. In the first row farthest to the left sits Louis De Geer himself. The man with the moustache, who is seated in the middle, is the successful Minister of Finance Johan August Gripenstedt, and to the right is the Minister of Foreign Affairs Ludvig Manderström.

The proposal, however, proved sufficiently conservative for the powers that wanted restraint and sufficiently radical for those who wanted change. The majority in favor of the proposal in the final voting in the Estate of the Nobility was not overwhelming; 361 nobles voted for the reform and 294 against. Certainly many cast their affirmative votes with heavy hearts. With the abolition of the Riksdag of the Estates, the nobility renounced its last significant political privilege.

Two chambers were to replace the four Estates, and a number of regulations went into effect concerning who should have the right to vote and who should be eligible to stand for election.

- The Second Chamber was to be chosen by general direct or indirect election. No one should have more than one vote, but in order to vote it was necessary to meet certain economic criteria which implied that nearly all workers and lower public officials and many small landowners were excluded. It was the farmers who were favored. The members were usually chosen by majority vote in one-candidate election districts. In the larger towns and cities voting was sometimes by means of lists in which the list receiving the greatest number of votes won. Women were not allowed to vote, nor were they eligible for election. The term of office was three years, and a small stipend was paid to the representatives.
- The First Chamber was to be elected indirectly by the county councils and the city councils in the larger towns and cities. Eligibility to the First Chamber required a large income and/or significant wealth. No stipends were paid to the representatives, and the candidate had to be at least 35 years of age. Only 6,000 of the country's four million inhabitants were eligible for election. The First Chamber was to be renewed successively, and the term of office was nine years.

The closing of the last Riksdag of the Estates on June 22, 1866. Woodcut by Oskar L. Andersson.

- The chambers were to be equal in principle. The approval of both chambers was needed for changes in the law. In questions concerning the budget and government finances, joint voting was to take place, if the chambers were unable to come to an agreement separately. The most important committees were joint committees. Until 1921 the King had the right to appoint the Speakers of the chambers. They were required to swear an oath before the King and to promise to "maintain and defend the Crown and the rights of the Riksdag with all my ability, so help me God..."
- The Riksdag was to convene every year instead of every third year. No other rule was more important for the position of the Riksdag.

The Speakers of the last Riksdag of the Estates in 1866: Count Gustaf Lagerbjelke, the Nobility; Archbishop Henrik Reuterdahl, the Clergy; the wholesaler Johan Gustaf Schwan, the Burghers; and the farm owner Nils Larsson from Tullus in the province of Jämtland, the Peasantry. *Ny Illustrerad Tidning*.

On December 7, 1865, when the results of the voting on the representation reform in the House of the Nobility were announced, people outside cheered. The lone clergyman, who is walking away from the crowd, is not taking part in the general jubilation. *Ny Illustrerad Tidning*.

The representation reform was received with enthusiasm in Stockholm. Sympathizers with the reform and radicals felt that they had won a great victory. The old Riksdag of the Estates had been abolished and replaced with "modern" popular representation.

The restrictions on voting rights and eligibility for office gave the new representatives a very conservative appearance. The First Chamber was filled by high public officials, owners of ironworks and manufactories and large landowners, often of noble birth, while the Second Chamber was dominated by farmers. The latter were favored at the expense of the growing working class. The workers were unable to meet either the wage or wealth requirements.

Still the representation reform should not be underestimated. No longer could anyone gain access to the Riksdag by right of birth. The cumbersome Riksdag of the Estates, which was a reflection of the old society, was replaced by a more effective bicameral Riksdag. For many of those who had worked with the reform it was important that the rules concerning voting rights and eligibility for office could be changed, and this is what eventually happened. Within the framework of the bicameral Riksdag universal and equal suffrage for men and women was later introduced. But this would take half a century.

The history of the Swedish Riksdag is not characterized by quick decisions. Measured by European standards Sweden was slow and cautious. By this time many countries had long since freed themselves from rule by Estates and had a far more radical form of representation than Sweden.

## The Representation Reform of 1866

THE 1865–66 RIKSDAG had to take a stand on the pending proposal for representation reform. The Burghers and the Peasantry approved it immediately, while the Clergy preferred to wait until the Nobility had reached its decision. The Minister of Justice Louis De Geer was first in the long line of speakers in the House of the Nobility:

> This proposal for the restructuring of national representation in Sweden, which has now been presented to be acted upon, has been the object of serious and many-sided scrutiny. For my own part I have had several occasions to speak in defense of this proposal. The present moment's formal solemnity now requires looking only at the matter in the larger perspective. Therefore I shall not go deeply into any ambitious study of the suggestions which have been made in opposition to the proposal, and even less, as the pending discussions will probably cause me to be called upon to take the floor again.
>
> I only wish to concisely present the stand, according to which I have been and still am in this moment firmly convinced of the proposal's acceptability, although I greatly feel the weight of my responsibility and have considered the doubts which have been expressed by men whose love of country I respect and whose astuteness I admire.
>
> What makes the constitution of the Estates so dear to the thinker is that it paints society as an organism and not as a mere aggregate of individuals, held together by arbitrary external bonds. But the pragmatic statesman cannot be satisfied only with beautiful forms. He must see that the form actually has the content that is intended. For him it is not enough that the organism has once had a full life. It is more crucial that it still lives and contains the requisites for continued health.
>
> No one can deny that the powerful tide of time has overwhelmingly worked toward and is still working toward the dissolution of the Estates, both their privileges, by which they have been protected by custom, and the foundation for their existence. Eventually the borders between the Estates disintegrated, so that now, with the exception of the Clergy, they have lost their significance in all but the question of the right to representation. At the same time the general concepts of mankind and citizen have become more significant.

Using the famed sculpture of Saint George and the Dragon by Bernt Notke in *Storkyrkan* as a model (see p. 21), this caricature was drawn portraying Louis De Geer as Saint George in a struggle against the four-headed dragon of the Estates. The dragon's Peasantry and Burgher heads have already been chopped off, but the Nobility and Clergy are still putting up a fight. The princess who is anxiously watching in the foreground is Mother Svea (a symbol of Swedish nationhood).

## The Riksdag and Its Meeting Places

The western façade of *Storkyrkan* prior to its renovation in the late 1730s. The Estate of the Clergy met here from the end of the sixteenth century. Watercolor by Johan Eberhard Carlberg.

FOR NEARLY THE ENTIRE EXISTENCE of the Riksdag in Sweden, finding suitable meeting places has been a problem. During the Riksdag of the Estates there were endless discussions about where the various Estates should meet; the nonnoble Estates first obtained a building on the little island of *Riddarholmen* in Stockholm in 1834.

The first meetings that had the character of a Riksdag took place under open skies. They were often informal meetings, where those who were gathered only had to give their ayes and nays to some royal proposal. When Gustav Vasa was chosen King at Strängnäs in 1523, the meeting took place in the town's churchyard, after which those assembled went to the King and swore a loyalty oath. The 1527 Riksdag in Västerås met in a hall in the Dominican monastery. It was so small that there was room for only a few of the three hundred delegates.

The Riksdag Act of 1617 gave more shape to the work of the Riksdag, but still none of the Estates had their own meeting place, and even less was there any building large enough for the entire Riksdag. One explanation has been that the meetings were short, sometimes only three or four weeks, and the periods that elapsed between the convening of the Riksdag could be long. Until 1812 the Riksdag also sometimes met in towns other than Stockholm.

The Nobility was the first Estate to get its own meeting place. The construction of the House of the Nobility, designed by the French architect Simon de la Vallée, began in 1640 in *Gamla Stan* (the Old Town) between *Helgeandsholmen* and *Riddarholmen*. In 1660 it was, in principle, ready. The building was a symbol of the power that the Nobility had gained under

Stockholm's Town Hall on *Stortorget* on a wash drawing by Erik Palmstedt from 1768. Shortly thereafter the building was replaced by the new Stock Exchange Building after having served as the meeting place for the Estate of the Burghers since the end of the sixteenth century.

The House of the Nobility in Stockholm was ready for the Riksdag in the fall of 1660. The architects were the Frenchmen Simon and Jean de la Vallée (father and son) and the Dutchman Justus Vingboons. The figures on the ridgepole represent war and the arts, the areas which the Nobility regarded as their foremost fields of service to society.

The Estate of the Peasantry met in *Bondeska palatset* between 1765 and 1834.

Gustav II Adolf and Axel Oxenstierna. The large hall is decorated with the shields of all the families which have been introduced into the House of the Nobility.

The remaining Estates used premises in various parts of *Gamla Stan*: the Clergy met in *Storkyrkan*, the Burghers in the assembly room of the Town Hall and the Peasantry in a medieval guild hall. The center of Riksdag life became the House of the Nobility, a building to which the meeting place of none of the other Estates could be compared. In the late eighteenth century the Burghers moved into the new Stock Exchange which was built on *Stortorget*. The Peasantry also found new premises in the new Town Hall (*Bondeska palatset*).

It seems strange that the powerful Estates were not able to arrange permanent meeting places during the Age of Liberty. Only the Nobility constructed its own building during the seventeenth century.

After 1809 the question of adequate locations for assembling were discussed on several occasions, but no decisions were made.

The Stock Exchange Building on *Stortorget* was finished in 1776, and the Estate of the Burghers held their meetings there until the 1830s.

The building of the Estates of the Realm on the small island of *Riddarholmen*. It was here that the Clergy, Burghers and Peasantry in 1834 had their own premises for the first time.

A motion that was introduced by three members of the Clergy during the 1828–30 Riksdag stated that it was unsatisfactory that the Estates had to bargain for their premises prior to every Riksdag and "both with humility and embarrassment negotiate for the necessary lodging." They proposed the provision of permanent meeting places for the nonnoble Estates. There was also a proposal which suggested that the discussions of the Riksdag should be open to the public, and that could not be realized with the locations then in use.

The motion was approved, and in 1834 the three lower Estates and all the committees except the Banking Committee were able to move into a building on *Riddarholmen*. The Clergy met on the first floor, and on the second, the Burghers and the Peasantry. All three halls were supplied with galleries for observers. There were many who bore witness to the fact that the new quarters were uncomfortable and not suitable for their purpose. The members had to push their way through crowds both inside and outside the meeting rooms.

The representation reform which went into effect in 1866 did not lead to any new construction, but rather to the two chambers moving to renovated premises on *Riddarholmen* which were still not particularly suitable. The rooms were crowded and warm and were regarded as simply unhealthy. A debate on a new Riksdag building continued from the 1870s onward.

One of the most distinctive characteristics of the new bicameral Riksdag was its economy with public funds. It became important for the farmers in the Second Chamber to oppose the various proposals which were presented for more or less stately Riksdag buildings, just as they tried to prevent other state expenditures. They preferred to sweat in the unpretentious building on *Riddarholmen*. In 1887 the Second Chamber, which was dominated by

The Riksdag Building on *Helgeandsholmen* the year it was inaugurated, 1905.

the Agrarian Party, defeated a proposal for new premises for both the Riksdag and the Bank of Sweden on *Helgeandsholmen* below the Royal Palace. The fact that the Riksdag would have to pay to move the King's stables, as well as for the construction of the building, contributed to the defeat of the measure.

In spite of the defeat, a new proposal for buildings on *Helgeandsholmen* for both the Riksdag and the Bank of Sweden was approved in 1888. There were no drawings, and a special committee was assigned the task of carrying out the project.

Throughout the 1890s there was lively discussion both within and outside the Riksdag concerning the appropriateness of constructing a large building on *Helgeandsholmen*. Some felt that it would look too small below the Royal Palace, while others argued that it would disturb the view of the palace.

In 1897 Oscar II laid the cornerstone of the new Riksdag building, and in 1905 the Riksdag could move in. The building, which was designed by the architect Aron Johansson, was not well received by the press or among the leading trendsetters. Taste had changed during the course of construction, and one architect called the new building "a frog without a front or a back." More serious, however, was the fact that from the very beginning it proved impractical for the daily work of the Riksdag.

The building on *Helgeandsholmen* served, however, as the chambers for the bicameral Riksdag until the bicameral system was replaced by the unicameral Riksdag in 1971. A provisional move was then made to a new building on *Sergels torg* owned by the City of Stockholm. The big question during the 1970s was whether these temporary facilities should be made permanent or whether the Riksdag should move somewhere else. The decision was finally made to move back to *Helgeandsholmen*, where the old Riksdag Building would be modernized and expanded by linking it with the building that had formerly housed the Bank of Sweden. The old administrative quarters in the vicinity were renovated to provide offices for members of the Riksdag.

The 1983 meeting of the Riksdag was opened on *Helgeandsholmen*. The Riksdag Building was again in service after a thorough renovation. One of the surprises in connection with the renovation was the archeological discovery that was made. Parts of old Stockholm appeared, and what had been proposed as a garage became an underground museum which shows fragments of the Swedish capital during the Middle Ages.

The Riksdag Building on *Helge-andsholmen* was reinaugurated in 1983 after its renovation and connection to the former Bank of Sweden Building.

FRIHET OCH RÄTT

ALLMÄN RÖSTRÄTT

NED MED BOLAGSVÄLDET

JORDEN ÅT FOLKET

RÄTTVISA ÅT DE SMÅ

RUSDRYCKS-FÖRBUD

NORMAL-ARBETSDAG!

BORT MED TULLARNA

KAMP MOT TRUSTERNA

FÖRFATT-NINGSRE-VISION

FRONT MOT MILITARISMEN

SKYDD ÅT BONDEN

ARBETETS FRUKTER ÅT DEM SOM AR-BETA.

FOLKET HERRE I EGET HUS

C·A·Jacobsson

Arbetarna tåga ut i valkampen.

# CHAPTER 8

# Toward Democracy and Parliamentary Government

T HE ABOLITION OF THE RIKSDAG of the four Estates and the creation of a new political system gave rise to broad expectations. But there were also voices of doubt. The day following the passage of the representation proposal one of the opponents of the reform, Count Henning Hamilton, spoke of the loss of the old Riksdag of the Estates, but still welcomed "the young Svea," the new Riksdag.

> Today for the first time I greet the young Svea. I do this with a sense of melancholy, as I loved her mother, who was buried yesterday, and beneath whose medieval costume, an eternally youthful Swedish heart always beat. I do it with anxiety, perhaps because I do not know her as well as I knew the old. In any event, as she is young, her first steps may be unsteady; it is then our duty to support her, and we should do it lovingly; perhaps she still needs some up-bringing; then it is our duty to give it to her, and to do so gently, but seriously, so that she may some day become what the departed was to us, so that she may become, not only as loved as the old, but also as happy, strong and free as she was.

The fears that Hamilton expressed would soon show themselves to be unfounded. In no way did the new Riksdag prove to be a playground for radical and democratic elements. The 1866 election displayed rather that the similarities between the new Riksdag and the old were conspicuous, at least as far as its composition was concerned.

A little clique of high-ranking officials and businessmen dominated the 125 members of the First Chamber. More than half of the members, 78, belonged to the nobility, and of these 42 were counts or barons. A member was not required to be a resident of his election district.

When it came into being, the Second Chamber had 190 members. The farmers became the leading faction, comprising more than half its members, and in 1867 they organized themselves in a Riksdag party, the Agrarian Party (*Lantmannapartiet*).

Count Henning Hamilton delivered a very emotional speech at the last meeting of the Estates. For many years Hamilton was one of the leading conservative politicians and a harsh critic of Louis De Geer's representation proposal. He is portrayed here as the Speaker of the Nobility in a watercolor by Fritz von Dardel.

*On the opposite page:* A Social Democratic poster from the 1911 election, the first with universal male suffrage. Hjalmar Branting and the Swedish Trade Union Confederation president Herman Lindqvist are marching in the lead. In the background may be seen the veteran August Palm who has a beard and is wearing a cap.

The Second Chamber during its first session in 1867 in the former assembly hall of the Estate of the Peasantry in the building on *Riddarholmen*. The Speaker of the Chamber is the Bishop of Karlstad, Anton Niklas Sundberg, later Archbishop and leading member of the First Chamber. *Ny Illustrerad Tidning*.

## Calm Debates in the New Chambers

For a couple of decades the elections to the Second Chamber caused very little excitement. In 1872 slightly more than 200,000 of the country's inhabitants, about 5.6 percent, were eligible to vote, but only a small proportion of them did so, about 20 percent or a total of 40,000 persons.

Election rallies were rare, and many men were elected to the Riksdag without having given voice to their political sympathies. The Agrarian Party was a Riksdag party and lacked a nationwide organization. The remaining political groups in the Riksdag were only loosely organized.

Activities were limited during the meetings of the Riksdag. During the 1883 meeting, for example, a total of 51 government bills were presented. Nor were the Riksdag members particularly active when it came to introducing motions (the members' formal written proposals) or to presenting interpellations (written queries) to the members of the government. At the same meeting 33 motions were presented to the First Chamber and 103 to the Second. By way of comparison, during the last meeting of the bicameral Riksdag (1969/70) 1,382 motions were presented in the First Chamber and 1,605 in the Second. During the period 1867 to 1886 there was one interpellation in every other Riksdag on the average in the First Chamber and somewhat more in the Second Chamber.

The last meetings of the Estates were characterized by lively debates that were often brilliant. Sometimes they were rather heated and could even degenerate into fistfights. There were young people in the Nobility who at times caused problems. By comparison, in 1876 the Second Chamber had only one member under the age of 30 and 105 were over 50 years of age. In 1873, 98 of the 128 members of the First Chamber were older than 50. The atmosphere in both chambers was calmer and more disciplined than it had been in the assemblies of the Estates.

The Committee of Supply (*stats-utskottet*) was the most powerful in the two-chamber Riksdag, because it had to take a stand on the final form of the budget. The committee had twelve members from each chamber. *Ny Illustrerad Tidning,* 1875.

During the period after 1809 the most fundamental question in the Riksdag that had sharpened wits and inspired the great speakers was the representation reform. Defense, tax questions and tariffs, which dominated the debates in the Riksdag after the introduction of the bicameral legislature, were certainly important issues, but not as dramatic as representation. Of course, even after the bicameral reform there were members who gave weight to the discussions and fired the imagination. The Liberal Adolf Hedin was one of the personalities who lent color to the Second Chamber during several decades.

## Increased Party Activity

It was not until the mid-1880s that political activity increased in the Riksdag and among the voters. Prime Minister Robert Themptander, who took office in 1884, was in favor of free trade, as was King Oscar II. Themptander was the first Prime Minister who became involved in an election campaign when he gave a speech in Göteborg in 1887. The office of Prime Minister had been established in 1876. Until that time, the head of government had also been Minister of Justice. Louis De Geer was appointed the first Prime Minister, and the Ministry of Justice received a special head.

In 1887, when the proponents of free trade lost their majority in the Second Chamber, the government, which shared this view, lost its base. The question was how this would affect the composition of the government. For the preservation of royal power it was important that the King should make the decision, not the Riksdag. Oscar II spoke constantly of the Council of State as "his advisers." If the government resigned, it would set a "parliamentary precedent"; the government would show its dependence on the Riksdag. Parliamentarism had won a victory in Norway in 1884 after a battle between the King and the majority in the legislature. Oscar II wanted to avoid a repetition of this in Sweden at all costs.

Oscar II on a one crown coin from 1876. In 1873 new currency was introduced in Sweden. The *riksdaler* was abandoned, and the main coin became the one crown piece (*krona*), which was divided into 100 *öre*.

## Adolf Hedin – the Tribune of the People

Adolf Hedin as drawn by Albert Engström, 1895.

THROUGHOUT THE CENTURIES a number of brilliant and interesting personalities have been part of the Swedish Riksdag. There have been good speakers with well-reasoned political arguments. Still, the typical Riksdag member is one of the group, one who does not stand out. Political groups and parties have been more prominent than individuals. Those who have had their own policies and thus influenced decisions in the Riksdag have been the exceptions.

Adolf Hedin (1834–1905), who held a seat in the Second Chamber at various times between 1870 and 1905, belonged to the prominent exceptions. He was a politician who thought independently and formulated his own political program. He was a captivating speaker and debater, a tribune of the people with the power to persuade. On the other hand, he was not a person who could cooperate and did not fit into any party. The New Liberal Party of the Second Chamber, in which he served as leader, was short-lived.

The bicameral legislature was greeted with great expectations by Hedin. He believed in a renewal and modernization of Swedish policy. He published "fifteen letters from a democrat to the members of the Swedish Riksdag," a brochure which dealt with popular expectations of the new representation. France and the ideals of equality of the French Revolution were central to Hedin. He argued for universal and equal suffrage and a stronger Riksdag. In contrast to many other radicals and liberals Hedin was in favor of a strong defense and warmly supported universal military conscription.

After Oscar II's accession to the throne in 1872 and as Germany became increasingly stronger, Sweden began to shift politically and culturally away from France and closer to Germany. Oscar II hastened this development, but Hedin criticized it. He generally opposed the Court and argued against increased allowances for the royal family. During the 1870 Riksdag the newly elected member of the Second Chamber said: "The thought comes to mind that the constitutional monarchy of today is so changed in importance in comparison with the monarchies of the past that it would do the wisest thing if it took a more humble position, if it had a more middle class stance."

Hedin played a central role in Swedish social debate until his death in 1905. He was a well-known political figure who irritated and upset many people during his active political life, which was during a conservative period that was favorable to the monarchy. He has a special place in Swedish social legislation, because as early as 1884 he submitted a motion concerning accident and old-age insurance for workers. The proposal led to various studies and eventually to legislation. Hedin was one of the country's first social liberals.

Oscar II speaks with Prime Minister Gillis Bildt during a meeting of the King in Council in 1888. In 1991, when Oscar II's great-great grandson Carl XVI Gustaf was King, Gillis Bildt's great-great grandson Carl Bildt became Prime Minister. *Ny Illustrerad Tidning.*

The victors in the 1887 election were conservative, and they were not interested in parliamentarism. However, they wanted someone who favored tariffs as a successor to Themptander. The problem was solved when Oscar II appointed Marshal of the Realm Gillis Bildt to be Prime Minister. He was acceptable to conservatives because he was a protectionist and a member of the First Chamber. What was of importance to the King was that he was the Marshal of the Realm and thus the member of the Court closest to him. Nor was there a complete shift in the government, and thus there was no "parliamentary precedent."

The government became steadily more dependent on the Riksdag anyway, although there was no discussion of parliamentarism because it was disliked by the King, the Prime Minister and the other members of the Council of State. There would not be a complete shift of government until 1905, but it became clearer that the government was just as dependent upon the Riksdag as upon the King.

Bildt's successor as Prime Minister, Gustaf Åkerhielm, was forced to resign in 1891 after he made a statement in a private meeting with the First Chamber in which he said that a better defense would make it easier for the country to speak Swedish both to the east and to the west. There were strong reactions to this in Sweden as well as in Norway, but the real reason for Åkerhielm's resignation was that he did not have sufficient support in the Riksdag.

The Agrarian Party had split into a free trade and a protectionist part over the tariff question. New party groups that were more or less loosely composed were later formed. In the Second Chamber a liberal popular party developed during the 1890s, while in the First Chamber a conservative majority party which favored tariffs played an important role. There was also a moderate party which favored free trade. The various party groups which existed around the turn of the century, however, lacked nationwide organizations and carried out political campaigns on a very limited basis.

The question of new tariffs caused lively discussions in the 1880s and at least partly cut across class lines. As a rule, however, conservatives favored tariffs, while liberals were opposed. Those who favored free trade argued that tariffs would cause higher food prices and thus primarily affect the workers and the little man. This woodcut is from the radical newspaper *Fäderneslandet*, 1888.

August Palm, a tailor by trade, was for many years one of the Social Democrats' most well-known popular speakers. In his memoirs *Ur en agitators liv* (From the Life of an Agitator) there is an illustration showing how he spoke to the people of Arboga from a rowboat in the river, because he had not been able to find a hall for his meeting in the town.

Essential to contact between the parties and the voters was the existence of a press which was close to the various parties. *Aftonbladet* had already played a direct role in Riksdag politics. Among the many newspapers which were founded toward the end of the nineteenth century most took a stand for one of the major political orientations: conservative, liberal or social democratic. Many journalists were also members of the Riksdag or the local assemblies. They became very important in the development of the party system.

During the 1880s Social Democratic agitators had become active in Sweden. They modeled their activities on developments in Germany and Denmark and founded local branches and party districts and published newspapers. The Social Democratic Party (*Socialdemokratiska arbetarepartiet*) was started in 1889, and, unlike the parties that had thus far existed in Sweden, it was a national party and not merely a party in the Riksdag.

The Social Democrats were opposed to revolution and wanted to reform society using democratic methods. Together with the Liberals they had as one of their foremost goals universal and equal suffrage. During the 1890s, together with the Liberals, they took part in two popular parliaments which had universal and equal

The first page of *Social-Demokraten* May 1, 1899. The newspaper was filled with slogans for the day's demonstration parade. With only a few interruptions Hjalmar Branting was editor-in-chief of *Social-Demokraten* from 1887 to 1917.

Hjalmar Branting giving a speech in Sickla, south of Stockholm, in July 1905. A few weeks earlier Norway had repudiated its union with Sweden, and Branting now demanded a peaceful solution to the crisis.

suffrage on the program. The close cooperation between the Social Democrats and the Liberals is also evidenced by the fact that the Social Democratic leader, Hjalmar Branting, was elected to the Riksdag on a Liberal ballot in 1896.

After the turn of the century both liberals and conservatives formed campaigning organizations, the National Liberal Society (*Frisinnade landsföreningen*, 1902) and the General Electoral Association (*Allmänna valmansförbundet*, 1904). During the period up until the First World War Sweden had a three-party system, and there was close cooperation between the Liberals and the Social Democrats in the Riksdag. The Liberal Party was favored by many within the middle class. It was supported by religious groups outside the state church and by temperance movements, as well as by "urban liberals," who differed from conservatives, not only because of their radical view on the right to vote, but also through their lack of interest in defense.

## Dissolution of the Union and Voting Rights Reform

With the exception of a few short intervals, the landowner Erik Gustaf Boström was Prime Minister from 1891 to 1905. He was not directly associated with any party but demonstrated great skill in balancing the various groups within the Riksdag against one another. A reform of the defense system was accepted by the Riksdag during this period, while two other central questions remained unresolved: the union with Norway and suffrage.

Prime Minister Erik Gustaf Boström favored tariffs, but was above all a typical pragmatic politician and became well-known for his ability to smoothly manage to get the necessary majorities in the Riksdag.

## Christian Lundeberg – a Conservative Leader

Christian Lundeberg.

CHRISTIAN LUNDEBERG (1842–1911), owner of a rural manufactory, was elected to the First Chamber by the council of the county of Gävleborg in 1885 and was to hold office until 1911. His name has gone down in history as he was Prime Minister during the union crisis of 1905 when the Swedish–Norwegian union was peacefully dissolved in a way that was acceptable to both countries. It was also the first time there was a shift of government; all ministers were replaced when he took office.

Lundeberg's heyday in the Riksdag was during the 1890s, when he was one of the leaders of the majority party in the First Chamber. The word party was used by the members themselves, but the majority party had little in common with the political parties of today. It could be most aptly described as a conservative gentlemen's club for high-ranking public officials, military officers, estate owners and industrial leaders. The party leader was Patric Reuterswärd, but he was older than Lundeberg and did not have Lundeberg's strength.

The most important issue for the majority party concerned tariffs or free trade. Lundeberg had his origins in a county which favored free trade, but he was a warm supporter not only of tariffs, but also of a strengthened defense and Swedish superiority in the union with Norway. He was opposed to modern ideas such as parliamentarism and universal and equal suffrage.

The Uppsala professor Oscar Alin, who was also a member of the First Chamber, was a close friend of Lundeberg. He had conducted research on the Kiel Treaty and the circumstances surrounding the origins of the union. His results were clear: Sweden should reign over Norway. With the help of his associate professors, academic colleagues and journalists around the country he organized a campaign against the Norwegian demands for independence.

The union issue became for the Conservatives, what the suffrage question was for the Liberals and the Social Democrats.

In spite of all the harsh words and judgements against the Norwegians, Lundeberg was able to accept the agreement concerning the dissolution of the union while he was Prime Minister in the "coalition government" in 1905. He understood that the game was lost. He realized finally that a split was the only alternative and that the union had no advantages for Sweden.

The social, economic and political gap between Norway and Sweden, as well as the different historical traditions, were apparent even when the Treaty of Kiel was signed. Norway had no upper class with a powerful nobility corresponding to that in Sweden, but rather there was a strong middle class that played a leading role in the Norwegian parliament. During the late nineteenth century the King's position was weakened in Norway, and the groups that wanted a dissolution of the union grew stronger.

During the 1890s the Union Committee with members from Sweden and Norway tried to find a solution to the disputes between the two countries, but it was not successful. It made four different proposals, none of which was accepted. In the Swedish Riksdag there were militant forces that wanted to put the Norwegians in their place, but both the Liberals and the Social Democrats sympathized with the Norwegian demands for independence. Norway was a politically progressive land with a well-developed party system and parliamentary government.

In 1905 the Norwegians renounced the union agreement, and the crisis between the two countries became acute. In Sweden a government was formed which included representatives of the various parties and political orientations in the Riksdag. The Conservative Christian Lundeberg was appointed Prime Minister, but the Liberal Party leader Karl Staaff also held a post in the government. In the Swedish town of Karlstad the two countries finally reached an agreement on complete separation.

Karl Staaff succeeded Lundeberg as Prime Minister after the success of the Liberals in the election to the Second Chamber in 1905. He submitted a proposal for a suffrage reform, but it was defeated by the First Chamber. Staaff resigned after less than a year as Prime Minister and was followed by Arvid Lindman, who headed a right-wing government. The latter proved to be more successful in the question of voting rights, and a reform was finally passed by the Riksdag in 1909.

The oldest known Swedish newsbill is from November 22, 1892. The advent of the telegraph, the telephone and the large news bureaus increased the speed of news communication in the late nineteenth century. The number of newspapers also grew. They became cheaper and reached an expanding public in broader social groups.

Oscar II at the opening of the extraordinary Riksdag which was summoned in 1905 as a result of the union crisis. Oscar II was the last Swedish King who appeared with a crown, mantle and scepter. In his speech from the throne the King requested that the government receive the authorization of the Riksdag to solve the union crisis. The government which was in office resigned and was replaced by a government with wide support among the various groups in the Riksdag.

The demonstration outside the People's Hall in Kiruna in 1909. The banners demand universal suffrage and an eight-hour workday.

Arvid Lindman portrayed by Carl Eldh in the main stairwell of the Riksdag Building, where a number of Swedish prime ministers have been honored with busts. Lindman represented an element of Swedish conservatism which was favorable to industry and business.

Swedish men thus received the right to vote, but they had to fulfill a number of qualifications before they could exercise that right. Women were still not allowed to vote.

Two principles were especially important to Lindman.

- The First Chamber should remain conservative in order to balance the Second Chamber. The differences between the two chambers became rather large: in 1918 the Conservatives still held 60 percent of the seats in the First Chamber, but only 25 percent of those in the Second Chamber.

- Proportional representation was preferred to majority elections, as the Conservatives could not count on getting the majority in many constituencies. The proportional system meant that the parties won seats in proportion to the number of votes they received within the respective constituencies. The composition of the Second Chamber would thus reflect the party sympathies of the voters.

The voting rights reform meant that the left-wing parties gained the majority in the Second Chamber in the 1911 election: the Social Democrats received 64 seats and the Liberals 102. The Conservatives won as many seats as the Social Democrats. Although the Conservatives still controlled the First Chamber, the election results led to the resignation of Lindman, and Karl Staaff formed a new Liberal government.

## The Palace Yard Crisis

The period prior to the First World War was a time of political unrest in many European countries. In Sweden the question of defense was the focal point. The Conservatives in the Riksdag and strong forces outside the parliament were opposed to the defense policy of the Staaff government. The threat from Russia was dramatized. In 1912 the explorer Sven Hedin wrote the pamphlet

Gustaf V speaks to the Farmers' Demonstration. Thousands of farmers came to Stockholm in February of 1914 to protest the Liberal government's defense policy. They assembled in the Palace Yard beneath the banners of their various provinces. The Farmers' Demonstration was a combination of a show of historical romanticism and a modern political mass movement.

*Ett varningsord* (A Word of Warning), which had a great effect on public opinion.

Staaff was construed by conservatives as a traitor to his country, when he did not appropriate the funds that to their way of thinking were necessary for an effective defense. In 1912 there was a fund-raising drive for a new armored ship. This venture was very successful and was a show of opposition to the government. In February 1914 there was also a demonstration against Staaff's defense policy: 30,000 farmers traveled to Stockholm and appealed to the King and his family from the Palace Yard.

Gustaf V addressed the farmers directly in a speech that received much notice:

> Those are not lacking in our land who are of the opinion that the question of the training time for the infantry should not be resolved now, but I do not share that opinion. Instead I am of the same opinion that you have just expressed, namely, that the defense question should be dealt with as a whole and a decision reached now, without delay and in one context. The demands for the army's readiness and preparedness for war, which those knowledgeable within my army have presented as indispensable, I do not depart from. ... For the carrying out of its great tasks not only should my fleet be maintained, but should also be significantly strengthened.

As the Liberal leader, Karl Staaff worked for universal and equal suffrage and for parliamentarism. He was a controversial politician and was subjected to several hate campaigns. Bust by Carl Eldh in the Riksdag Building.

The speech polemicized directly against the Riksdag and the Liberal government. The Prime Minister had not been able to influence its content. Two days later a counter demonstration was held consisting of 40,000 workers. They gathered outside the government offices, and Hjalmar Branting addressed Staaff:

> The working people of this country, suffering from high prices, unemployment and heavy taxes of various types and still lacking the social and democratic reforms for which they have fought for decades oppose most decidedly an increased military burden. To the government and the Riksdag we submit a strong plea, not to allow the continued reckless agitation for armaments to cause you to betray the promises which have been given to the people in the election. The breaking of these vows is not consistent with the demands for political trust and honor.

In this 1909 photograph the Social Democratic leader Hjalmar Branting, hat in hand, speaks with King Gustaf V. The picture may be interpreted symbolically in a number of ways. One is that the King accepts the representative of the labor movement. Another is that the Social Democratic leader shows his loyalty to the existing order, and that the King could be at ease even if the Social Democrats gained power.

In addition, with reference to recent events, we would like to emphasize that the Swedish people will never submit to the demands of a monarch, but rather they are confident that they will always with all their might uphold democracy's ancient, fundamental principle that the people's will alone shall rule in the country of Sweden.

Staaff thanked Branting for his words, and he also took up the battle with Gustaf V. The Prime Minister demanded that the King should declare that the speech in the Palace Yard was not an official act, because it had not been approved by the government. The King refused, and the Liberal government resigned. The King had won a short-term triumph, and the governor of the county of Uppsala, Hjalmar Hammarskjöld, was asked to form a government, with the support of the King.

The Farmers' Demonstration and Staaff's resignation were victories for the Conservatives. They showed that they too could mobilize the masses. Until that time such a display of strength had always been the province of the Liberals and the Social Democrats. The Farmers' Demonstration had an old-fashioned strain, but it was also a modern political weapon directed against the radical elements in society.

The new government was not directly associated with a political party, but generally conservative and favorable to defense. Its first act was to dissolve the Second Chamber and announce a new election. The election campaign, which was very heated, focused on defense and constitutional questions. Voter participation was greater than ever before; nearly 70 percent of those eligible cast votes. The results spelled success for both the Conservatives and the Social Democrats, while the Liberals lost ground. Hammarskjöld felt that he could retain his post as Prime Minister, and he received help from developments in Europe.

A company of the Royal Svea Life Guards marching through Stockholm to a maneuver in 1915. With the outbreak of the First World War in the fall of 1914 the Riksdag greatly increased military appropriations.

The First World War broke out in August 1914. Those who had warned about the danger of a full-scale war were shown to be right. The hostilities which now began had a different character, however, from those that Sven Hedin and other supporters of a strong defense had feared. Russia, which had been painted as the greatest threat, had no expansive power. The political parties in Sweden buried their differences when war was a fact; it was important to keep the country out of war. Karl Staaff and Hjalmar Branting promised to support the government in the serious situation which had arisen.

## Democracy and Parliamentarism

The Hammarskjöld government was able to remain in office until 1917 in spite of internal controversies and sharp criticism from the outside. At that time unrest arose in Swedish domestic policy, which affected both the parties and the sitting government.

Since the 1880s there had been two phalanxes among the socialists: one reformist, which wanted to change society within the existing system, and one which felt that a revolution was the only way to reach a socialist society. In May 1917 the left wing founded the Social Democratic Left Party (*Socialdemokratiska vänsterpartiet*). A number of well-known Social Democrats joined. They conducted revolutionary agitation and hoped to attract a majority of the working class.

The success of the new revolutionary party was limited. In the province of Norrbotten it was able to win a majority within the previously Social Democratic district and managed to take over the Social Democratic newspaper *Norrskensflamman* (the Flare of the Northern Lights), but otherwise it gained little support. In the election to the Second Chamber in 1917 the new party received 8.1 percent of the votes, while the Social Democratic Party received 31.1 percent. The new party would later decline and split; in 1921 the Swedish Communist Party (*Sveriges kommunistiska parti*) was formed, which became a section of the Communist International.

Another change in the party system was the establishment of two agrarian parties, the Agrarian Union (*Bondeförbundet*) in 1913 and the National Agricultural Federation (*Jordbrukarnas riksförbund*) in 1915. These organizations had their roots both in the old Agrarian Party in the Second Chamber and in the Farmers' Demonstration. They joined forces in 1922 under the name of the Agrarian Union. The party had a strong organization and support from a number of newspapers. In the 1924 election the Agrarian Union received 10.8 percent of the votes.

Hjalmar Hammarskjöld's government was followed in 1917 by a right-wing government headed by the wholesaler from Norr-

The riots at *Gustav Adolfs torg* in central Stockholm on June 5, 1917. At the same time that local voting rights were being debated in the Riksdag, there were large demonstrations, and fights broke out between the police and the demonstrators. The man with the cane between the mounted police is Hjalmar Branting who left the debate in the Riksdag to calm down the excited masses.

Nils Edén, a history professor from Uppsala, succeeded Karl Staaff as the leader of the Liberals in 1915. He was Prime Minister in a Liberal–Social Democratic coalition government during the period 1917–1920. This government marked the definitive breakthrough for parliamentarism in Sweden.

köping Carl Swartz. This government did not last long, however, and resigned after the Conservatives' defeat in the Riksdag election in the fall of 1917. They lost more than 10 percentage points in the Second Chamber, while the Liberals and the Social Democrats had great success. The Swartz government was succeeded by a coalition composed of Liberals and Social Democrats. Nils Edén, who was named leader of the Liberal Party after Karl Staaff's death in 1915, became the Prime Minister, and Hjalmar Branting was a member of the government, along with three other Social Democrats.

The shift in the government in the fall of 1917 was a decisive moment in the history of the Swedish Riksdag. It showed that the King was no longer able to influence the composition of the government with the support of different groups or actions outside the Riksdag, in spite of various attempts. Since that time parliamentarism has reigned in Sweden.

The two constitutional questions which the Social Democrats and the Liberals had struggled for during three decades were parliamentary government and universal and equal suffrage. Parliamentarism had been accepted with the formation of the government after the 1917 election. The issue of universal and equal voting rights remained. It was necessary not only to change the qualifications for participating in elections to the Second Chamber, but also to reform the election of the First Chamber. Income and wealth determined the number of votes each person had in the elections to the local bodies, the county councils and certain city councils, which, in turn, appointed the members of the First Chamber. After the 1909 reform the maximum number of ballots per eligible voter was set at 40, the forty-degree scale, but persons with high incomes were still favored, and the First Chamber had a clearly conservative character.

Shortly after taking office the left-wing government submitted a proposal for a constitutional reform, but it was voted down by the First Chamber. Not until the fall of 1918 a decision on the democratization of elections to both chambers would be settled.

Events outside the country's borders would once again influence developments in Sweden. The Russian Revolution inspired supporters of radical social change. The unrest that was in evidence in several parts of the country in 1917 had its origins there, as well as in the failure of reforms and the lack of food. The spirit of the times had certainly changed in Sweden from the winter of 1914, when the drama of the Palace Yard took place.

In November of 1918 the parties came to an agreement on a thorough reform of voting rights. Women received the same voting rights as men. This was the result of a long struggle by several women's organizations. The forty-degree scale was abolished, but there were still certain restrictions. People who had gone into bankruptcy, been declared incapable of managing their own affairs or received poor relief were not allowed to vote. The voting age was also rather high: 23 years for the Second Chamber and 27 years for the county councils and the city councils which appointed the members of the First Chamber.

Parliamentarism and democracy came late to Sweden. The slow and undramatic process may be characterized as typically Swedish. There was a powerful upper class composed of high public officials, estate owners, managers of rural manufacturing communities and factory owners. They had a strong position in the First Chamber and constituted a restraining element.

The campaign for women's suffrage was also seen on Christmas cards. The banner reads "Suffrage for women."

The meeting with the central committee of the National Association for Women's Suffrage in 1911. The struggle for women's voting rights did not result in riots in Sweden, as was the case in several other countries, for instance England. However, the struggle attracted many women, especially Liberals and Social Democrats, and was of great importance.

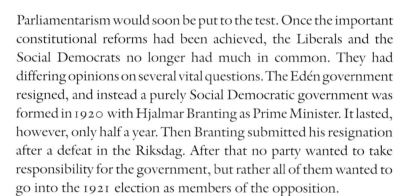

MINISTÄREN BRANTING

Branting's first government in 1920. The man beating the drum is the Minister of Defense Per Albin Hansson, and the sack of money is supporting the Minister of Finance, Fredrik Thorsson, the shoemaker from Ystad, who was known for his thrift.

## Minority Governments and Strong Committees

The first women were elected to the Swedish Riksdag in 1921. Kerstin Hesselgren became a member of the First Chamber. An additional four women won seats in the Second Chamber.

Elisabeth Tamm.          Bertha Wellin.

Agda Östlund.          Nelly Thüring.

Parliamentarism would soon be put to the test. Once the important constitutional reforms had been achieved, the Liberals and the Social Democrats no longer had much in common. They had differing opinions on several vital questions. The Edén government resigned, and instead a purely Social Democratic government was formed in 1920 with Hjalmar Branting as Prime Minister. It lasted, however, only half a year. Then Branting submitted his resignation after a defeat in the Riksdag. After that no party wanted to take responsibility for the government, but rather all of them wanted to go into the 1921 election as members of the opposition.

Thus a caretaker government was appointed consisting mainly of persons who were not members of the Riksdag, but who had knowledge in their respective fields. A county governor acted as Prime Minister.

By the election to the Second Chamber in September 1921 the number of eligible voters had increased from 20.4 to 54.3 percent of the population. A majority of the new voters were women. Voter participation was a disappointment, however, for those who had fought for a broader franchise. Only 54 percent of the eligible voters cast ballots in the election. This was a low figure in comparison with voter participation in other European democracies at the time. The proportion of women voting was especially small; only 47.2 percent of those entitled to vote exercised their rights, compared with 62 percent of the men.

The 1921 election involved 230 seats in the Second Chamber. From 1924 onward the term of office was four years, and the proportional representation system that had been introduced in 1909 was still in effect.

Only five women occupied seats in the Riksdag in 1922. Kerstin Hesselgren was elected to the First Chamber as an independent by the Liberals and the Social Democrats. The other four were elected to the

Second Chamber: Bertha Wellin (Conservative), Elisabeth Tamm (Liberal), Nelly Thüring (Social Democrat) and Agda Östlund (Social Democrat). The number of women in the Riksdag long remained small. In 1942 five percent of the members were women, and in 1971 they still numbered only 14 percent. (After the 1994 election 42 percent of the members of the Riksdag were women.)

The party system had developed slowly but surely during the preceding decades, and it maintained great stability. In the 1921 election the Social Democrats became the largest party with more than 36 percent of the votes, and it held its position thereafter. The next largest party was the Conservatives (the present Moderate Party, *Moderata samlingspartiet*) with 25.8 percent of the votes, followed by the Liberals (today the Liberal Party, *Folkpartiet liberalerna*) with 19.1 percent. It was not until 1988 that a new party (the Green Party, *Miljöpartiet de gröna*) would manage to gain seats in the Riksdag under its own steam. Sweden is one of the few democracies in the world where the party system in the parliament has remained unchanged for as long as seventy years.

The 1920s would, however, be unstable; it was the decade of government crises and minority governments. During the twelve years after the fall of Edén in 1920 until the Social Democrat Per Albin Hansson took over the reins of government in 1932, the holder of the post of Prime Minister changed no fewer than twelve times.

One of the reasons for the unstable parliamentary conditions during the 1920s was that the position of the Liberals had been weakened. There had earlier been a number of factions in the party, but the gaps had been bridged by unity in the struggle for democracy and parliamentary government. When these victories had been won, other issues came to the fore, such as prohibition of alcohol.

The "prohibitionist" wing, which included the members of religious groups outside the state church and those who favored temperance, wanted alcohol forbidden, while the "urban liberals" regarded the current restrictions as sufficient, that is, limitations of purchase (a ration book) and the requirement that food be consumed along with alcohol in restaurants. In 1923 the Liberal Coalition Party (*Liberala samlingspartiet*) split and was succeeded by the Liberal People's Party (*Frisinnade folkpartiet*) and the Liberal Party (*Liberala partiet*). In spite of the fact that both had limited support among the voters, they played a central role in the parliamentary game.

The leader of the Liberal People's Party, Carl Gustaf Ekman, who was Prime Minister during two periods between 1926 and 1932, would show great skill when it came to alternately gaining support from the Conservatives and the Social Democrats. Decisions were often made through compromises in the committees, which during the 1920s had greater power than at any time before or later in the history of the bicameral legislature. There was talk of "committee parliamentarism."

Albert Engström's poster from the prohibition referendum in 1922 has become a classic. The implication is that a national delicacy, crayfish, cannot be eaten without spirits.

Ration books for alcohol purchases became compulsory throughout the country in 1919 and were not abolished until 1955.

A demonstration against the Ekman government's labor legislation in May 1928. During the 1920s Sweden had a large number of labor conflicts. One of the proposals of the Ekman government was the establishment of a labor court along international lines. This opposition banner encouraged people to "Ward off Ekman's attack on the trade union movement." The proposal was passed despite the protests, and the court is still in existence.

A peace demonstration in Stockholm in 1924. Hjalmar Branting, to the right in the picture, won an international reputation for his work for peace, especially within the framework of the League of Nations in Geneva. The banner cried out: "No more war!" Branting was awarded the Nobel Peace Prize in 1921.

The Riksdag was far from paralyzed. In the mid-1920s a defense reform was carried out which meant significant disarmament, although not as extensive as the Social Democrats had hoped for. The Ekman government, together with the Social Democrats, also managed to get a reform of the school system approved. Despite the opposition of the Social Democrats, the Riksdag passed legislation concerning strike injunctions and the creation of a labor court. Ekman had support from the right on these issues.

The retrospective evaluation of the policies of the 1920s has been rendered by those who came to power after 1932. The Social Democrats regarded the 1920s much as Gustav III did the Age of Liberty: a period of decline, primarily characterized by lack of decisiveness on the part of the government. Liberals of various hues, however, have had another point of view. They have pointed to the number of reforms that were carried out and emphasized that there was strength in the fact that the minority governments had to take the opinions of the Riksdag into consideration. The rule by committees meant that both the right and the left had a part in exercising power.

## A Shift in the Political System

Neither the representation reform of 1866 nor the fundamental amendments to the constitution which were adopted around 1920 brought about any rapid changes in Swedish politics. Louis De Geer's reform was protected by so many restrictions that it would take decades before Sweden developed modern political parties and a functioning parliamentarism. Nor did the reform of voting rights lead to any radical changes in the decade that followed. Many who had been granted suffrage did not bother to exercise their right.

EN VAR "ARBETAREPARTIET" SOM RÖSTAR PÅ RÖSTAR FÖR MOSKVA.

The 1928 election has become known to history as the "Cossack election." In some places there was local cooperation between the Social Democrats and the Communists, which gave the Conservatives reason to represent the Social Democrats as allied with the Communists. The poster with the Cossack played on the centuries old fear of Russia in Sweden.

During the period 1866 to 1933 the Riksdag played a more central role for the country than the Riksdag of the Estates did after the Age of Liberty. The power of the King was weakened, and the Riksdag became more representative of the people.

Sweden underwent fundamental change. The old agrarian country was transformed into a modern industrial society. The changes did not occur wholly without economic, social and political unrest. The 1920s was the decade of strikes. During a peaceful strike demonstration in Ådalen in 1931 five persons were shot to death and five wounded by members of the military. This event led to one of the most heated debates in the Swedish Riksdag in modern history.

The long-term development was largely peaceful for two fundamental reasons.

- Although there were extremists among the Conservatives, they never formed a majority. They could be restrained by forces of moderation. Leading men of the right supported both the dissolution of the union in 1905 and the suffrage reforms of 1907–1909. The bitter atmosphere which characterized the "Cossack election" in 1928, when the Social Democrats were accused of wanting to bring about "a socialist society," was the exception.
- A similar situation existed on the left. There were radical, revolutionary elements which were very vociferous, but they never dominated. While in office, Hjalmar Branting cooperated with the Liberals, and, although a certain amount of radicalization occurred after the death of Branting, in 1933 the Social Democratic Prime Minister Per Albin Hansson cooperated closely with a nonsocialist party.

## The Riksdag on the Ådalen Riots

The demonstration in Ådalen, a valley in the province of Ångermanland, in May 1931, shortly before the shots were fired. This event led to a heated debate in the Riksdag.

ON WEDNESDAY, MAY 13, 1931 a meeting for workers was scheduled at the athletic field in the little town of Kramfors. It was arranged by a Communist group, and its purpose was to voice opposition to the use of strikebreakers for unloading and loading goods. The meeting concluded with a march to Lunde, where the strikebreakers were located. The demonstrators broke through a police cordon and attacked the strikebreakers, who were beaten.

A military unit was ordered to come from the regiment in Sollefteå, as the police feared that they could not protect the strikebreakers. The following day, Ascension Day, a new meeting was held which also ended with a march which was headed for Lunde. It was stopped when the soldiers opened fire; five persons were killed and five injured.

The Ådalen riots received much attention and caused great indignation throughout the country. The events reached the floor of the Riksdag, although Ådalen was not on the agenda. In his memoirs the Social Democrat Ernst Wigforss, a member of the Riksdag from 1919 to 1947 and Minister of Finance for many years, called the Ådalen debate "the most impassioned dispute between the parties which I can remember during my days in the Riksdag."

The dividing line was not only between the Liberal Prime Minister C.G. Ekman and the socialist opposition; there was also a split between the Social Democrats and the Communists. In contrast to the Communists, the Social Democrats did not accept violence, not even against strikebreakers. Per Albin Hansson, a Social Democrat, said the following in the debate:

I can understand that in a heated situation people do rash things, and it is possible and very probable, that among the participants in the acts of violence on Thursday there were also people who allowed themselves to be misled in that way. But I also know that there are others who promote propaganda which advocates acts of violence, and I must say to the Communists, that their words here and their protests would have made a totally different impression, if they could say with a clear conscience that they do not bear any burden of guilt for what happened. I dare argue that the entire course of action from the Communist side and the way in which they use the mood of indignation mean that, when those responsible are being sought, the Communists must be placed on the side of the employers and the strikebreakers. The position which the party that I represent takes and which, moreover, the entire labor movement takes in the question of violence has been clear from the beginning.

The Communists had to fight a two-front war. They primarily attacked Prime Minister Ekman because he did not stop the strikebreakers and for summoning the troops, but they also condemned the Social Democrats, because they did not show complete solidarity with the demonstrators and their actions. The Speaker of the Second Chamber, the farm owner Per Nilsson from Bonarp in the province of Skåne, had to intervene repeatedly, interrupt the speakers and demand a "more moderate" use of language. The Communist August Spångberg was reprimanded twice as he spoke, but he would not stop. He characterized the strikebreakers thus:

> No, I maintain and I emphasize the opinion, that such people have no right to exist. They are scabby animals. They have no more right to exist than a diseased, mangy dog, than a reptile. They should not be protected. They have no right to live from the workers' point of view. People who behave in this way should be interned. And if they are free, then the workers must have the possibility to defend themselves. Just as I defend myself against a mad dog, I have the right to defend myself against a mad animal with two legs...

At that point the Speaker of the Chamber not only pounded the gavel decisively, but also made the following statement:

> As it appears that the speaker intends to continue using such expressions, I thus move to ascertain if the Chamber wishes to adjourn.

The Chamber accepted the Speaker's proposal. It is the only occasion on which a meeting in the Swedish bicameral Riksdag was adjourned because the Speaker of the Chamber was not obeyed.

# CHAPTER 9

# The Modern Riksdag

THE YEAR 1933 was the starting point for a period of stability in Swedish political life. For more than fifty years the same political parties would struggle for power, and one of them, the Social Democrats, would hold the post of Prime Minister for most of the era.

The position of the government and the Riksdag had undergone drastic changes in the beginning of the twentieth century, but this did not lead to any thorough revision of the Instrument of Government and the Riksdag Act. There was early a demand for such a revision, but the parties were slow in coming to an agreement on a new constitution. The results of several extensive studies and investigations on constitutional questions were the two reforms which were carried out in 1969 and 1974. The bicameral Riksdag was replaced by a unicameral legislature, and parliamentarism and democracy were written into the constitution.

From the 1930s onward political decision-making dealt largely with the public sector and its growth. National and local government received increasing responsibility. There was surprisingly often consensus among the parties in questions concerning the build-up of the welfare state. The conflicts were about the rate and extent of the expansion rather than about the basic principles.

Of course, other topics also played an important role in political debate. During the Second World War foreign policy was paramount. Defense, the constitution, nuclear power and education later became the major issues, but it is striking that even in these areas compromises were worked out.

## Per Albin Hansson and Axel Pehrsson-Bramstorp

In the 1932 election campaign the Social Democrats were on the offensive in an entirely different way than they had been earlier. The Conservatives did not have the initiative, as was the case in 1928. The mood of the country was also more favorable for the Social Democrats. Memories of the Ådalen incident were still fresh. The financier Ivar Kreuger, who had been a symbol of the new successful capitalism, shot himself in Paris and left behind a

*On the opposite page:* Today's Swedish Riksdag makes laws and determines what taxes will be levied and what expenditures the state will make. The government of the country must have the confidence of a majority in the Riksdag.

Overcrowding and poor hygienic conditions were still vast social problems during the 1930s. They became central issues in the political struggles of that era.

legacy of bankruptcy. The Liberal Prime Minister and parliamentary tightrope artist Carl Gustaf Ekman had to leave his post in August after it was revealed that his party had accepted financial support from Kreuger.

Sweden was in the midst of an economic crisis. Unemployment was high, and many families lived in real destitution. Discontent was rife, both within the Agrarian Union and among the Social Democrats. Bankruptcies among farmers were common, and competition from abroad increased. The voters wanted to hear new and positive proposals for solutions to the crisis.

The problems and the mood were similar in the USA, Sweden and several other European countries. The American President tried to calm the voters by promising that "happiness is just around the corner." It was only necessary to wait, and it would come. The Democrat Franklin D. Roosevelt entered the 1932 presidential election with a program which contained a number of active measures to get the economy moving. The main message was that there was no way in which saving would solve the crisis, and with that message the Democrats won the election.

The Conservatives and the Liberal People's Party in Sweden held ideas similar to those of the Republicans in the USA. The Social Democrats, on the other hand, advocated active government intervention in the economy. They wanted to increase public relief work and to pay those who were employed regular wages. They proposed a number of other measures which would be expensive for the state, but which could be defended because they would promote growth and thus bring the economy into balance.

A larger proportion of the eligible voters, 68.6 percent, took part in the 1932 election. The main losers were the Conservatives,

## Per Albin and the Welfare State

DURING THE RIKSDAG DEBATE on January 18, 1928 the Social Democratic leader Per Albin Hansson used a term or metaphor for Swedish society which would gain significance in future political debate – *folkhemmet*. This term, which might literally be translated as "the home of the people," came to represent the modern welfare state for Swedes. Per Albin spoke during a time of political and economic crisis. The Social Democrats were accused of trying to introduce socialism on a Soviet model. Per Albin's speech may be regarded as a response to these accusations. The metaphor was later often used by Social Democratic leaders, especially Olof Palme.

Toward the end of the 1930s areas with simple single homes were built in Swedish towns and cities. They came to symbolize the Swedish welfare state, as the buildings were partially financed with state and municipal funds. Here is a sample of such homes in Långängen, Stockholm.

The foundation of the home is a sense of community and belonging. The good home does not recognize some who are privileged, while others are neglected, no favorites and no step-children. One does not look down on the other nor does anyone try to gain advantages at the expense of others; the strong do not oppress and plunder the weak. In a good home equality, consideration, cooperation and helpfulness reign. Applied to the great home of the people and citizens this means that all social and economic barriers must be broken down which divide citizens into the privileged and the underprivileged, the masters and the mastered, the rich and the poor, the propertied and the propertyless, the plunderers and the plundered.

Swedish society is still not a good home for its people. Certainly there is formal equality here, equality in terms of political rights, but socially, a class society still exists, and economically, the dictatorship of the few. The inequality is sometimes flagrant. While a few live in palaces, many regard themselves lucky if they can live in a garden shack during the cold winter. While some live in luxury, many go from door to door to get a bit of bread, and the poor are anxious about tomorrow, where sickness, unemployment and other misfortunes may be lurking.

If Swedish society is to be a good home for its people, class differences must be banished, social conscience must be developed, an economic leveling must occur, the workers must be given a share in management of the economy, and democracy must be realized and applied socially and economically.

The objection might be raised that social and economic equalization has long been making progress and is still continuing to do so. A liberal economist a while ago made much of the fact that since the 1860s the pay of unskilled laborers and agricultural workers has risen more quickly than those of lecturers and judges. That certainly is not proof that we have reached a state where we can sit back. Although there is less poverty and deprivation than earlier, they are still daily visitors in thousands of Swedish homes, a fact which some circles think of only at Christmas time.

## Olof Olsson from Kullenbergstorp – Agrarian Leader

Olof Olsson from Kullen-bergstorp in the province of Skåne. A caricature by Nils Melander.

OLOF OLSSON from Kullenbergstorp (1859–1934) first won a seat in the Riksdag in 1909. He was in many ways typical of agrarian politicians, who long played a major role in the history of the Swedish Riksdag. He began on the local level and held a number of posts in various agrarian organizations. He was spokesman for the people of Skåne during the Farmers' Demonstration in 1914.

From today's viewpoint "the man from Kullenbergstorp" may be said to have been wrong about almost everything. He was the only person in the Second Chamber who voted against the entire proposal for universal suffrage in local elections. He was definitely opposed to allowing people to vote who had not been able to pay their taxes in time; the voting restriction concerning tax debts should remain.

According to Mr. Olsson from Kullenbergstorp, obligations should be part and parcel of rights. That should also be the case as far as voting rights were concerned. A citizen should have paid his taxes to be allowed to vote for members of the Riksdag; military service should have been completed as well. Olsson was also opposed to female suffrage. There were certainly many who shared his opinions, but they understood that such views could not possibly gain ground.

During the Riksdag meetings of the 1920s Olof Olsson was very active as an initiator of motions and participant in debates. Agriculture and everything related to it were the focus of his interest. The reforms which he proposed were aimed at preservation of the old society, for example, facilitating the inheritance of farms in a family or preventing the impoverishment of the countryside through emigration. In the large number of letters he wrote home to his sons, he consciously described what happened in the Riksdag and in the capital city.

In 1929, when Olof Olsson was 70 years old, he was elected chairman of both the national committee of the party and the party's Riksdag group. This must be regarded as one of the strangest party leader elections in modern history. The Agrarian Union elected a person who was totally out of touch with his time in a situation when the country was faced with major problems and changes.

In spite of the frequent shifts in government during these years Olsson never accepted a post as minister. He had received offers but in a 1930 debate declared: "It is difficult for farmers to participate in big-time politics, because then they will be deceived." This agrarian leader did not lack self-confidence, however.

Olof Olsson's political career came to an unfortunate end. The crisis settlement with the Social Democrats in 1933 was an idea totally alien to him, and the agreement was made behind his back. In 1934 he resigned as party leader and was replaced by the much more modern Axel Pehrsson-Bramstorp, who definitely did not feel that farmers should keep out of "big-time politics."

Per Albin Hansson together with his government colleagues during the quincentennial celebration of the Riksdag in 1935. The Prime Minister had reason to look pleased. The government which he had formed in 1932 had worked well. It had a stable majority in the Riksdag, and the recurrent crises of the 1920s had been brought to an end.

Ernst Wigforss was the Minister of Finance during the periods 1925–1926 and 1932–1949 (with the exception of the summer of 1936). He was one of Sweden's foremost promoters of the economic theories of John Maynard Keynes. According to Keynes, as in many countries the economic crisis in Sweden in the beginning of the 1930s could not be solved by saving, but rather by different investments by the state "to get the ball rolling."

although the two liberal parties also lost ground, while the Social Democrats and the Agrarian Union gained. The Social Democratic Party increased by more than 4 percent from the previous Riksdag election and received in excess of 40 percent of the votes.

The Social Democrat Per Albin Hansson was asked to form a government. Ernst Wigforss, the architect of the new economic program, became the Minister of Finance. The problem, however, was that the government did not have a majority in the Second Chamber, still less in the First. The contrast with the USA was significant. Roosevelt won the election there, and could, as President, immediately begin with his new policy, the New Deal. The Social Democrats did have the largest number of votes of any party in the Second Chamber, but the government which was formed seemed to be only one in a series of minority governments.

In retrospect, cooperation between the Agrarian Union and the Social Democrats may seem to have been the obvious choice, but it was not apparent to the contemporary world. The Agrarian Union had its roots in the old agrarian movement, which had supported the Farmers' Demonstration. Its leader, Olof Olsson from Kullenbergstorp, was conservative and feared the Social Democrats. On top of that, the farmers represented producers and the workers, consumers. In an economic crisis, could the latter be expected to agree to measures that would lead to more expensive goods?

Everything indicated that minority parliamentarism would continue in its old form. However, the farmers and the Social Democrats did have common interests which made it possible for them to overcome the differences of opinion. Olsson from Kullenbergstorp was pushed aside, and Axel Pehrsson-Bramstorp became the real leader of the farmers. He was among the younger members of the Agrarian Union and was typical of politicians who want results. He realized that there would be advantages for the farmers if the Social

A satirical drawing by the artist who used the pseudonym Jac. The drawing portrays the agreement between the Social Democrats and the Agrarian Union in 1933, which has gone down in history as the "horse trade." Under the supervision of the shepherds Per Albin Hansson and Axel Pehrsson-Bramstorp the lambs graze among the resting lions.

A campaign poster for the Conservatives in 1936. During the spring the question of defense led to a government crisis and played an important role in the intense election campaign. The election resulted in great losses for the Conservatives.

Democrats stopped the free importation of agricultural products. An agreement was reached which had its roots in the election program of the Social Democrats and was complemented by the demands from the farmers. Its opponents called it the "horse trade."

Cooperation between the Social Democrats and the Agrarian Union was a success. Bramstorp took over as party leader from Olsson in 1934, and the two parties which had made the crisis agreement realized that they could also work together on a number of other questions. By the spring of 1936, however, everything seemed to be back where it had been before. Just as during the First World War, the controversial issue was defense. The Social Democrats did not want to go as far as other parties in arming the country. They were not even willing to agree to the compromise which the Liberal Party (*Folkpartiet* – the two liberal groups joined forces under this name in 1934) and the Agrarian Union had worked out. The government resigned in June when it was defeated in the Riksdag on a pension issue.

After making some inquiries the King assigned Bramstorp the task of forming an Agrarian Union government, the equivalent of the earlier minority governments. However, Bramstorp's government was even more short-lived than any of the earlier ones and resigned after one hundred days. It never met the Riksdag. The Social Democrats were again victorious in the election of 1936, but the Conservatives lost. It was then clear that the task of forming a government would be in the hands of the Social Democrats.

## A Strong Coalition Government

Per Albin Hansson had learned important lessons from the four years during which he was head of the government. He understood that it would be more suitable to take the Agrarian Union into the government than to work with the party informally or within the framework of the Riksdag committees. The Agrarian Union shared this view, and for the first time since 1920 Sweden had a majority government. The new government worked well, and the Riksdag thus acquired a new position. The major issues were solved within the government, and the committees lost their central role. All proposals, of course, were presented in the Riksdag and treated as usual, but this did not usually lead to any radical changes.

The main job of the Riksdag became one of giving the government a stable foundation. The opposition parties could certainly make interpellations and submit motions, but they had little chance of influencing larger issues.

The foreign policy situation grew increasingly serious. Members of the left wing in Sweden took an active interest in the civil war in Spain, which had been going on since 1936, and volunteers fought there against the fascists. Italy initiated a war with Abyssinia, the present-day Ethiopia, in 1935, which struck a deep chord in Swedish public opinion. Sweden helped the sick and wounded by sending an ambulance and medical personnel. Most serious, however, was the development in Germany.

German influence on Sweden had long been great. Not only middle class circles, businessmen, high public officials, military officers and academics, received their most important impulses from Germany: even the Social Democrats had close contact with their German counterparts. Germany had about the same importance for Sweden between 1875 and 1940, as the USA has had since the Second World War.

National Socialism did not have any significant support in Sweden. There were small, vociferous Nazi organizations, but they do not appear to have been as large as in most other countries in Europe. The Conservatives broke with their own youth organization, the National Youth League (*Sveriges nationella ungdomsförbund*), when the group displayed Nazi sympathies. An association called the Young Swedes (*Ungsvenskarna*) was organized instead. At about the same time the right became unified in the Conservative Party through the merger of the General Electoral

Sweden contributed medical aid when Abyssinia was attacked by Italy in 1935. In an air attack by an Italian fighter plane one of the Swedish medical workers was killed in the car which is seen in the picture. The Abyssinian War may be regarded as the first Third World conflict which generated strong reactions in Swedish public opinion.

The chairman of the Swedish Trade Union Confederation (*LO*), August Lindberg, and the chairman of the Swedish Employers' Confederation (*SAF*), Sigfrid Edström, sign the agreement between the parties on the labor market, the so-called Saltsjöbaden Agreement, at the Grand Hotel in Saltsjöbaden outside Stockholm on December 20, 1938.

Association and the two conservative groups from the First and the Second Chamber. No Nazi was ever elected to the Swedish Riksdag. The stability which was created in the political and trade union arenas during the 1930s meant that there was no seedbed for antidemocratic tendencies.

The stability was further strengthened by what became known as the Saltsjöbaden Agreement which was reached in 1938 between the opposing sides in the labor market. It initiated a period of cooperation between laborers and employers.

The local elections of 1938 gave the Social Democrats a majority among the voters, 50.4 percent. The election results meant that Per Albin Hansson's government gained an even stronger position. Its policy seemed to have support among a wide range of people.

## The Riksdag during the War Years

Immediately after the outbreak of war in September 1939 a demand for a national coalition government was made by the Agrarian Union. The Agrarian Union thought that more parties should share the responsibility for the many interventions in the daily life of people which had to be made as a result of the war. The extensive criticism of the Hammarskjöld government during the First World War was still a fresh memory.

Sweden was faced with great problems in supplying the country with food and other necessities when cut off from the outside world by the Second World War. Shortly after the outbreak of the war rationing cards for gasoline were issued, and thereafter also for the purchase of other goods, such as coffee, tea, sugar, flour, bread and fats.

It would not be until December that a national coalition government was formed headed by Per Albin Hansson. In addition to the Social Democrats, there were members of the Conservative Party, the Liberal Party and the Agrarian Union; only the small Communist Party was not included. The leaders of all parties participated in the government. Christian Günther, Sweden's ambassador to Oslo, was appointed Foreign Minister.

The position of the Riksdag had changed with the crisis agreement and the coalition government between the Social Democrats and the Agrarian Union. The government had an entirely different role than during the period of minority parliamentarism. Agreements were no longer reached in the committees and chambers, but rather among the members of the government. With the

Per Albin Hansson's national coalition government in December 1939. In the government there were representatives of the Social Democrats and of the three nonsocialist parties, the Conservative Party, the Liberal Party and the Agrarian Union. Furthermore, the government included two ministers without party affiliation.

national coalition government this characteristic became even more prominent. The important foreign policy questions were still treated by the party groups, but it was nearly impossible for them to change decisions made by the government. That was especially true in the beginning of the war.

The national coalition government had an exceptional position of power, and it was said that the Riksdag had been converted into a "transportation company." Some Riksdag members complained of their inability to exert influence on events. Others felt that the information they received on developments was insufficient.

The powerlessness of the Riksdag should not be exaggerated, however. There was an opposition, and in certain crises Per Albin had to use all of his political talent to get the Social Democrats in the Riksdag to go along with the government line. At midsummer 1941, after intensive and heated debates, the government and the Riksdag allowed a German division to be transported from Norway to Finland on the Swedish railway. Other German demands were only partially accepted; the basic rule was not to relinquish more than was absolutely necessary.

German soldiers being transported through Sweden. Between 1940 and 1943 a total of two million persons and 200,000 tons of equipment were transported on Swedish railways for the German government.

Sweden also, however, acquiesced to certain German demands to intervene against Swedish newspapers. Freedom of the press was one of the most important issues in the Riksdag debates during the war. In this context the First Chamber played a role which both warranted attention and won respect for its independence.

The press was still very much party-oriented during the Second World War, while radio was neutral; the independent journalist did not exist in principle. The mass media generally did not attempt to play the role of a third branch of the government, as is the case today. The Swedish News Agency (*Tidningarnas Telegrambyrå, TT*) was responsible for the news broadcasts on the radio. In the newspapers ties to parties were seen, not only on the editorial page, but also in the columns, in news articles, in satires and on the family page. A person was born and died in a newspaper with the "right" political color.

The leading editors were also party politicians. During the Second World War about 10 percent of all Riksdag members were

On May 1, 1940 the normal Social Democratic May Day parade was transformed into a demonstration of support for the national coalition government with a blue and yellow flag in the front and banners hailing a staunch will to defend the country. Here the leader of the Conservatives, Gösta Bagge, is seen walking side-by-side with the Social Democratic Prime Minister Per Albin Hansson.

The Communist Party's election poster from the party's record election in 1944. The clenched left fist was met by the "punch from the right" of the Conservatives in the same campaign.

newspapermen. The chairman of the town or city council was also often an editor. As a rule the newspapers were the long arm of the party, which left its mark on their reporting. It was also natural to take a stand in the headlines and the news accounts. There were conflicts between the press and the government during the war, but on the whole there was consensus among the leading politicians and most of the newspapers.

The majority of Swedish opinion also supported government policy. In the 1940 election the Social Democrats received 53.8 percent of the votes, which may be seen as a vote of confidence for both Per Albin Hansson and the national coalition government. The voters did not want a policy of heroic struggle, but rather a policy of adaptation which did not lead to capitulation.

No new political parties were formed during the Second World War. Something sensational happened, however, in the 1944 election when the Communist Party, which had been regarded as almost treasonable earlier in the war, had its greatest success. The number of Communist seats in the Second Chamber increased from three to fifteen (10.3 percent of the votes). The progress may be explained by the Soviet Union's victories in the war, but also by a certain dissatisfaction with the Social Democratic cooperation with the nonsocialist parties and a radicalization of the political climate in Sweden.

The Communists, however, soon lost the confidence which had been placed in them. They took over leadership of the largest trade union, the Metal Workers' Union, and in the spring of 1945 called a strike which was very extensive and costly for the strikers. The strike was a failure, and the Communists lost both trade union and political support. In addition, events outside the country, the Cold War, the iron curtain and the Communist takeover of Czechoslovakia in 1948, all affected the Swedish Communists negatively.

The radical winds which were blowing at the end of the war also reached the Social Democrats. In 1944 a 27-point postwar domestic program was adopted; the socialist harvest was to come. Fundamental to the Social Democratic program was that the state should take on many of society's problems. There was a desire for full employment and a fair distribution of incomes among citizens. However, there were also demands for socialization and for greater influence on the production process for the working man.

There were obvious differences of opinion in the Social Democratic Party by the end of the war. Per Albin Hansson, who was the unchallenged leader of the Social Democrats, made it clear on several occasions that a national coalition government could also have advantages for the country in peace time. This view was totally alien to the younger and more radical wing of the party. The election results in 1944, when the Social Democrats lost ground and the Communists had great success, could be interpreted as a warning; a continuation of the coalition government could cause the Social Democrats to be identified with nonsocialist groups. In the summer of 1945 the coalition was replaced by a purely Social Democratic government.

The Swedish Riksdag and the Swedish government were much more successful during the Second World War than during the First. Nevertheless, there was criticism of appeasement of Germany. However, the Prime Minister retained his post, and all the leading Social Democrats who had held positions in the coalition government shifted to the one-party government. The new Foreign Minister was Östen Undén, and among the other new members of the government were found Gunnar Sträng and Gunnar Myrdal.

In October 1946 Per Albin Hansson died suddenly of a heart attack and was succeeded as Prime Minister and party leader by Tage Erlander.

## The Social Democrats in Power

After the First World War Sweden and the rest of the world suffered from a severe economic downturn, and many thought that the same thing would happen after the Second World War. The Swedish economy was good, however, even if inflation became extensive. In contrast to the situation in many of the warring nations, industry in Sweden was intact, which gave great advantages on the export market. Production increased and continued to do so during the 1950s and 1960s.

Every year the pie which was to be divided grew larger. Even in the first years after the war important reforms were carried out: larger pensions, three weeks' vacation, general child allowances and a public health insurance, which in principle guaranteed free medical care for all citizens. These reforms were prepared in committees with participants who represented both the Social Democrats and the nonsocialist parties. Decisions could thus be

The pseudonym EWK drew this caricature of Tage Erlander for his sixtieth birthday in 1961. Erlander was the son of an elementary school teacher from the province of Värmland and, as did Wigforss, he came into contact with Social Democratic ideas while studying at the university in Lund.

Typical for family policy since the Second World War is its general application. For example, all children give a family the right to child allowances of the same size, regardless of the family's income.

VALÅRET 1948

utan kvinnor inget folkstyre

A poster from the 1948 election campaign printed by the Committee for Increased Female Representation and designed to get more women to vote.

made with a significant amount of unity. There were no great differences of opinion concerning the general welfare policy.

After the war political debate concentrated on two areas: socialization and taxes. It was on these issues that the nonsocialist opposition attacked the Social Democratic government. The attack was based on the postwar program which advocated some socialization but also on the results of various governmental studies and evaluations.

The discussions in the Riksdag once more received a great deal of attention and often became heated. The debates in the two chambers were characterized by different styles. In the First Chamber there was greater formality, and the mode of expression was more academic than in the Second Chamber. The government was accused of retaining unnecessary regulations from the war and introducing new ones, as well as wanting to socialize the country. The opposition not only talked of a Sweden where everything was difficult and complicated, but also of economic mismanagement.

The opposition had strong support in the daily press which was dominated by the nonsocialist newspapers. The tone also became harsher in the newspaper debates, not least due to the style which was introduced by Herbert Tingsten, the editor of *Dagens Nyheter* after the war. In contrast to many other editors-in-chief, Tingsten was not a party man, but, as a rule, he supported the Liberal Party, not least in the election campaigns. In certain issues, however, he deviated from the Liberal Party line, such as when he advocated joining the Atlantic Pact.

The election of the Second Chamber in 1948 appeared to be a turning point, and the opposition, especially the Liberal Party,

Voting in the First Chamber of the Riksdag on *Helgeandsholmen* during a session in the 1950s.

looked optimistically toward the future, while the Social Democrats were on the defensive. In 1944 the Liberal Party elected a new leader, the economist Bertil Ohlin, who was a modern party leader with a liberal social policy. Tage Erlander had succeeded Per Albin Hansson as Prime Minister and leader of the Social Democratic Party. During the war he had been an undersecretary in the Ministry of Health and Social Affairs, and after the new government was formed, he became head of the Ministry of Education and Ecclesiastical Affairs. He was unknown to people in general, and many regarded him as a less significant politician than his predecessor.

Bertil Ohlin on the rostrum of the Second Chamber, while his main opponent, Tage Erlander, listens. On the bench behind Erlander is seen the young Olof Palme.

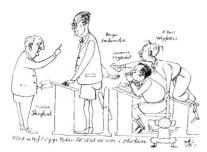

Erlander's lack of political experience when he assumed the post of Prime Minister provided much material for satires. This drawing by Anders Sten in 1946 represents the new Prime Minister as a schoolboy who manages to pass questioning by the Conservative politician Martin Skoglund from Doverstorp only by means of slips of papers and whispers from his colleagues, the ministers Gunnar Myrdal and Ernst Wigforss.

Tage Erlander and Gunnar Hedlund shake hands when agreement was reached on the 1951 coalition government.

Social Democratic women demonstrating against Swedish atomic weapons on May 1, 1955. Several leading Social Democrats at that time argued in favor of supplying the Swedish military with atomic weapons.

The results of the election were positive for the Liberal Party; it doubled its number of seats in the Second Chamber. But the right lost ground, and the Social Democrats did not suffer the losses that the opposition had counted on. Voter participation was higher than ever before, 82.7 percent.

The Social Democrats were able to remain in power even though the position of the government had been weakened in the Riksdag. The idea of forming a coalition with the Agrarian Union existed, and such cooperation was regarded as positive in many ways. It would give a more stable majority in the Riksdag and make a nonsocialist three-party government impossible. The discussions which were carried out in 1948 brought no results, but the question was kept alive. In 1949 Pehrsson-Bramstorp was followed as leader of the Agrarian Union by the farmer and Doctor of Laws Gunnar Hedlund, and the discussions which were resumed in 1951 led to a new coalition government. The Social Democrats promised not to push any demands for socialization, and the Agrarian Union gained support for its agricultural policy.

The 1950s were characterized by strong economic growth and political stability. The coalition between the Social Democrats and the Agrarian Union contributed to this situation, as did the situation outside the country. The Cold War and the Korean War were experienced by many as the prelude to a new world war which would be even more terrible because of atomic weapons.

For the government and the Riksdag the coalition meant a return to the situation which had existed between 1936 and 1939. The Liberal and Conservative parties comprised the nonsocialist opposition. The Conservatives named a new leader in 1950, the business executive Jarl Hjalmarson. He had served as secretary to Arvid Lindman and in a similar manner would bring the Conservative Party closer to the people.

The coalition worked without serious friction during the first years, but after the 1956 election a crisis arose, as the Social Democrats and the Agrarian Union both lost ground to the Liberal and Conservative parties. Cooperation came to an end in 1957. Thereafter a new political pattern emerged in the Riksdag: bloc politics.

The question of a national supplementary pension (ATP) became the overriding political issue at the end of the 1950s. Although the nonsocialists were divided between two alternatives, they were all opposed to the model supported by the Social Democrats, which advocated a public insurance model. The supplementary pension proposal was a bold venture on the part of the Social Democrats. It seems strange that this complicated issue, which initially was regarded more as a technical economic question, not only became the focus of political debate, but in the fall of 1957 also became the object of a referendum.

In some countries referenda are used rather frequently as an alternative to decisions by parliament. In Sweden referenda of an advisory nature had been used only twice before. On both occasions, the topic concerned matters that were not bound to party positions: prohibition of wine and spirits in 1922 and conversion from left-hand to right-hand traffic in 1955. The supplementary pension issue was tied to the positions of the political parties.

Domestic politics, which otherwise lacked color in the 1950s, took a dramatic turn at the end of the decade. The result of the referendum was not clear. This caused the Social Democrats to call for a new election, which is as uncommon in Swedish political life as a referendum. Nor did the election produce any clear-cut results; the votes were relatively evenly split between those who favored and those who opposed the proposed pension. The seats in the Second Chamber were divided so that the Social Democrats and the Communists received 116, while the three nonsocialist parties had 115. Because the Speaker of the Chamber, who did not have the

Posters from the referendum on the supplementary pension system. Alternative one was that of the Social Democrats and proposed a state-financed insurance system, which was later carried out. The second alternative was the purely voluntary one, which was supported by the Center Party/Agrarian Union. The third alternative, backed by the Swedish Employers' Confederation, and the Conservative and Liberal parties, proposed agreements between employees and employers.

The result of the vote in the Second Chamber on May 14, 1959: yes, 114; no, 115; abstentions, 1; absent, 0. A "yes" vote meant a vote in favor of the opposition's rejection of the government's proposal. The abstention of the Liberal Party member Ture Königson gave the majority to the Social Democratic Party alternative.

## Olivia Nordgren – Working Class Woman and Riksdag Veteran

WOMEN were long poorly represented in the Riksdag. One of the first female members was Olivia Nordgren (1880–1969). Per Albin Hansson reputedly said that, if any woman was able to become a member of the government, she would be the one. Olivia Nordgren was the kind of woman he admired. Not only was she from Skåne as he was, but she had also climbed the ladder the hard way both in the trade union and in politics. Furthermore, she was no "feminist."

Olivia Nordgren entered working life in 1894, with little education, as a typographer for the newspaper *Trelleborgs Allehanda*. She was the first female typographer in town. She explained later that in her political career she had been able to make use of her experience as the only woman in a group of men. She also learned a great deal about politics by working on the newspaper, especially because of trade union activities in the Typographers' Union. She had soon reached positions in the local and the regional trade union and political movements.

The time she spent as a typographer was no short transition period for Olivia Nordgren. She worked in her trade seventeen years before she became entirely involved in trade union activities and politics. In 1924 she was elected a member of the national committee of the Social Democratic Party, where she was long the only woman. She was elected to the Riksdag in 1925, succeeding the former Minister of Finance Fredrik Thorsson, and was to remain a member of the Second Chamber until 1952.

In feminist questions, Olivia Nordgren showed restraint. She declared many times that it was best for children if the mother was at home. She did not accept a seat in the Riksdag until her three children were rather grown-up. Her maiden speech in the Riksdag in 1926, however, dealt with the position of the woman on the labor market. She stated

Olivia Nordgren surrounded by her male colleagues in a temporary committee about 1930.

that the right to work should exist "regardless of civil status or sex," but at the same time that it would "from society's point of view be unfortunate if too many married women were taken from their homes and placed in the labor market."

Social problems formed the focus of Olivia Nordgren's interest. During the war she was also known as the sole woman on the important Food Commission.

Olivia Nordgren represents in many ways a large group of Social Democratic Riksdag members. She began by serving actively in her trade union and continued in different posts in the party organization; she was a member of local and regional boards of the Typographers' Union, the Federation of Social Democratic Women and the Social Democratic Party. She was also a member of the town council and the county council. She maintained her local contacts even when she entered the Riksdag.

In an interview in the newspaper *Dagens Nyheter* on her seventieth birthday, she complained that her political work had taken most of her time. She had never had any leisure time, and there had been no time for trips, besides those she made to Stockholm. She could only remember one four-day journey to Dalarna.

right to vote, was a Social Democrat, this made the division even. In this stalemate a member of the Liberal Party, Ture Königson, departed from the party line, and thus the Social Democratic proposal received a majority of the votes.

## The Constitution in Focus

The Social Democrats remained in control of the government during the 1960s. They did not have an absolute majority, but they could depend on the support of the Communists in the Riksdag. Giving the Communists seats in the government was never considered, but on all the important questions, they voted with the Social Democrats. There were times when the Communists were not willing to go along, as in 1959 on the issue of the introduction of a general four percent sales tax (later transformed into a value-added tax, VAT), but in the end they supported the Social Democratic policy. It was a victory for the Social Democrats, but especially for the Minister of Finance Gunnar Sträng. He was to hold this post for 21 years and had a leading position in the Social Democratic governments.

After the election that focused on the supplementary pension issue, the Social Democratic dominance seemed impossible to budge. However, the political climate did change, especially because of the role which the mass media gained in politics. The political loyalty of the newspapers declined, at least as far as the reporting of news was concerned, and radio and television began to practice active political journalism. In the province of Skåne the newspaper *Sydsvenska Dagbladet* spearheaded a new local political group, Citizens' Coalition (*Medborgerlig samling*), an attempt to promote cooperation among the Conservative Party, the Liberal

Minister of Finance Gunnar Sträng conversing with Minister of Labor Ingemund Bengtsson, later Speaker of the Riksdag. The man beside Ingemund Bengtsson is Minister of Justice Lennart Geijer.

The bicameral system was out-of-date, as were the premises which accommodated the two chambers. In this picture, which was arranged, we see the Riksdag members working in the common typing room. By moving to *Sergels torg* in 1971 for the first time the members of the Riksdag all got their own offices.

Prime Minister Tage Erlander together with King Gustaf VI Adolf in 1969. The constitutional reform of 1974 left the Swedish monarch with primarily ceremonial functions.

Party and the Center Party (the Agrarian Union changed its name to the Center Party, *Centerpartiet*, in 1957).

Election campaigns became increasingly concentrated to debates and interviews on radio and television. The 1966 local elections reflected this trend, and the results showed that the Social Democrats were vulnerable after all. They received only 42.2 percent of the votes, which was a decline of 5 percentage points compared with the election to the Second Chamber two years earlier.

One of the explanations of this result was that the Social Democrats had not made a sufficiently good impression in the mass media. Questions concerning the housing shortage and the increased tax pressure had dominated, and the nonsocialist parties were on the offensive. In spite of economic growth and extensive reforms, there was evidently decreased confidence in the ruling Social Democrats. Tage Erlander called this "the discontent of rising expectations."

One of the areas of great importance to the nonsocialist parties was the constitution – the structure of the Riksdag and the election system. These issues were especially emphasized by the Liberal Party, which maintained that the constitution was unjust in several respects and might even be considered undemocratic. The bicameral system was described as old-fashioned, and the election system was said to favor the Social Democrats. Criticism was directed especially at the First Chamber, which was painted as reflecting an earlier state of electoral opinion as it was renewed successively.

The government had begun to study the question as early as 1954 with the appointment of the Commission on the Constitution, whose task was to modernize the constitution. The commission took its time, and its first proposal was not ready until 1963. The group, however, was divided on two of the central issues: the number of chambers and the election system.

After the 1966 election, when the constitutional question played an important role in the opposition's criticism of the government, everything moved more quickly. A Commission on the Fundamental Laws was appointed, and its proposal for a unicameral Riksdag and a new election system was presented in 1967. It was passed by the Riksdag in 1968 and 1969.

The 1969 changes were adopted as amendments to the 1809 Instrument of Government and the 1866 Riksdag Act. The work on the new constitution continued, and in 1974 Sweden received a new Instrument of Government and a new Riksdag Act.

## The Introduction of the Unicameral Riksdag

The various constitutional changes which were finally adopted in 1969 created new prerequisites for political life. Bertil Ohlin stated in 1964 that there were "strong democratic arguments" for giving the voters "the opportunity to determine the composition of the Riksdag and the government of the nation in one and the same election." Ohlin's wish was fulfilled. In 1970 Sweden got a unicameral legislature with 350 members (349 from 1976 onward) and an election system in which the parties were given a number of seats corresponding to the percentage of votes cast. In order to be represented in the Riksdag, a party had to receive at least 4 percent of the total votes or 12 percent of the votes in one constituency.

The Social Democrats wanted to maintain a "local connection," a connection between national and local elections, in the new system with a directly elected unicameral legislature. (Previously local assemblies had appointed the members of the First Chamber.) This demand was met by scheduling the national and local elections at the same time. The term of office was reduced to three years.

The system of Riksdag committees was also modified by the constitutional reform. In the old Riksdag the organization had been based on two fundamental functions, legislation and budgetary issues. For instance, there had been three committees on the law, a committee on the constitution, a committee on taxation, and

The meeting room of the Committee on Finance in the Riksdag Building. The room has been retained intact since the days of the bicameral legislature, when it served as a reference library.

The Advisory Council on Foreign Affairs meets in the Royal Palace under the chairmanship of King Carl XVI Gustaf.

a ways and means committee. Certain "special" committees also existed, such as an agricultural committee and a committee on foreign affairs.

In today's Riksdag there are 16 committees which generally reflect areas covered by the existing ministries, for example, the Committee on Education, the Committee on Cultural Affairs and the Committee on Finance. When necessary, a special committee may be appointed, which occurred in 1992 when the Riksdag was to deal with the agreements with the European Communities concerning European economic cooperation, the EEA Treaty.

Until 1921 foreign policy questions were taken up in special secret committees. These were replaced at that time by the Advisory Council on Foreign Affairs, chaired by the King. A Committee on Foreign Affairs was established in 1937 which had the same members as the Advisory Council with the exception that a member of the Riksdag functioned as chairman. The 1974 Instrument of Government limited the number of members in the Advisory Council, and coordination with the Committee on Foreign Affairs ceased; the composition of the council and the committee is only partially the same.

The meetings of the committees are not public. However, since 1988 it has been possible to arrange public hearings.

As in the old Riksdag, the committees are the focus of daily activity. Most decisions are made in the committees, and often compromises between the parties are worked out there. When a proposal is presented to the Riksdag for voting, in practice the decision has been made and the voting is a confirmation of viewpoints that are already well-known. This is one of the reasons why the debates and the voting in the Riksdag do not generally attract much attention. Attempts have been made to increase

The Plenary Chamber of the temporary quarters of the Riksdag during the period 1971 to 1983.

interest in the work of the Riksdag in different ways, for instance by having sessions geared to discussion of issues of current interest.

The parties play a dominant role both in the constitution and in political work. All important questions are first discussed in the various party caucuses in the Riksdag, and their judgement is often crucial for the future decision. The meetings of the party caucuses are not public, but the viewpoints presented and the decisions reached are often quickly spread by the mass media. The position of the party leaders is central both within and outside the party.

When the Riksdag moved to temporary premises near *Sergels torg* in Stockholm in 1971, working conditions for the members improved considerably. They received their own offices and a certain amount of secretarial help. Such facilities are also available in the present buildings on *Helgeandsholmen*. Riksdag administration has grown significantly, and now greatly increased services are available to the members.

The party offices have been strengthened by assistance from the state. Since 1965 financial support is also given to each party in proportion to its numbers in the Riksdag.

The changes in the fundamental laws made in 1969 were worked into the new constitution which was adopted by the Riksdag in 1973 and 1974 and which has been in force since January 1, 1975. Thus the 1809 Instrument of Government ceased to be valid.

The 1974 Instrument of Government limited the position of the King as head of state to purely ceremonial duties. The Speaker of the Riksdag assumed the King's task of requesting the formation of a new government. When a new Prime Minister is to be appointed, the Speaker confers with representatives of the various parties and thereafter proposes a candidate to the Riksdag. The proposal is approved if no more than half of the members of the Riksdag vote against the candidate. The person who is appointed

King Carl XVI Gustaf and Queen Silvia arriving at the opening of the Riksdag in 1993 and being greeted by Speaker of the Riksdag Ingegerd Troedsson. In the background behind the Queen is seen the Prime Minister, Carl Bildt, leader of the Moderate Party.

Prime Minister thus does not need the support of a majority in the Riksdag. (Only the 39 members of the Riksdag belonging to the Liberal Party voted for their party leader Ola Ullsten when he was elected Prime Minister in the fall of 1978.)

During its meetings the Riksdag may express its dissatisfaction and bring about the fall of a government. Through a vote of no confidence a particular minister may also be forced to resign.

In addition the new constitution means that the results of the elections, which are held in September, are immediately reflected in the composition of the Riksdag. Earlier, the new Riksdag first met in January, while it now opens in October.

## The Era of Bloc Politics

The social climate underwent a change at the end of the 1960s, when a general radicalization occurred which had its origins partly in the Vietnam War and the opposition to USA's involvement. The protest movements which developed in 1968 and the years that followed did not directly affect the party system or the Riksdag. No new party was formed. There was a change in the leadership of the

Communist Party in 1964, and Carl-Henrik Hermansson represented a "more modern" brand of communism than the old leader,
Hilding Hagberg. The party gained a great deal of strength in 1966
and changed its name to the Left Party Communists (*Vänsterpartiet kommunisterna*) in 1967. The proportion of the votes the
party received was cut in half in 1968, however. One of the main
reasons was the Soviet Union's invasion of Czechoslovakia in
August of the same year.

It is remarkable that the most established party, the Social
Democrats, won the 1968 election in spite of the opposition
movements. The party had been activated after the poor election
results in 1966. Tage Erlander took part in his last election as Prime
Minister and was enormously popular. The student protests and
the attack on Czechoslovakia gave an advantage to the ruling party,
which reaped more benefit than harm from the savage criticism
from various radical groups.

In 1969 the Social Democrats gained a new leader, Olof Palme.
His position was very close to that of Tage Erlander on the major
issues, and he had been the former Prime Minister's closest collab-
orator since 1953. On the other hand, his personality was quite
different from that of his predecessor. He evoked greater enthusiasm and fighting spirit, but also considerable resistance from the
opposition.

The first election held according to the new rules was in 1970.
The Social Democrats lost ground but were able to hold their
government position with the support of the Left Party Communists. The following election caused considerable problems for the
Riksdag and the government. The polarization between a nonsocialist and a socialist bloc had increased. The Center Party was
riding on a wave of popular issues and also attracted voters outside
its traditional support groups in the countryside, partly due to its
emphasis on environmental questions.

The result of the 1973 election was a balanced Riksdag; the blocs
received an equal number of seats. The Palme government remained in power, however, and a number of questions were
decided by lottery. The Riksdag period from 1973 to 1976 may be
evaluated in different ways. It was strange that the Riksdag was
able to retain much of its authority, although chance decided the
outcome of important issues. One of the reasons was that the
parties made a real effort to compromise through negotiations and
in the committees to avoid deciding issues by lottery.

From 1932 to 1976 the government was headed by Social Democrats. In no other democratic country has one party remained in
power so long. The turning point came in 1976, when the nonsocialist parties received the majority and formed a majority
government headed by the Center Party leader Thorbjörn Fälldin
and with the Moderate Party leader Gösta Bohman as Minister of

Prime Minister Olof Palme at an
appearance on the island of Gotland
in 1980. Olof Palme was an intense
speaker who was able to come into
close contact with his audience. His
rhetorical skills were exceptional
among Swedish politicians. His
speeches were characterized by im-
provisation, forcefully formulated
phrases and pointed remarks.

The leaders of the nonsocialist coalition in 1976: Thorbjörn Fälldin,
the Center Party, Per Ahlmark, the
Liberal Party, and Gösta Bohman,
the Moderate Party. The Social
Democrats had lost the power to
govern which they had exercised
alone or in coalitions with other
parties since 1932 (with a short
break for one hundred days in
the summer of 1936).

The government crisis in 1978,
which would lead to the fall of the
first Fälldin government, took place
largely in front of the TV cameras.
After a number of attempts within
the government at compromise concerning the nuclear energy issue, it
was necessary to admit at last that
the differences of opinion were too
great. – To the right in the picture
is Ola Ullsten who replaced Per
Ahlmark as the head of the Liberal
Party in 1978.

Economics and the leader of the Liberal Party Per Ahlmark as
Minister of Labor and Deputy Prime Minister. It was an historic
government, not only because the Social Democrats' hold on the
government was broken, but also because for the first time the
three nonsocialist parties governed together.

The new government would face a number of trials. The first was
the nuclear power question. The Center Party had categorically
promised in the election campaigns not to allow the arming of new
reactors. After a number of conflicts the three-party government
fell in October of 1978 because of a lack of agreement in the energy
question. It was followed by a Liberal Party minority government
under the new party leader Ola Ullsten. Initially the new government had a significant amount of success, but difficulties arose
during the spring of 1979, when it suffered from the repercussions
of the nuclear power plant accident in Harrisburg, Pennsylvania,
USA. An energy proposal that had been worked out in collabora-
tion with the Social Democrats had to be withdrawn, and instead
the parties agreed to a referendum on the nuclear power question
which would be held in the spring of 1980.

The nonsocialist parties also won a majority in the 1979 election,
and a three-party government was formed again under Thorbjörn
Fälldin.

The referendum of 1980, the fourth in Swedish history, dealt with
the question of the future of nuclear power. The voters had to take
a stand on three proposals. All were for a retreat from dependence
on nuclear power, but the difference was in the timing. The position
which supported the most gradual dismantling of nuclear reactors
won. From the point of view of the Riksdag, it might be said that the
representative body was not able to deal with a problem which did
not follow the traditional right–left political scale.

The governing parties had different views in the nuclear power
referendum, but they were able to remain unified. Instead the
government fell in 1981, when the "middle-of-the-road" parties,

that is the Center Party and the Liberal Party, collaborated with the Social Democrats on a tax reform. The three-party government was followed by a two-party government consisting of the Center Party and the Liberal Party. Fälldin retained the post of Prime Minister.

What role did the Riksdag play during the years of nonsocialist government? With the support of the trade union movement the Social Democrats built up a large office as a center for its Riksdag group. Many former government officials moved there, and the goal was to make the opposition as professional as the government. The position of the Riksdag, however, became less strong than it had been during the days of the balanced Riksdag. The bills that were presented were often the result of long negotiations within the government, and there was therefore little room for compromises in the committees.

Striking is the eagerness with which the nonsocialist governments showed that they did not want to destroy the welfare programs which had been built up during the years of Social Democratic rule, in spite of growing economic problems with an increasing budget deficit. They borrowed outside the country to avoid cuts and attempted a number of different measures to prevent an increase in unemployment. When the government proposed that the value-added tax should be raised in the late summer of 1980 the Social Democrats requested an extraordinary meeting of the Riksdag. At the meeting the increase in the value-added tax was accepted.

Karin Söder became the first female Foreign Minister in Sweden in 1976 and, when elected head of the Center Party in 1985, the first female party leader.

In the 1982 election the Social Democrats again took power, and a new Palme government was formed with Kjell-Olof Feldt as Minister of Finance. A 16 percent devaluation of the Swedish crown, which was added to the 10 percent devaluation of the earlier two-party government, led to a sharp rise in exports. In the 1985 election the Social Democrats received somewhat less support, but they were able to remain in power. The Liberal Party with its new leader, Bengt Westerberg, was the only party which increased, growing from 21 to 51 seats.

The uncertain parliamentary support became an increasing problem for the Social Democrats. The social composition of the Left Party Communists had changed, and under the party leader Lars Werner it retained more independence in relation to the Social Democrats. It was no longer clear that the Left Party Communists would routinely support Social Democratic proposals. Rather, in certain cases the party demanded first negotiations and then concessions from the Social Democrats.

A question which had been an encumbrance for the Social Democrats since the 1970s was the so-called wage-earners' investment funds. The original proposal came from the Swedish Trade Union Confederation, and one of the goals was to increase the influence of employees in their companies. The nonsocialist parties regarded the

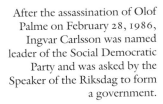

After the assassination of Olof Palme on February 28, 1986, Ingvar Carlsson was named leader of the Social Democratic Party and was asked by the Speaker of the Riksdag to form a government.

funds as a step in the process of socialization. The funds were introduced in a modified form by the Social Democratic government but were later dismantled when the nonsocialist parties were in power.

The assassination of Olof Palme on February 28, 1986 did not lead to any new policy. Palme's successor Ingvar Carlsson had earlier been Deputy Prime Minister and was one of those who had been closest to Palme politically. However, the climate of public debate was influenced by the assassination; the country was nearly in a state of shock. The public opinion polls noted a rise in the popularity of the Social Democrats, which can scarcely be explained by an increase in support for their policies; it had more to do with the mood of the country following the assassination.

During his entire career as a politician Olof Palme had been deeply involved in international politics. He was a spokesman for the people of the Third World and intensely condemned USA's war in Southeast Asia. At the time of his death he was hailed as a statesman of great international importance.

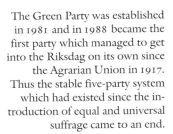

The Green Party was established in 1981 and in 1988 became the first party which managed to get into the Riksdag on its own since the Agrarian Union in 1917. Thus the stable five-party system which had existed since the introduction of equal and universal suffrage came to an end.

## The End of the Five-Party System

The Social Democrats were able to remain in power after the election of 1988, but the traditional Swedish party system changed when the Green Party passed the four percent threshold and gained 20 seats in the Riksdag.

During the 1980s the welfare state was challenged as never before. Reference was made more frequently to its negative aspects, the high level of taxation and a costly and, it was claimed, ineffective public sector. Competition and private solutions were presented as alternatives.

Around 1990 domestic politics focused on taxes. Until 1991 taxpayers with average incomes had to pay a tax amounting to 60–70 percent of their excess income. After extensive negotiations, but without public debate, the Social Democratic government made an agreement with the Liberal Party on a comprehensive tax reform which went into effect during 1991. A large part of the state's income today comes from indirect taxes. There is a value-added tax on practically all goods and services.

The decision on a tax reform was passed in the Riksdag, but it can still serve to illustrate how an important measure was worked out by means of more or less informal discussions among representatives of different parties. Formally the Riksdag played a decisive role but in reality could only accept or reject the proposal which was presented. On the other hand, the party caucuses were able to take stands and influence the proposal.

The foreign policy debate was dominated by the far-reaching changes in Eastern Europe and the question of Sweden's relationship to European cooperation. On June 14, 1991 Prime Minister Ingvar Carlsson presented a declaration to the Riksdag which stated that the government intended to seek membership in the European Communities. All parties except the Left Party (the Left Party Communists changed its name to the Left Party, *Vänsterpartiet*, in 1990) and the Green Party supported the government, and the application was submitted on July 1, 1991.

Prior to the 1991 election the Social Democrats had such low ratings in the opinion polls that they feared not only losing control of the government but also having the worst election results in more than 50 years. At the same time the nonsocialist parties were united, and the Moderate Party especially had high ratings in the opinion polls. The two questions which had split the earlier nonsocialist governments – taxes and nuclear power – were no longer on the political agenda. The election was a victory for the Moderate Party, which increased its seats by 14, and a loss for the Social Democrats, who lost 18 seats.

Two new parties entered the Riksdag, the Christian Democratic Party (*Kristdemokratiska samhällspartiet*) and New Democracy (*Ny*

Alf Svensson was named the head of the Christian Democratic Party in 1973, and in 1997 he is the party leader who has retained his position the longest.

*demokrati*), while the Green Party disappeared. The Christian Democratic Party had been in existence for more than twenty years, but had never earlier been able to make it across the four percent threshold. New Democracy was scarcely a year old but during the months before the election had been given a great deal of attention in the media.

A four-party minority government was formed with the Moderate Party leader Carl Bildt at its head. In addition to the Moderate Party, the Liberal Party, the Center Party and the Christian Democratic Party made up the government. New Democracy held the balance in the same way that the Left Party Communists had done during the Social Democratic governments.

The government worked well in the beginning in parliamentary terms. New Democracy played an unobtrusive role in the Riksdag and as a rule, sometimes more or less under protest, gave the government proposals its support without any concessions.

The economic crisis which had its beginning in the 1970s and continued during the 1980s deepened. Unemployment increased and was not stopped by the nonsocialist government. In the fall of 1992 the Swedish crown suffered from a wave of speculation which led to economic tensions with strong political connotations.

Various so-called crisis agreements between the government and the Social Democrats contained measures which were intended to create faith in the Swedish economy abroad. The parties had to accept a number of uncomfortable decisions: qualifying days and personal fees for sickness insurance, decreased support to developing countries, cancellation of tax reductions, decreased defense spending and lower employer contributions.

During the acute economic crisis the government and the Social Democrats cooperated, but the climate soon became chillier. The government had to depend on New Democracy instead. It made changes in the social insurance system, introduced a house doctor system and abolished the wage-earners' investment funds.

The Speaker of the Riksdag Thage G. Peterson asked Carl Bildt, the head of the Moderate Party, to form a four-party government after the 1991 election.

A difficult area for both the government and the opposition was refugee policy. The war in the former Yugoslavia caused a great influx of refugees which meant that the existing regulations concerning asylum and the solution of placing refugees in special premises were called into question.

Foreign policy was not a political issue during the years that the nonsocialist government was in power 1991–1994, just as it had not been between 1976 and 1982. The most important stand that was taken was on the issue of Swedish membership in the European Union. However, the definitive decision had to wait until the fall of 1994, when a referendum was scheduled for November following the elections.

In spite of different political strains the nonsocialist government under Carl Bildt was able to keep together until the 1994 election. The Center Party leader, Olof Johansson, left the government in June of the same year when he could not accept participating in a government which approved a bridge over Öresund between Sweden and Denmark. This did not significantly disturb the harmony, however. The other Center Party ministers remained.

In the area of constitutional questions a decision was made in 1994 to increase the term of office for members of both the Riksdag and the local government from three to four years. There was general agreement that a three-year period was too short for both the voters and the office holders. Governments were forced to consider the next election all too soon.

The crisis in government finances – a very large budget deficit and a rapidly growing national debt which resulted in high interest rates and a weak currency – caused the 1994 election campaign to concentrate on economic problems. None of the parties promised new reforms. Instead the debate centered on the measures that should be taken to decrease unemployment and reduce the budget deficit and national debt without a rise in inflation.

The most striking changes in the party picture in the 1994 Riksdag election affected the Social Democrats. Their support increased from 37.7 to 45.2 percent of the votes. The Liberal Party and the Center Party declined and the Christian Democratic Party nearly lost its right to seats in the Riksdag. The election was a catastrophe for New Democracy; the party received a little over one percent of the votes. The Left Party, however, showed good results, 6.2 percent, and demonstrated a changed profile with its new party leader, Gudrun Schyman. The Green Party again gained seats in the Riksdag with 5 percent of the votes.

The results of the election caused Carl Bildt and his government to resign, and Ingvar Carlsson formed a purely Social Democratic government. Göran Persson was appointed Minister of Finance, and he carried on the tradition of strong leaders in that office.

Olof Johansson became the head of the Center Party in 1987. He held several posts in Fälldin's governments, including that of Minister of Energy.

In 1993 Gudrun Schyman became the first female leader of the Left Party. Under her leadership the party had good results in the 1994 election, and she has tried to come to terms with the party's communist past.

The Riksdag election and the change in government yielded an increase in female representation for both. Today 42 percent of the members of the Riksdag and one half of the appointed ministers are women. When Maria Leissner succeeded Bengt Westerberg as head of the Liberal Party in 1994 it meant that two of the party leaders in the Riksdag were women, as well as one of the two spokesmen for the Green Party.

The referendum concerning whether or not Sweden should join the European Union was preceded by similar votes in Austria and Finland, where the outcomes, as expected, were clearly positive to joining. In Norway, where the opposition was thought to be strongest, a referendum gave negative results a few weeks later. Formally the vote in Sweden was only advisory, but all the parties had promised to act in accordance with the outcome.

The EU referendum may be compared with the nuclear power referendum. There were significant splits within the parties in both cases, and the traditional right–left scale made itself felt only to a limited extent.

The campaigns prior to the referendum were characterized largely by opposing groups that were not formed along the lines of party affiliation. Most politicians within the establishment, representatives of the business community and much of the press were in favor of membership. The reasons varied somewhat, but the major arguments were partly economic, partly political. It was often emphasized that it was better to be a member and participate in decision-making than to stand on the outside and be forced to make accommodations to EU decisions.

Two parties, the Left Party and the Green Party, were opposed, as were many Social Democrats and Center Party members. They stressed questions of sovereignty: Sweden should defend its right to determine the fate of its own national territory. The opponents also pointed out that EU was the rich man's club which excluded the poor world.

A majority, 52.3 percent, voted in favor of EU membership, while 46.8 percent were opposed and only 0.9 percent left their

The 1994 election was characterized by the fact that women gained a stronger position than ever before in the Riksdag. The female members of parliament are gathered here behind the Speaker of the Riksdag, Birgitta Dahl.

ballots blank. A little over 83 percent of the voters participated, which was somewhat lower than in the latest Riksdag election (ca. 87 percent). Yet, it was regarded as satisfactory, because referenda normally mobilize fewer voters.

The Carlsson government came to be characterized by a strict economic policy and reduction of a number of benefits within the welfare system. It led to some improvements in government finances, but also to a trying debate within the Social Democratic Party. The terms "reformers" and "preservationists" were coined, where the latter opposed what they saw as the dismantling of the welfare state which Social Democracy had built. The reformers argued that the greatest threat to the welfare state lay in the guarding of costly social programs. Sweden had to borrow from outside the country to maintain these programs.

In spite of its election victory the Social Democratic government did not have a majority in the Riksdag. In the fall of 1994, however, after negotiations, it was possible to get a number of proposals passed with the support of the Left Party. But cooperation with the left wing soon came to an end and was replaced by more formalized cooperation with the Center Party. This changed the political picture by splitting the nonsocialist bloc.

In the fall of 1995 Ingvar Carlsson announced that he intended to resign as party leader and Prime Minister and that a new party leader (and thus Prime Minister) would have to be named at an extraordinary party congress in March of 1996. Carlsson's resignation led to the intensification of conflicts of principle within the party. There was also a comprehensive discussion as to the successor. This resulted in the naming of Minister of Finance Göran Persson as leader of the Social Democratic Party. The extraordinary party congress which elected Persson, in spite of a number of signs to the contrary, was characterized by unity. The party rallied around its new chairman. In March 1996 Göran Persson was named Prime Minister by the Riksdag.

Persson made significant changes in the government. Erik Åsbrink became the Minister of Finance. The policy of reconstruc-

Göran Persson, who was then Minister of Finance, was named leader of the Social Democratic Party in the spring of 1996 and thereafter became Prime Minister. Unlike his predecessors, he had earlier held leading political positions at the local level.

tion of government finances would continue, but it would be combined with measures to improve employment. The goal was to cut unemployment in half by the turn of the century.

## Stability?

Stability has been the foremost characteristic of the Riksdag since the 1930s. During the decades directly following the Second World War the Social Democrats held the dominant position in Swedish politics. This period was distinguished by a strongly increasing public sector and a sharp rise in government spending which was financed by comprehensive direct and indirect taxes.

The long period of Social Democratic governments is unique. There is no simple explanation, and it is remarkable that the party was able to maintain power in spite of the great social and economic changes in the country. The Social Democratic electoral base, the workers, decreased, while salaried employees and members of service occupations increased.

At the end of the 1970s and during the 1980s rivalry grew among the parties, and the Social Democrats partly lost their role as "the governing party." One of the reasons was that the country's income had not expanded at the same rate as expenditures. There was no longer a growing pie to be cut.

The new unicameral legislature and the new election system which came into being in 1970 meant that the struggle for government power was the focus of the elections to a greater extent than previously. The central question became which groups or which bloc could form a governing majority. The weaknesses of this system were demonstrated during the period of nonsocialist governments from 1976 to 1982.

After the 1988 election a new party gained seats in the Riksdag for the first time in decades. The old five-party system ceased to exist, and Sweden thus began to resemble other European countries more closely. This resemblance became even more clear after the 1991 and 1994 elections. On the other hand, the Social Democrats again came to power after the nonsocialist losses in 1994. There was a great deal of speculation about a coalition, first between the Social Democrats and the Liberal Party, and later between the Social Democrats and the Center Party. The government, however, chose to cooperate first with the Left Party and later, in a more comprehensive and formalized way, with the Center Party.

Lars Leijonborg was elected chairman of the Liberal Party in 1997. With the 1998 election approaching he has declared that it is natural for the Liberal Party to cooperate with the Moderate Party in the government.

The dominant question following the 1994 election was if bloc politics, which had characterized the period of the unicameral legislature, would gain ground, or if the cooperation between the Social Democrats and the Center Party would develop.

## Popular Representation Debated

The Social Democrat Birgitta Dahl became Speaker of the Riksdag after the 1994 election. She succeeded Inge-gerd Troedsson, a member of the Moderate Party, who in 1991 was the first woman to occupy the post.

IN SWEDEN, as in nearly all countries with popular representation, there is an ongoing debate concerning the parliament and its role in society. The representativity of the Riksdag, its organization and the way it functions are often challenged and discussed in the media. This debate and the media's reporting and reviews of the parliament are an important and necessary part of a democratic society. The Swedish tradition of openness and of public access to official records has also left its imprint on the relationship of the Riksdag to the sur-rounding world. Increasing numbers of de-bates and hearings are broadcast live on TV, and new technology has contributed to mak-ing information about the work of the Riksdag more and more accessible to a broader public.

A problem, which Sweden shares with many other countries, is the distrust of politicians at all levels of society. This development is expressed, for example, in a decline in involvement in political parties. Thus far participation in elections has not been affected and still remains high when interna-tional comparisons are made; 87 percent of the eligible voters took part in the 1994 election.

Within the Riksdag there are continual dis-cussions about changes in work routines to increase accessibility to and interest in debates and decisions, especially among youth. In re-cent years a number of studies have also been completed which deal with the election sys-tem, the work of the Riksdag committees, members' right to submit motions and the number of members of the Riksdag. Recent changes have included a lengthening of the term of office from three to four years. A decision has also been made to increase the element of voting for candidates on the basis of personal qualifications in the 1998 election. The process of drawing up the national budget has been radically revamped.

Sweden's membership in the EU has clearly modified the work routines of the Riksdag. An Advisory Committee on EU Affairs has been established for consultations between the Riksdag and the government. On the whole there has been an internationalization of the work of the Riksdag in recent years in the form of increased contacts and involvement, also with countries outside of Europe.

# Distribution of Seats in the Riksdag 1922–1997

The Riksdag which convened in 1922 was the first elected by universal suffrage.
Election to the Second Chamber then occurred in principle every fourth year.
The First Chamber was chosen by means of indirect elections and was successively
restructured by the annual renewal of one eighth of its members.

## First Chamber 1922–1970

| Year | Conserva-tives | Agrarian Union/ Center Party | Liberals | Social Democrats | Socialists/ Communists | Total |
|------|------|------|------|------|------|------|
| 1922 | 41 | 18 | 38 | 50 | 3 | 150 |
| 1925 | 44 | 18 | 35 | 52 | 1 | 150 |
| 1929 | 49 | 17 | 31 | 52 | 1 | 150 |
| 1933 | 50 | 18 | 23 | 58 | 1 | 150 |
| 1937 | 45 | 22 | 16 | 66 | 1 | 150 |
| 1941 | 35 | 24 | 15 | 75 | 1 | 150 |
| 1945 | 30 | 21 | 14 | 83 | 2 | 150 |
| 1949 | 24 | 21 | 18 | 84 | 3 | 150 |
| 1953 | 20 | 25 | 22 | 79 | 4 | 150 |
| 1957 | 13 | 25 | 30 | 79 | 3 | 150 |
| 1958 | 16 | 24 | 29 | 79 | 3 | 151 |
| 1961 | 19 | 20 | 33 | 77 | 2 | 151 |
| 1965 | 26 | 19 | 26 | 78 | 2 | 151 |
| 1969 | 24 | 21 | 26 | 79 | 1 | 151 |

## Second Chamber 1922–1970

| Year | Conserva-tives | Agrarian Union/ Center Party | Liberals | Social Democrats | Socialists/ Communists | Total |
|------|------|------|------|------|------|------|
| 1922 | 62 | 21 | 41 | 93 | 13 | 230 |
| 1925 | 65 | 23 | 33 | 104 | 5 | 230 |
| 1929 | 73 | 27 | 32 | 90 | 8 | 230 |
| 1933 | 58 | 36 | 24 | 104 | 8 | 230 |
| 1937 | 44 | 36 | 27 | 112 | 11 | 230 |
| 1941 | 42 | 28 | 23 | 134 | 3 | 230 |
| 1945 | 39 | 35 | 26 | 115 | 15 | 230 |
| 1949 | 23 | 30 | 57 | 112 | 8 | 230 |
| 1953 | 31 | 26 | 58 | 110 | 5 | 230 |
| 1957 | 42 | 19 | 58 | 106 | 6 | 231 |
| 1958 | 45 | 32 | 38 | 111 | 5 | 231 |
| 1961 | 39 | 34 | 40 | 114 | 5 | 232 |
| 1965 | 33 | 36[1] | 43 | 113 | 8 | 233 |
| 1969 | 32 | 39 | 34 | 125 | 3 | 233 |

## The Riksdag 1971–1997

| Year | Moderate Party | Center Party | Liberal Party | Social Democrats | Left Party Communists/ Left Party | Green Party | Christian Democrats | New Democracy | Total |
|------|------|------|------|------|------|------|------|------|------|
| 1971 | 41 | 71 | 58 | 163 | 17 | – | – | – | 350 |
| 1974 | 51 | 90 | 34 | 156 | 19 | – | – | – | 350 |
| 1976 | 55 | 86 | 39 | 152 | 17 | – | – | – | 349 |
| 1979 | 73 | 64 | 38 | 154 | 20 | – | – | – | 349 |
| 1982 | 86 | 56 | 21 | 166 | 20 | – | – | – | 349 |
| 1985 | 76 | 44[2] | 51 | 159 | 19 | – | – | – | 349 |
| 1988 | 66 | 42 | 44 | 156 | 21 | 20 | – | – | 349 |
| 1991 | 80 | 31 | 33 | 138 | 16 | – | 26 | 25 | 349 |
| 1994 | 80 | 27 | 26 | 161 | 22 | 18 | 15 | – | 349 |

[1] Of whom one is a representative of the Citizens' Coalition.
[2] Of whom one is a representative of the Christian Democratic Party.

# Prime Ministers 1876–1997

The list below contains the names of Sweden's heads of government from the year 1876, when the office of Prime Minister was established. Also included are the names of the political parties which participated in the various governments after the breakthrough of parliamentarism in 1917.

| | |
|---|---|
| Louis De Geer | 1876–1880 |
| Arvid Posse | 1880–1883 |
| Carl Johan Thyselius | 1883–1884 |
| Robert Themptander | 1884–1888 |
| Gillis Bildt | 1888–1889 |
| Gustaf Åkerhielm | 1889–1891 |
| Erik Gustaf Boström | 1891–1900 |
| Fredrik von Otter | 1900–1902 |
| Erik Gustaf Boström | 1902–1905 |
| Johan Ramstedt | 1905 |
| Christian Lundeberg | 1905 |
| Karl Staaff | 1905–1906 |
| Arvid Lindman | 1906–1911 |
| Karl Staaff | 1911–1914 |
| Hjalmar Hammarskjöld | 1914–1917 |
| Carl Swartz | 1917 |
| Nils Edén (Liberals, Social Democratic Party) | 1917–1920 |
| Hjalmar Branting (Social Democratic Party) | 1920 |
| Louis De Geer the Younger (Nonpolitical) | 1920–1921 |
| Oscar von Sydow (Nonpolitical) | 1921 |
| Hjalmar Branting (Social Democratic Party) | 1921–1923 |
| Ernst Trygger (Conservatives) | 1923–1924 |
| Hjalmar Branting (Social Democratic Party) | 1924–1925 |
| Rickard Sandler (Social Democratic Party) | 1925–1926 |
| Carl Gustaf Ekman (Liberal People's Party, Liberal Party) | 1926–1928 |
| Arvid Lindman (Conservatives) | 1928–1930 |
| Carl Gustaf Ekman (Liberal People's Party) | 1930–1932 |
| Felix Hamrin (Liberal People's Party) | 1932 |
| Per Albin Hansson (Social Democratic Party) | 1932–1936 |
| Axel Pehrsson-Bramstorp (Agrarian Union) | 1936 |
| Per Albin Hansson (Social Democratic Party, Agrarian Union) | 1936–1939 |
| Per Albin Hansson (Social Democratic Party, Conservatives, Agrarian Union, Liberal Party) | 1939–1945 |
| Per Albin Hansson (Social Democratic Party) | 1945–1946 |
| Tage Erlander (Social Democratic Party) | 1946–1951 |
| Tage Erlander (Social Democratic Party, Agrarian Union) | 1951–1957 |
| Tage Erlander (Social Democratic Party) | 1957–1969 |
| Olof Palme (Social Democratic Party) | 1969–1976 |
| Thorbjörn Fälldin (Center Party, Moderate Party, Liberal Party) | 1976–1978 |
| Ola Ullsten (Liberal Party) | 1978–1979 |
| Thorbjörn Fälldin (Center Party, Moderate Party, Liberal Party) | 1979–1981 |
| Thorbjörn Fälldin (Center Party, Liberal Party) | 1981–1982 |
| Olof Palme (Social Democratic Party) | 1982–1986 |
| Ingvar Carlsson (Social Democratic Party) | 1986–1990 |
| Ingvar Carlsson (Social Democratic Party) | 1990–1991 |
| Carl Bildt (Moderate Party, Liberal Party, Center Party, Christian Democratic Party) | 1991–1994 |
| Ingvar Carlsson (Social Democratic Party) | 1994–1996 |
| Göran Persson (Social Democratic Party) | 1996– |

The dates given for the regents during the Middle Ages (until 1520) are sometimes uncertain. There were also periods when two rulers were struggling for power.

| | | | |
|---|---|---|---|
| Birger Jarl | 1250–1266 | Sigismund | 1592–1599 |
| Valdemar Birgersson | (1250)–1275 | Karl IX | (1599)–1611 |
| Magnus Ladulås (Barnlock) | 1275–1290 | Gustav II Adolf | 1611–1632 |
| Birger Magnusson's regency | 1290–1298 | Kristina's regency | 1632–1644 |
| Birger Magnusson | 1298–1318 | Kristina | 1644–1654 |
| Magnus Eriksson's regency | 1319–1332 | Karl X Gustav | 1654–1660 |
| Magnus Eriksson | 1332–1364 | Karl XI's regency | 1660–1672 |
| Albrekt of Mecklenburg | 1364–1389 | Karl XI | 1672–1697 |
| Margareta | 1389–1412 | Karl XII's regency | 1697 |
| Erik of Pomerania | (1397)–1439 | Karl XII | 1697–1718 |
| Kristofer of Bavaria | 1441–1448 | Ulrika Eleonora | 1719–1720 |
| Karl Knutsson (Bonde) | 1448–1457 | Fredrik I | 1720–1751 |
| Kristian I | 1457–1464 | Adolf Fredrik | 1751–1771 |
| Karl Knutsson (Bonde) | 1464–1465 | Gustav III | 1771–1792 |
| Karl Knutsson (Bonde) | 1467–1470 | Gustav IV Adolf's regency | 1792–1796 |
| Sten Sture the Elder | 1471–1497 | Gustav IV Adolf | 1796–1809 |
| Hans | 1497–1501 | Karl XIII | 1809–1818 |
| Sten Sture the Elder | 1501–1503 | Karl XIV Johan | 1818–1844 |
| Svante Nilsson Sture | 1504–1511 | Oscar I | 1844–1859 |
| Sten Sture the Younger | 1512–1520 | Karl XV | 1859–1872 |
| Kristian II | 1520–1523 | Oscar II | 1872–1907 |
| Gustav (Eriksson) Vasa | (1521)–1560 | Gustaf V | 1907–1950 |
| Erik XIV | 1560–1568 | Gustaf VI Adolf | 1950–1973 |
| Johan III | 1568–1592 | Carl XVI Gustaf | 1973– |

The map below shows all the provinces of Sweden as well as the position of selected geographical places mentioned in the book. Smaller villages have not been included, but their location is usually clear from the text.

Ambrosiani, Björn, Stockholm 17
Antikvarisk-topografiska arkivet,
    Stockholm 18, 32; Sören Hallgren
    20, 25
Arbetarrörelsens arkiv, Stockholm
    159, 170, 176, 179, 182, 183, 184, 188
Armémuseum, Stockholm 114

Berlingska boktryckeriet, Lund 108
Bernadottebiblioteket, Kungl. Slottet,
    Stockholm 161
Bibliothèque nationale, Paris 8
Bildservice, Göteborg 65
Borås turistbyrå 23

Dagens Nyheter, Stockholm 11
Dalarnas museum, Falun;
    Olle Norling 94, 112

Ekströmer, Jonas, Stockholm 202

Finlands nationalmuseum, Helsinki;
    Syrjänen 128; Gunnari 130
Foto-Hernried, Stockholm 187, 189

Glase, Gösta, Stockholm 79, 116
GullersBild, Uppsala 194

Hallgren, Sören, Enskede 19
Hasselberg, Lars, Vara 20
HSB:s bildarkiv, Stockholm 177

International Magazine Service,
    Stockholm; Mathias Hansen 141

Kalmar läns museum, Kalmar;
    Rolf Lind 41
Kiruna kommuns bildarkiv;
    Borg Mesch 162
Det Kongelige Bibliotek,
    Copenhagen 35
Kristdemokraten, Stockholm 202
Kulturen, Lund 83, 138
Kungl. Biblioteket, Stockholm 58, 89,
    95, 102, 146, 158
    *Handskriftssektionen* 8, 21, 38, 39,
    43, 49
    *Kart- och bildsektionen* 19, 50, 58, 67,
    74, 97, 118, 128, 131, 142, 143, 144,
    145, 154, 155, 156, 157, 167
    *Sektionen för okatalogiserat tryck* 152,
    169, 171, 180, 184, 189
    *Tidningssektionen* 102, 141, 157
Kungl. Husgerådskammaren, Stock-
    holm; Håkan Lind 137

Kungl. Myntkabinettet, Stockholm
    13, 42, 80, 139, 155; Gabriel Hilde-
    brand 11, 44, 56, 64, 80, 81, 99

Lindroth, Kurt, Borlänge 126
Livrustkammaren, Stockholm 72, 93;
    Karl Erik Granath 62; Lennart
    Nilsson 59; Göran Schmidt 35, 116
Loewe, Walter, Stockholm 135
Lunds universitetsbibliotek 135, 158
Länsmuseet i Gävleborgs län, Gävle
    112, 115

Malmström, Åke, Stockholm;
    Axel Malmström 164, 166, 179
Malmö museer; Lena Wilhelmsson
    117

Nordiska museet, Stockholm 74, 84,
    142, 169, 186; Sören Hallgren 88,
    115; Hans Koegel 182; Mats Lan-
    din 77, 116

Pica, Stockholm; Leif R. Jansson
    195; Ulf Palm 203, 205; Kent Öst-
    lund 203
Posten Frimärken, Stockholm 10
Pressens bild, Stockholm 159, 166,
    170; Bernt Claesson 197; Jan
    Collsiöö 191; Hans T. Dahlskog
    204, 207; Bertil Ericson 198; Lasse
    Hedberg 200; Tommy Pedersen
    198; Rudolf Södergren 172; Ola
    Torkelsson 206

Qwarnström, Anders, Stockholm 16,
    21

Regeringskansliets centralarkiv,
    Stockholm; Kurt Eriksson 15
Reportagebild, Stockholm 183, 192;
    Bibbi Johansson 200
Riddarhuset, Stockholm; Sven G.
    Andersson 148
Riksarkivet, Stockholm; Kurt Eriks-
    son 31, 42, 43, 48, 51, 56, 63, 66, 75,
    78, 87, 88, 91, 92, 99, 110, 123, 124,
    130 (Bonniers bildarkiv), 161
Riksdagen, Stockholm 150, 160, 167,
    168, 190, 199; Folke Hellberg 192;
    Tord Lund 27; Sven Nilsson 7, 14,
    70, 100, 115, 128, 129, 144, 149, 162,
    163; Peter de Ru 125; Holger
    Staffansson 148; Thomas Svensson
    6, 9, 151, 174, 193, 196

Scandibild, Uppsala; Sven G.
    Andersson 29
Skansen, Stockholm; Marie
    Andersson 71
Skattkammaren, Kungl. Slottet,
    Stockholm; Karl Erik Granath 44
Skoklosters slott, Bålsta 52
Statens konstmuseer, Stockholm 49,
    106, 114; Hans Thorwid 64, 68
    *Nationalmuseum* 34, 62, 82, 83, 92,
    104, 105, 110, 111, 119, 129, 132; Per
    Jalkman 72 (Bonniers bildarkiv);
    Åsa Lundén 85, 133; Hans Thorwid
    36, 153
    *Statens porträttsamling på Gripsholm*
    45, 53, 55, 59, 69, 75, 98, 136; Bodil
    Karlsson 72
    *Svenska porträttarkivet* 56, 98, 101,
    103, 119, 121, 129, 133, 134
Stiernspetz, Karl-Henrik, Vaxholm
    71, 91
Stockholms stadsmuseum 49, 86,
    134, 139, 147, 164; Francis Bruun
    57, 117, 148; Sören Hallgren 26;
    Axel Malmström 163
Svenska röda korset, Stockholm 181

Törnell, Lennart, Göteborg 48, 109
    (from "Gamla stan förr och nu" by
    Rune Lindgren, 1992)

Uppsala-Bild; Rolf Nodén 46
Uppsala universitet 40; Tommy
    Westberg 68
Uppsala universitetsbibliotek 7, 22,
    23, 25, 28, 33, 73, 77, 90, 136

Västmanlands läns museum,
    Västerås 60

Zornsamlingarna, Mora 37

Östergötlands länsmuseum,
    Linköping 54

Most of the pictures included in the photomontage on the cover are taken from the book and are found in the list of illustrations above.

The map on page 24 was drawn by Arne Olovsson, Stockholm, and those on pages 65 and 214 by Kerstin Kåve-rud, Nacka.

*For further information:*

Sveriges riksdag / The Swedish Parliament
SE-100 12 Stockholm, Sweden

Phone exchange: +46 8 786 40 00
Fax: +46 8 786 61 45
E-mail: riksdagsinformation@riksdagen.se
Web site location: http://www.riksdagen.se